The Other Side of The Island: 52 Spots to Explore Long Island's Natural Places

Two Spirit Press
© 2014 M.C. Hayes

The Other Side of The Island:
52 Spots to Explore Long Island's Natural Places

TABLE OF CONTENTS

March 2012 - June 2012
1) Shu Swamp (Mill Neck) 11
2) Tackapausha (Seaford)..16
3) Lakeland Preserve (Islandia)..24
4) West Hills (Melville)..29
5) Jamaica Bay National Wildlife Refuge (Queens)..................35
6) Cranberry Bogs Preserve (Riverhead)...................................41
7) Target Rock Wildlife Refuge (Lloyds Neck).........................46
8) Muttontown Preserve (Muttontown).....................................51
9) Wertheim (Mastic)..56
10) Orient State Park (Orient)..61
11) Cold Spring Harbor and
Upland Farms Preserve (Cold Spring Harbor).........................67
12) Randall Preserve (Ridge)...73

June 2012 - September 2012
13) Massapequa Preserve (Massapequa)....................................78
14) Caleb Smith Preserve (Smithtown)......................................84
15) Cedar Point (East Hampton)..88
16) Marine Nature Study Area (Oceanside)...............................94
17) Sunken Meadow (King's Park)..99
18) Avalon (Stony Brook)...106
19) Stillwell Woods (Syosset)...111
20) Caumsett State Park (Lloyd's Neck)...................................116
21) Sunken Forest (Fire Island)..122
22) Wildwood State Park (Wading River)................................127
23) Manorville Hills (Manorville)..132
24) Marine Park (Brooklyn)...138
25) Tiffany Creek (Oyster Bay)..144
26) Otis Pike Fire Island Wilderness Area 148

September 2012 - December 2012
27) Blydenburgh Park (Smithtown)...............................153
28) Hubbard County Park (Flanders).........................158
29) Udall's Cove (Douglaston)..................................164
30) Robert Cushman Murphy Park (Calverton).......................167
31) Mashomack (Shelter Island)..172
32) Mill Pond (Bellmore)...178
33) Edgewood Preserve (Brentwood)..182
34) Prosser Pines (Middle Island)..187
35) Heckshire State Park (Islip)..191
36) Sands Point Preserve (Port Washington)............................195
37) Pine Meadow Preserve (Riverhead)..................................199

December 2012 - March 2013
38) Gardiner County Park (Bay Shore)....................................204
39) Dwarf Pine Plains (Westhampton).....................................208
40) Forest Park Preserve (Queens)...212
41) Garvies Point (Glen Cove)..216
42) Arthur Kunz Preserve (Smithtown)....................................221
43) Cupsogue Beach (Westhampton Beach)...........................226
44) Brookhaven State Park (Ridge)..230
45) Connetquot State Park (Oakdale)..235
46) Twin Lakes Preserve (Wantagh)..240
47) David Sarnoff Preserve (Riverhead)..................................244
48) Sears Bellows Preserve (Flanders).....................................248
49) Hallock State Park (Jamesport)..253
50) Montauk Point/Camp Hero (Montauk).............................257
51) Wellwyn Preserve (Glen Cove)...262
52) West Meadow Beach (East Setauket)................................266

INTRODUCTION

Adventure begins with curiosity. I developed an interest in hiking a few years back, and wondered how many places I could go and be face to face with nature on Long Island. With whatever information I could gather, I started exploring them one by one. As I became more familiar with the natural side of the Island, I realized that I needed to share my experiences. When people think of Long Island they don't think of hiking and nature. They think of seven and a half million people, the expressway, and a string of enjoyable, but crowded, beaches. Feeling a yearning to commune with nature, some Long Islanders travel long distances at considerable expense to find a piece of nature in some other part of the country, completely overlooking the natural world around them. I've heard people say you can't really hike on Long Island, because it's all flat, and there are no mountains. Have these people ever enjoyed walking along the ocean? If you believe that experiencing nature requires you to travel someplace unpopulated and remote, have you ever seen weeds growing out of cracks in the sidewalk? Better yet, have you ever seen them bloom? Nature doesn't take an all or nothing approach, so why should we? Nature slips in wherever it can find an opening. Look beyond the strip malls and tract housing, and you will be amazed. This book is about long Island's often overlooked wild side.

This book serves as a guide. Each chapter covers a different preserve. The different locations provide examples of the various habitats found on Long Island. Starting the first day of spring of 2012 and ending the first day of spring of 2013, the book cronicles the subtle changes going on around us as the seasons progress through the year. I explored the beaches, the pine barrens, the estuaries, the rivers, the hills, and the open fields. I explored areas untouched by development, and reclaimed by nature after farming, dredging, building and other types human intervention. The book highlights plants, animals and habitats common on, and in some cases, unique to Long Island.

In some cases, invasive species have become so prevalent, that they've become the new environment. When farms and estates return to nature, they still leave their mark. Prosser Pines and the Norway spruce in Muttontown preserve show that groves of trees planted for decorative or commercial purposes can, over time, become beautiful forests in their own right. Mute swans, one of the largest birds capable of flight were brought over from Europe, and now peacefully share the ponds with indigenous geese and ducks.

As the seasons change, flowers bloom, trees bear fruit and leaves change color and fall. Animals go in and out of hibernation. Some birds leave the island for the winter, and some visit from much further north during the winter months. My intention is to provide you with a practical guide to places to go, and an idea of what to look for when they get there.

I selected hikes and locations for their unique value, choosing some shorter hikes, because they offer a unique and valuable connection with different aspects of the natural world. The preserves in this book incorporate many sections of the eighteen mile Nassau-Suffolk Greenbelt, the thirty-two mile Long Island Greenbelt, and 125 mile Paumanok Path.

I also made sure to include a few locations in Queens and Brooklyn. Their natural areas get overlooked. The streams feeding into Jamaica Bay have been diverted into underground culverts, but they still flow, as they have been for thousands of years. Extensive restoration efforts have been successful in Jamaica Bay, Gerritsen Creek, and elsewhere in the city. Forest Park Preserve offers a rare view of what Queens looked like before we smoothed over the moraines to more easily build. Udall's Cove remains a quiet monument to the tenacity of local residents who cared enough to petition the city for twenty years and save an irreplaceable piece of wetlands on the North Shore.

    Nature slowly reclaims Nassau County's old estates. On a recent visit to Muttontown Preserve, I saw two white tailed deer run through its spruce forest. Several preserves on the South Shore protect small creeks essential to the surrounding communities for drainage. I grew up half way between Tackapausha Preserve and Massapequa Preserve, not realizing that acres of Atlantic white cedar once covered the area. Now, the only specimens remaining in Nassau County grow in Tackapausha Preserve. Salt marshes once covered most of the area south of Merrick Road, and that that were filled in developers decided to build here in the nineteen forties and fifties. Today these areas flood occasionally.

    Out in Suffolk, you will find the best hiking. The oak brush plains in western Suffolk gradually change into pitch pine forests further east. You'll find a colony of bank swallows nesting in the bluffs at Target Rock, and an extensive colony of prickly pear cactus in a remote part of Caumsett State Park. Further east, you'll find hoodoos on the beach and wild turkeys in the woods. You'll discover the Nissequogue, Carman, Connetquot and Peconic Rivers. At the eastern end, the Island comes to an end with its two forks. The sand at Orient Point slowly fades into the water, and beyond it you'll see Plum Island. Montauk Point faces the Atlantic with dramatic bluffs, and huge ocean waves. Between them, Gardiner's Island, owned by the same family since colonial times, remains off limits to all but invited guests. Shelter Island can be reached by a quick ferry ride. Mashomack Preserve, managed by the Nature Conservancy, covers about a third of Shelter Island, and has become a valuable location for serious research concerning the Peconic Bay. Fire Island, and the other barrier beaches on the South Shore contain some of the best beaches in the country. Away from the crowds, you can walk along the ocean, hand in hand with nature.

Hiking isn't about the distance traveled, as much as it is about exploring the environment, and developing a firsthand understanding of local plants and animals. To give an example, The Marine Nature Center in Oceanside, with less than a mile of trails, offers the best bird watching on the South Shore. If your goal is to observe or photograph birds and other wild life, pick a spot and stand still. The animals will come out, once they see you as part of the environment.

Diversity abounds. 180 different species of bird breed on Long Island, and many more winter here, or pass through on their migrations. Homo sapiens lounge on the beaches during the summer, and harbor seals enjoy the same beaches in the winter. Nearly one hundred native tree species can be found. Hundreds of types of flowers bloom from when skunk cabbage emerge from the swamp in early February to when witch hazel extends its thin yellow flowers in late November and early December. Crabs, mussels, oysters, and fish fill the bays and sound. You can visit the desert like habitat of the barrier beaches, where only the strongest survive, and then later in the day seek out a maple swamp somewhere along the south shore. We have a globally rare dwarf pine forest growing along Sunrise Highway in Westhampton. We have an equally rare maritime holly forest growing on Fire Island. Central Nassau even once contained one of the few prairies which existed east of the Appalachian Mountains. You'll find the few remaining acres left of the Hempstead Plains next to a dilapidated hockey stadium built in the 1970's.

Pine barrens cover much of the interior of Suffolk County, protecting our groundwater. Rainwater filters through the sand, recharging a series of aquifers underneath the Island. These aquifers bring fresh water into the Great South Bay, and feed the rivers and streams on the Island. Along the North Shore, two ridges stretch along the length of the Island, pushed here by glaciers between ten and twenty thousand years ago. At the time, the Long Island Sound was dry, connecting the Island to the mainland. The whole region was once the outwash of a river delta. The river in question flowed roughly from what is now the Mohawk River and Hudson River. The formation and erosion of glacial moraines in this location has been going on for millions of years, with successive ice ages coming and going. Our island simply rests on the most recent set of glacial moraines. The Harbor Hill Moraine stretches from Queens to Orient Point and beyond. The Ronkonkoma Moraine Starts in Woodbury, and extends eastward to Montauk Point. The northwest portion of Queens sits directly on bedrock. The area south of the moraines is simply the lighter sands which water and wind erode into the sea.

  We recently saw nature's will in action with the extensive flooding Hurricane Sandy brought to the South Shore. The storm re-arranged the barrier beaches. The chapter on The Otis Pike High Dunes Wilderness Area provides a before and after account of the breach at Old Inlet. I live about a mile from the Great South Bay, on land which was once a salt marsh. During the storm I watched the high tide rise into my living room, and continue up the street. When spring came around again, you could see the damage salt water did to the landscaping in the neighborhood. Very few people use native trees and shrubs to decorate their yards. Nobody uses plants which can handle being inundated by salt water. The salt water destroyed people's shrubbery. Leaves on the evergreens turned orange. Some of the deciduous trees never pushed out leaves in the spring. Some grew thin and frail looking crowns. The summer following Sandy, I walked barefoot on my back porch at night and noticed there were no garden slugs. Maybe the salt did them in.

More and more I realize that I am a part of the natural world, in spite of my many attempts to distance myself from that reality through electric lighting, automobiles and processed foods. In order to live one on one with nature, and develop an understanding of the natural world, I couldn't put it on a pedestal. I couldn't treat it as a consumer commodity. I couldn't go on a strict diet of organic food, or buy every plastic item with a picture of a tree silk screened on it. I needed to get out there and befriend it, visit it regularly, and watch it change and grow. I needed to watch it adapt to human influence with a will of its own.

From Brooklyn to Montauk, the Island is 118 miles long. It's 23 miles at its widest point, and covers an area of 14,000 square miles. If you're out hiking, you'll find very little to be afraid of. Long Island is home to about 7.6 million people (about 5000 per square mile), you can usually count on one or two of them being around. Even if you get lost, you will usually be within earshot of a major road, and near a cell phone tower. Bring water, wear comfortable shoes, dress for the weather, use insect repellent. Watch out for poison ivy, remember, "leaves of three...let it be". Ticks are probably the biggest natural threat, beside humans. Check yourself for ticks when you get home. Avoid areas with high grass, because the high grass attracts ticks. Most importantly, enjoy yourself.

MARCH

Glacial Erratics Resting Under the Trees

SHU SWAMP
Charles T. Church Preserve

March 20th

    Unless you get your information from a groundhog, today is the first day of spring. From some perspectives, spring starts quietly in early February when the first green shoots poke up through the dirt. It's early morning, the chill is gone from the air, and an extremely heavy fog, appropriate for a swamp, rests on the ground. The fog adds to the mystique and allure of the low places. Shu Swamp offers a variety of plants, and can be hiked in about an hour and a half. Two trails circle the 60 acre preserve. The larger is the blue trail and the smaller is the red trail. Because of its small size getting lost is impossible, even with heavy fog cover. Both the red and blue trails overlap briefly and start behind the information kiosk in the parking lot. The trails themselves aren't marked, so you have to study the map in the kiosk before venturing into the murky wilderness.

    Approximately half of the preserve consists of "old growth" which has never been farmed or developed. Very few pristine places are left on the Island anymore, especially in Nassau County. The swamp has been in Mother Nature's caring hands from time immemorial. As far as it concerns the activities and affairs of the Island's current residents, The North Shore Wildlife Sanctuary keeps an eye on it today.

    Springs feed the swamp. The sand forming Long Island holds millions of gallons of rainwater. In Shu Swamp, the land rests low enough, and the water table reaches high enough, that water seeps out through springs creating the swamp. Water forms streams, flowing into Beaver Pond on the opposite side of the railroad tracks from the swamp.

Beavers no longer live in the pond or brooks, but evidence suggests a family of otters currently live in the preserve. Once common on Long Island, otters were last seen in the 1960's. In recent years, they have slowly been returning from across the sound. Although the otters haven't been seen in Shu Swamp, or anywhere else in Nassau, a deposit of scat was found here in 2008.

Immediately upon entering the trail, several large grey boulders, older than the swamp itself, rest in the mud. Deposited before the first raindrop started filtering through the sand, the boulders sit in quiet contemplation, as they've been doing since glaciers deposited them about 20,000 years ago. The trail remains dry through most of the preserve. The real swampy parts are on the left and right side of the trial. Volunteers placed planks and walkways across the streams running through the preserve.

Skunk cabbages, the first flower of spring, push through the mud. Common in wet areas, you can spot them easily. They are stout green waxy looking plants with purple and red spots. Up close, they give off a rotten aroma, attracting flies that pollinate them, hence the name skunk cabbage. Two Februarys ago, I came through here after a light snow, and they were in bloom. Snow and ice melted around the plants, which maintain a constant temperature of about sixty degrees.

A short distance into the preserve the red and blue trails split. The blue trail branches to the left over a wooden walkway and into some tall grass. I follow the red trail. The streams run clear. Some foam rests on top, and sand lines the bottom of the streams. Water moves quick. Although the trees still sleep, the undergrowth starts to stir. The sticker bushes have their leaves out. Common in the preserve you'll find a bush called "hearts-a-bustin". Rare elsewhere in New York State, this endangered bush can be found throughout the swamp. Later in the year, their red berries will emerge, and break open, looking like tiny broken hearts. Most of the trees haven't started to bud yet, but are about to. In a few weeks the leaves will start coming out.

Various evergreens scatter around, providing some color, and beech still hold onto their dead brown leaves from autumn. Without the foliage, you can see the ground contours, and all the little streams flowing through the swamp. A flock of red winged black birds congregates in the branches above, back from their winter home. Within the next few days, the flock will disperse. The birds nest individually, and will congregate again in the fall. Six weeks from now, the swamp will be so overgrown, you won't be able to see the ground, except for on the paths. Tulip trees are the biggest trees you'll find, and easiest to identify without foliage. Their flowers look like little yellow and orange tulips, and bloom in April and May. The larger ones in the preserve have trunks with a diameter of approximately five feet. The stands of trees grow on drier mounds rising above the mud in little hammock areas. Water flows around their roots.

The trail turns right at an upland area. A hill rises on the left, and a pond sits on the right. Fresh duckweed covers the surface of the pond. The trail brings you up to the hill, and follows a fence, until it reaches the train tracks, and heads back into the swamp. A boardwalk and bench allow you to rest and get a good view of the pond. Behind the boardwalk train tracks mark the edge of the preserve. A culvert going under the tracks allows water to flow into Beaver Pond. Normally, a variety of waterfowl swim on the lake, but today there is only one Canadian Honker. The rest of his flock congregate on the on the other side of the tracks, out of sight, but not out of ear shot. Looking through the grass on the edge of the pond, you can see a mute swan building up her nest. Looking into the pond, I see a single trout, a little over two feet long swimming close to the surface. Following the trail a short distance returns me to the parking lot.

Having walked the red trail in about forty minutes, I decide to walk the blue trail. The blue trail follows Beaver Brook, the main stream feeding into the swamp. The stream flows quickly on the left and the swamp sits quietly on the right. Along the stream, yellow buttercups bloom. Throughout the year different wildflowers emerge and disappear. In the fall, mushrooms will emerge and disappear like wildflowers. The brook passes under a manmade rise that used to be "Old Swamp Road". The trail follows the stream to Giambrino Pond, surrounded by English ivy and named after a man who loved and frequented this preserve. The ivy contrasts with the surrounding undergrowth, staying green all winter. As you approach the pond, you cross over a wooden bridge. A very old tulip tree guards the bridge, drinking from the stream. The trunk measures twelve feet around. Several tulip trees this size and age occupy the area around the stream. Quite a few smaller ones also populate the preserve. Considered "old growth" tulip trees, may live as long as 600 years; although, these trees aren't quite that old. [1]

The blue trail turns left at Frost Mill Road, leading back to the parking lot. Along the side, violets bloom through the grass in the ground. Catbrier already starts growing in. Spring awakes, preparing for the year ahead. Preparing for birds to return, preparing for flowers to bloom, preparing for summer heat, preparing for

---

[1] The Queens Giant is a tulip tree that is 133 feet high, and has a circumference of 18'. Estimates place it at 400 years old. The city fenced in the Queens Giant to protect it from hooligans. A sign near the tree reminds visitors "...Treat this oldest Sylvan citizen of our City with the respect that it deserves. It has survived miraculously from a time when native Maneticock people trod softly beneath it to an age when automobiles roar by oblivious to its presence. If we leave it undisturbed, it may live among us for another hundred years or so."

mosquitoes to come to life, preparing for flowers to turn to fruit, preparing for the leaves to change color and fall to the ground, so the world can sleep once again.

Directions:

Shu Swamp is located on Frost Mill Road in Mill Neck.
From Route 25a, proceed north on Wolver Hollow Road.
Make a right on Chicken Valley Road.
Make a right on Frost Mill Road.
You'll find the parking lot immediately before the train tracks.

Skunk Cabbage

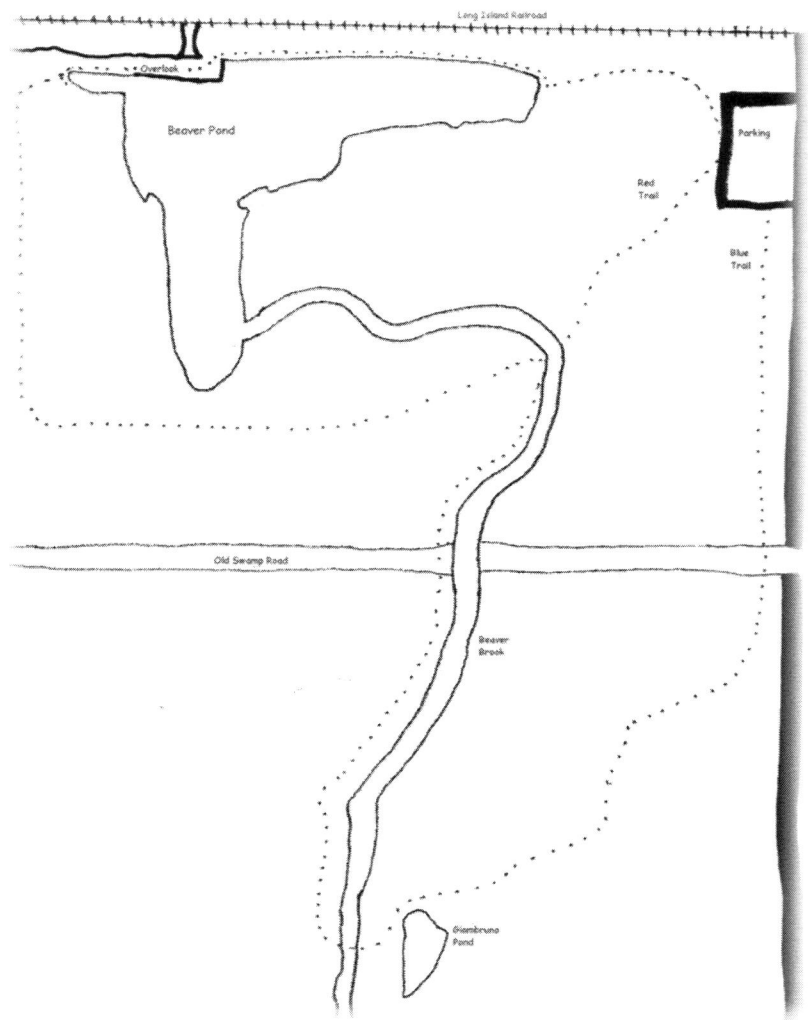

Figure 1 Shu Swamp

TAKAPAUSHA

March 31st

Takapausha preserve surrounds Seaford Creek, marking the vague boundary between Seaford and Massapequa. It offers a small oasis between the houses visible on either side of the preserve. Its narrow eighty five acres runs from Merrick Road to Jerusalem Avenue. The Seaford Creek, fed by springs under Jerusalem Avenue, serves as the primary drainage area for the communities on either side of the preserve. Intersecting roads divide the preserve into three sections. The southernmost goes from Merrick Road to Sunrise Highway. The middle section goes from Sunrise Highway to Clark Street, and the Northern section goes from Clark Street to Jerusalem Avenue. The main trails loop around, and smaller trails side trails cross the preserve. A parking lot and museum can be found on Jefferson Avenue at the south end of the preserve. You'll also find a manmade pond at the corner of Seaford Avenue and Merrick Road, where Seaford Creek flows under Merrick Road, and out to the bay. I grew up a short distance from here, and my first one on one experiences with local nature happened in this preserve. The museum once kept injured hawks and owls in an enclosure behind the museum. Even though the preserve is narrow enough that you can always see the backyards and streets along the edges, it somehow manages to be big enough to allow you to tune all that out, and allow you to just enjoy the stream and wildlife.

The pond at the south end is the only landscaped area of the preserve. A few mallards and Canadian geese swim in the shallow pond. In a few weeks, they will nest, and shortly after that swim around the pond with their new families. South of Merrick Road, Seaford Creek continues into an estuary and flows into the bay. The water changes from freshwater to saltwater as it gets closer to the bay. Because of the mix of salt and fresh water, a diverse assortment of waterfowl lives here during spring and summer. Signs around the pond remind people to not feed the waterfowl. Parents often come here with their kids to feed stale bread to the ducks. Nature provides plenty for the animals to eat. Feeding wildlife harms the animals more than it helps. When people feed the ducks, they stop feeding on the plants and animals in their natural ecosystems, and become malnourished. The ducks, fish and turtles don't go to the corner store and drink bottled water; they drink the water in the pond. Uneaten human food and excessive duck poo promote germs and sickens the animals.

    From a bridge on the north east corner of the pond you can see a stand of Atlantic white cedar with tops nearly eighty feet tall. The stand used to be much bigger, over the years they've been falling one by one. Atlantic white cedar once covered 60,000 acres on the south shore. These trees love swamps. People harvested their wood for ship masts, because the trees grow pin straight and very tall. Cedar also naturally resists most insects, mold, bacteria and other agents of decomposition, making the wood ideally suited for various types of construction. Atlantic white cedar still grows in the wetter areas of Suffolk, including a fairly large forest in the Cranberry Bogs Preserve in Riverhead. The ones in Takapausha are the only ones left in Nassau County. Up until several years ago, there were two in Brookside preserve in Baldwin, but they recently died. The ones in Takapausha will likely fall within the next several years, and there are no saplings to replace them.

    The trail, marked by yellow and white blazes, begins at the northwest corner of the pond. At the start of the trail, I notice two holly trees on the right side slowly being covered with vines. English ivy covers the ground.

Raspberry bushes and catbrier begin pushing their leaf buds out. The streams run from the north to the south through here. South of Sunrise Highway, the trail loops around two bridges, which cross over the streams.

  A large wooden bridge close to Sunrise Highway crosses over a marsh area. Today, you can see the results of a recent fire which burned the marsh grass down to the mud. With the grass burned down, you get a view of the twists and turns of the stream, and an idea of exactly how big the marsh grass area is. As you might expect, a few too many empty beer cans litter the ground. Green shoots, just under a foot in height, push up through the charred ground. Before summer arrives, the marsh grass will reach seven or eight feet high, and grow thick enough to once again hide the curves of the stream, the contours of the ground, and the accumulated trash.

  At the very north end of this section of the preserve the culvert directing Seaford Creek under Sunrise Highway opens up. Through most of the year, painted turtles and fish stay this area. I look in the water today, as I always do when passing here, and see a red-eared slider swimming in the stream.

  Once north of Sunrise, the trail goes through some brush and leads under the railroad tracks. Once you pass under the railroad tracks, the preserve opens up. The brickwork and rusted machinery on your left remain from the turn of the last century. It used to be part of a system that pumped water into Brooklyn. A shallow, spring fed pond appears right in front of you. Giant koi swim in this pond, most likely released from someone's aquarium. A grassy area on the southeast corner of the pond provides a habitat for toads, which call out, croaking during the summer. Several egrets also call this pond home.

  The middle section of the preserve fluctuates between being a little muddy, and completely submerged, depending on the amount rainfall we've been getting.

Today, it is fairly dry. Just like the area south of Sunrise, there isn't just one stream, but several streams that meander through here. Yellow flowers bloom along the streams.

Less than a mile past the railroad tracks, the trail crosses over Clark Boulevard into the Northern part of the preserve. A few mountain laurels line the side of the path. Ivy covers the ground and violets bloom. The trees are waking up, pushing out leaf buds. As I pass through here in the later part of the afternoon, spring peepers chirp loudly. Spring peepers are small frogs, nearly impossible to see. Their high pitched calls blend together in a loud rhythmless harmony.

I continue up the trail on the west side of the preserve. Between the maple and beech, several types of evergreens, including holly and yew, grow. The yew most likely escaped from someone's front lawn. Eventually the trail reaches a raised stand of white pine. How this stand got here remains a mystery. Somebody probably planted it at some time in the past, and the pine trees now thrive as if they always belonged here. Under the pine rests a soft fragrant layer of needles, beneath that, sand.

Once past the pines, the trail leads to the northern end of the preserve. Once summer reaches its peak, the undergrowth grows so thick, the trail becomes barely passable. At the northern end of the preserve, Seaford Creek trickles from a culvert under Jerusalem Avenue into a stream bed which is completely dry today. The traffic on Jerusalem Avenue provides a sudden reminder that I am in the middle of a heavily populated and developed area. Several fallen, uprooted maple trees in the stream bed sprout tenacious little buds from the newer branches. The older branches lying in the stream bed hold debris caught in their branches, including a dead and decaying opossum.

A wood walkway crosses the stream bed, and the trail continues south down the east side of the preserve. The environmental version of the British Invasion, English ivy grows up the sides of trees, gradually pulling them down. Walking south along the east side of the preserve, you'll find the crumbling remains of ivy covered sidewalks. They are left over from residential lots developers never sold. The trail proceeds south, through upland areas consisting mainly of maple and oak, getting muddier the further south you go, until you return to the pond at Merrick Road.

Directions:

From Route 135, travel east on Merrick Road.
Make a Left on Washington Avenue.
The entrance to the Museum and Parking lot will be on the right. The Pond is located on the corner of Merrick Road and Seaford Avenue.

Mallards on The Pond

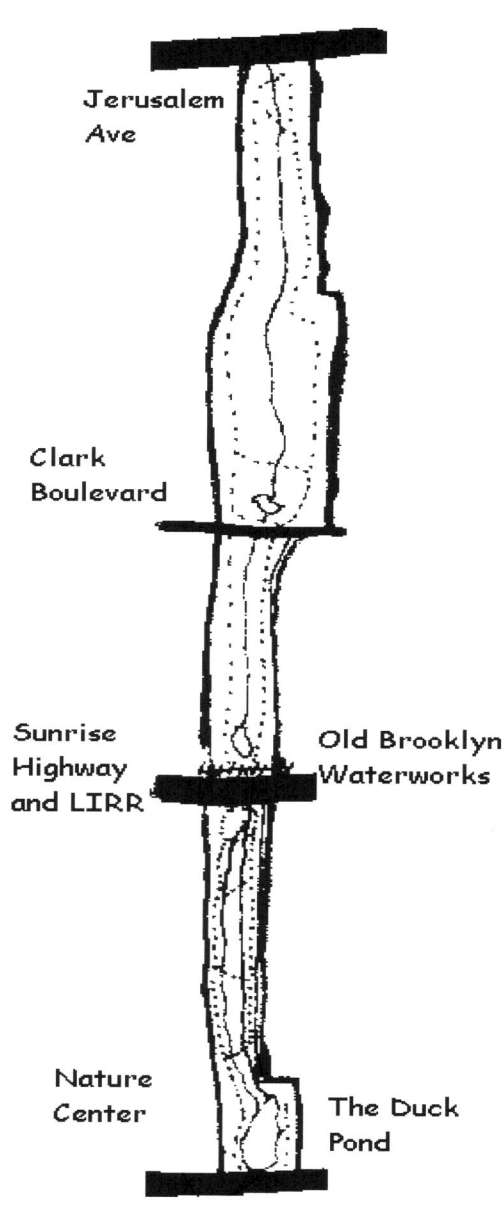

Figure 2 Tackapausha

APRIL

Bullfrog in the Sun

LAKELAND PRESERVE

April 8th

Lakeland Preserve connects with the northern part of Connetquot State Park. Although other, smaller, trails lead to different parts of the preserve, the only marked trail is the section of the Long Island Greenbelt passing through the preserve. A section of the Greenbelt stretching slightly over a mile extends from the parking lot on Johnson Avenue to Veteran's Memorial Highway. You can spend several hours exploring the county run preserve, and the northern Section of Connetquot State Park, or you can simply enjoy a brief stroll within Lakeland Preserve. Developers almost turned the preserve into an industrial park, but the local community spoke up, and convinced politicians to stop development, and leave this little preserve under Mother Nature's care. Consider what a polluted mess the area downstream, including Connetquot State Park and the Bayard Cutting Arboretum, would have been had the land been developed for industrial use.

The trail begins with a system of wheelchair accessible boardwalks leading over the springs. The boardwalks remain one of the best kept secrets among Long Island's many nature trails. Without this boardwalk area, this type of habitat would be completely inaccessible without waders. The walkway goes through the swamp, springs, and the accompanying Honeysuckle Pond. Some twists and turns on the boardwalk make it feel bigger than it is. Water reaches depths of about two feet. At the bottom, a mix of mud, algae and sand give the swamp a much deeper appearance. You can casually stroll the whole network of boardwalks in less than an hour. Benches and secluded areas make it fairly easy to find some solitude and seclusion here.

Fishing is legal with the correct permit. Trout and sunfish are common. Turtles, muskrats, and a variety of waterfowl also live in the pond. A small group of wood ducks and mallards swim around, and a pair of blue jays chase each other. Duckweed covers the stiller, swampy, areas. Stands of maple and beech trees grab hold of the edges of the pond. On the more upland areas surrounding the pond, pitch pine and oak mix, as they do throughout the pine barrens.

Honeysuckle Pond rests at the base of the Ronkonkoma Moraine. The water here, along with some connected swamps further south, forms the headwaters for the Connetquot River. Springs similar to the type found at Lakeland feed all the rivers on Long Island. Water pushes up through a layer of sand, until it reaches the surface, and then flows out to the bay. Connetquot Brook grows into Connetquot River, draining into the Great South Bay east of Heckscher State Park in Islip. The water fell as rain at one point, and remained in the sand for decades before being pushed back up to the surface in this particular spot.

Once past the pond area, the Long Island Greenbelt Trail continues for a short way through some pine and oak uplands and proceeds under the railroad tracks. Once past the railroad tracks, you enter the northern section of Connetquot State Park. Proceeding south, I notice an area that was recently burned in a small brushfire. The tracks from the trucks that came in to put it out are still new, and the smell of charred wood hangs in the air. Several fire breaks and a paved road divide the area, and also provide for some relaxed hiking. The paved road runs parallel to Vet's Highway, and crosses over the beginnings of the river. Smaller trails cross this section of the preserve as well. With a little creativity, you can create your own loop trail. This section of the preserve is big enough to enjoy, but small enough that it is hard to get lost in. The soil on the trails consists mainly of sand and rock.

Moss covers the ground, although it seems a bit drier than normal. The swampy low areas, referred to by some as "The Dismal Swamp", aren't as damp as they usually are. Shrubs just starting to bud, and smaller plants, just beginning to emerge, offer a little green. In a few weeks, the undergrowth will be thick, particularly in the wetter low lying areas. On previous visits, I have seen deer tracks and deer scat, but I have yet to see any deer on this side of Vet's Highway. On the other side of Veteran's Memorial Highway, in Connetquot State park, a sizable herd of white tailed deer takes up residence. The fence along Vet's Highway keeps them off the road and out of harm's way. Eventually, you reach the south gate at Veteran's Highway. You may cross the highway here, and explore the rest of Connetquot State Park, or you may turn back.

If you hike with a friend, and want to cover a longer stretch of the Long Island Greenbelt, you can park one car on the shoulder of Vet's Highway, and another at your destination, and avoid having to back track over areas you've already hiked through. The parking lot at Lakeland is good for that purpose also. Using the parking lot at Lakeland Park as a starting point, you can head south. Sunrise Highway, at the south end of Connetquot is approximately five miles away. Montauk Highway is a little more than six miles away, and Heckscher Park at the Great South Bay is about ten and a half miles away. Heading north, three miles brings you to the top of the Ronkonkoma Moraine, slightly north of Motor Parkway. Two benches mark the spot, and the view is worth the hike. Nearly five miles to the north, the Nissequogue River emerges quietly from a swamp. Stump Pond, a dammed up section of the Nissequogue, sits ten miles away, and the Nissequogue River ultimately empties into the sound at Sunken Meadow State Park twenty miles north, if you follow the trail.

Directions:

From exit 58 on the Long Island Expressway (Old Nichols Road), head south.
Make a left on Johnson Avenue.
The Preserve is 1/2 of a mile down the road on the right side.
You can also park on the north side Veteran's Memorial Highway, and access the preserve through Connetquot State Park.

Daffodils

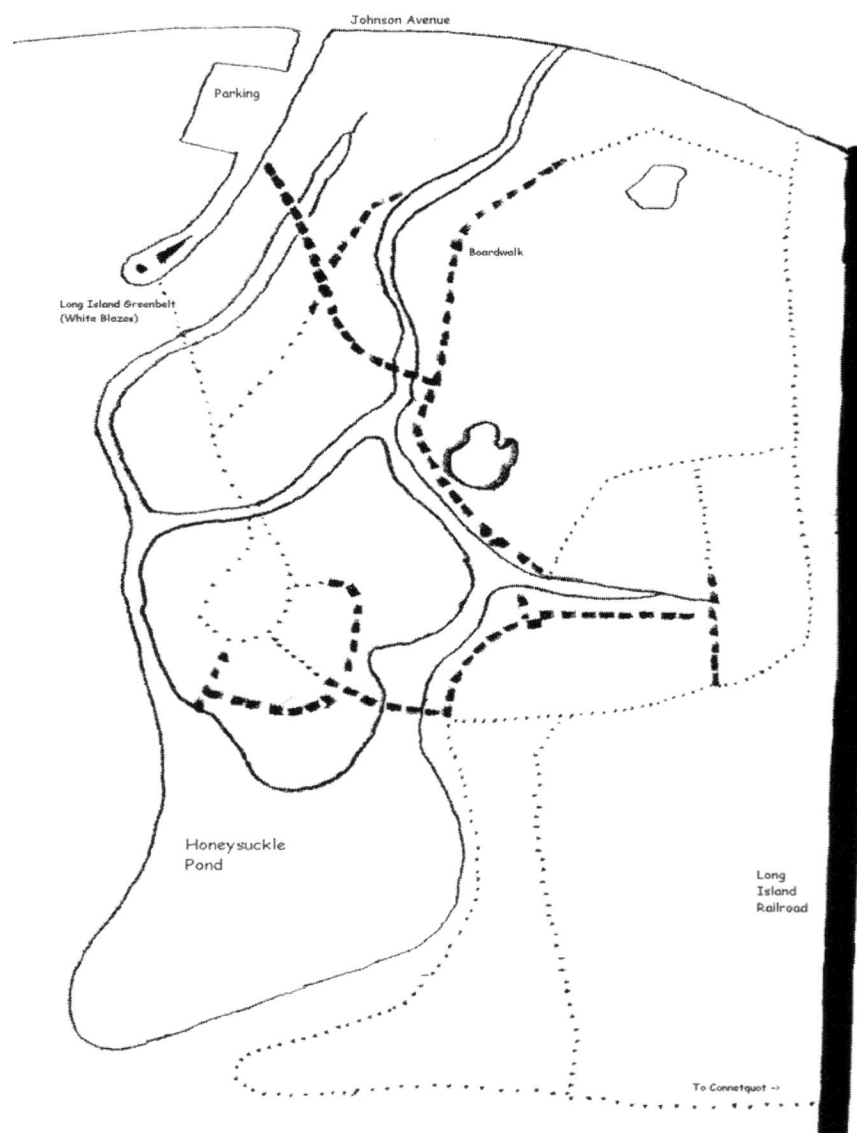

Figure 3 Lakeland Preserve

West Hills

April 15th

Mystery surrounds these hills. One can only speculate as to why West Hills lies east of East Hills. The name itself isn't as important as the fact that this place exists. The hills constitute one of the more elevated areas along the Ronkonkoma Moraine. In addition to encountering wildlife, you may encounter a visitor from another realm. Various local legends claim ghosts and tortured spirits inhabit these hills, particularly the area around Mount Misery. Two main parking areas allow for access to the park. One is accessible from Round Swamp Road, and the other located on Sweet Hollow Road. Suffolk County manages the preserve, allowing hiking, horseback riding, dog walking and camping at a fairly large camp ground available to Scout Groups, and other youth organizations. As the name suggests, it is all hills and upland areas, although a few ponds can be found. This contrasts with most of Long Islands other preserves, located on the water, around streams, or in generally flat areas.

    Walt Whitman was born in a house that still stands at the bottom of Jayne's Hill on the east side of the preserve. You can walk these trails and imagine yourself in the shoes of the poet, traveling back in time and visualizing the island as he saw it, walking to the top of Jayne's Hill, which, at 401 feet above sea level is the highest spot on Long Island. A much less demanding climb than Mount Everest, you won't need a Sherpa to guide you on your assent. Instead, you can bring your dog.

    Many trails cross the preserve. Most are poorly marked, if they are marked at all. You can get disoriented and lost, or you can bring a compass and practice orienteering. The variety of trails, and size of the preserve offer hikers a completely different experience on each visit. Just make sure you leave the preserve before the sun sets and the spirits roam the woods.

Today is the first truly warm day this season. A bright red cardinal stands out against maple and oak branches starting to bud. Portions of the forest constitute a climax oak forest with a mountain laurel understory. Beech and maple populate parts of the preserve as well. Through the winter, there's been little precipitation, leaving fallen branches quite dry. Last week, a brush fire burned four acres worth of forest near Mount Misery Road. In time, it will grow back.

The red dot trail, a two mile loop, starts at the parking lot near Round Swamp Road and the visitor's center. It branches off, and loops around at several points. Red cedar scatter around a portion of the trail. A garter snake cautiously makes its way across the path. It slithers for a bit, stops, looks around, continues, stops again, and returns to the leaves. Proceeding further, I reach two straight lines of spruce planted years ago. They continue for several hundred feet, ascending straight to the sky. Soon, the trail leads through the camping area. Tent and lean-to sites, bear the names of long gone local tribes. After passing through the camping area, the trail crosses a mowed activity field. A little white butterfly flies around the red cedar in the middle of the field. Past the field, the red dot trail proceeds up a hill, and back to the park's visitor center.

In another section of the preserve, the white/blue trail begins at the parking lot off of Sweet Hollow Road, leads up Jayne's Hill, and around the perimeter of the eastern third of preserve. A ridge comes up on the east side of the preserve, and roughly parallels route 110. This ridge faces east providing one of the best views of Long Island. You can start up the hill and loop around, or you can go to the North end of the parking lot, and look for the white blazes. Horses use the wider, sandy, trails. Mountain laurel covers the sides of the hills. Their woody branches twist around, with a shredded bark, similar to cedar. An evergreen with oval and waxy leaves, mountain laurels remain visible during winter. Springtime brings white and pink flowers to the tips of their branches. On the taller hills, you get a real sense of their height in comparison to the surrounding areas. The trees haven't completely leafed out yet, so you can still get a good view of the contours of the land, just like you would during the winter, but with bits of green starting to poke through the leaf litter. Eventually you reach an ascending section of the trail with logs laid across it like steps. The ascent is gradual. Not nearly as strenuous as the hills in Cold Spring Harbor, Jayne's hill is a very easy stroll by comparison.

  Walking up to the highest point on Long Island, I wonder, what should I expect…The bearded ghost of Walt Whitman letting me in on the meaning of life? I get to the top. A few feet away from a USGS marker, a graffitied boulder, and two park benches mark the spot. I try for a view towards the southeast, but a water tower is in the way. Next to the water tower, a cell phone tower blocks more of the view. Walt Whitman never had to worry about cell phone towers blocking his view. In Whitman's day, this area was all fields, so he was able to see the Atlantic Ocean and the Long Island Sound. Over the last one hundred and fifty years, the woods won, and the fields reverted back into woodland. Today, the trees grow thick enough to block any meaningful view.

  I proceed down the hill. The descent from the top of Jayne's hill is as gradual as the climb. As with the rest of the park, small hills and ridges, give you a little workout, but none of it really wears you out. The trail reaches a low spot between two hills where water collects, and drains down. It is not quite a stream, but more of a mud patch expanding into a small shallow pond. Skunk cabbages, rare in West Hills, grow out of the mud. At the end of the pond, a lone tulip tree sucks up the water, and the land starts to rise again. After a short distance, the path crosses Reservoir Road, and inexplicably, the markings change from white to light blue. The trail follows behind some people's homes and up the ridge running parallel to Route 110. If you were to take any of the trails heading down the hill, it would return you to the parking lot and picnic area where the blue and white trail begin.

      Some amazing views can be enjoyed along this ridge. My favorite is in a spot where you'll find a steep drop off, at the bottom of which sits the foundation for an abandoned building. Because of the drop off, there are no trees obstructing your immediate view. It's difficult to estimate how far you can see from here. Without binoculars, the radio towers in Hauppauge are clearly visible, and a water tower which might be Smithtown, or is at least in that direction is easily within sight. The view goes much further than that. Trees on the ground hide most of the development, so the view appears very natural. Today, because the leaves are new, mostly I see greenish yellow. Later in the summer, the greens will get darker, until fall arrives, when you will see more red and orange. As I stand here, a woodpecker lands on the tree above me and gets to work. It is time for me to go back down the hill. I guarantee that if you make the trip to this spot, you won't be disappointed, and will return, most likely with a friend.

      The hauntings reported in the preserve occur in the less traveled section located south of the Northern State Parkway, between Sweet Hollow and Mount Misery Roads. There isn't a parking lot, but you can park on the east side of Sweet Hollow Road, next to the cemetery. Long Island's native tribes considered this area cursed. The ghosts roaming this area include a spectral woman dressed in white robes, and a disheveled looking man carrying a basket of severed heads. According to local legend, an insane asylum burned down at some point in the past, with all the crazies locked inside of course. All that remained was a pile of roasted nuts. On cold nights, you can still hear their screams echoing through the forest. Some people who stop here for a park and spark report seeing U.F.Os, and other strange lights. Try not to get lost on the numerous trails crossing through this section of the preserve. None of them are marked. My compass wasn't working reliably on the day I visited here, so I relied on my intuition and my memory to find my way around.

    From the entrance across from the cemetery, the trail can take you either left, right, or straight ahead. White pines stand in a straight line on your left. White pine predominate this portion of woods. Red cedar and other trees and shrubs mix in with the pine. Young poison ivy plants, with a reddish tinge to their leaves emerge through the cover of pine needles on the forest floor. Up the hill, oak and mountain laurel crowd out the white pine. At the top of the hill, you can hear the Northern State Parkway below, but trees block any view of the parkway. You easily forget the preserve stands in the middle of a heavily populated area. Like the ridge along route 110, you can see a good distance, but the top of this hill faces north, instead of east.

    As I descend the hill, I pass through a section recently burned in a brush fire. By fire nature, is wholly regenerated. Unlike the pitch pine forests out east, oak forests do not rely on periodic fires to reproduce. In a severe fire oak trees will burn, but root systems stay intact, and new shoots emerge from the stumps and start over. It doesn't appear that this fire did a tremendous amount of damage. Some of the oak are severely burned, and will probably die, but most of the trees, scorched around their bases, push out leaf buds from their branches.

As understory trees, the mountain laurel bore the brunt of the blaze. Although a threat to homeowners in the area, occasional fires are a necessary part of nature. They clean the forest floor, and rejuvenate the sandy soil. Before the trail loops back around into the white pine area, it goes through a section with more new growth, in the form of birch and aspen. Referred to as pioneer species, these trees show a transition between farmer's old fields, and more mature oak and pine forests.

I covered an area of about two miles in this section of the preserve, and, in truth, barely covered a third of the Mount Misery area. Much to my disappointment, there were no UFOs, no Mothman sightings, no ghosts, and I didn't see anybody walking around with a basket of severed heads. Maybe I'll have better luck on my next visit.

Directions:

From The L.I.E, head North on Route 110.
Make a left on Old Country Road.
Make a Right on Sweet Hollow Road.
A Cemetery on the right side of the road stands across from the entrance to the Mount Misery section of the preserve. Follow Sweet Hollow Road across Gwynne Road, and a large parking lot will be on the right. You can access the blue and white trail and Jayne's Hill from this parking lot.

To park at the High Hold Drive Entrance:
From the L.I.E., head North on Round Swamp Road, and make a right on High Hold Road. A small parking lot will be on your left. You can access the Red Trail here.

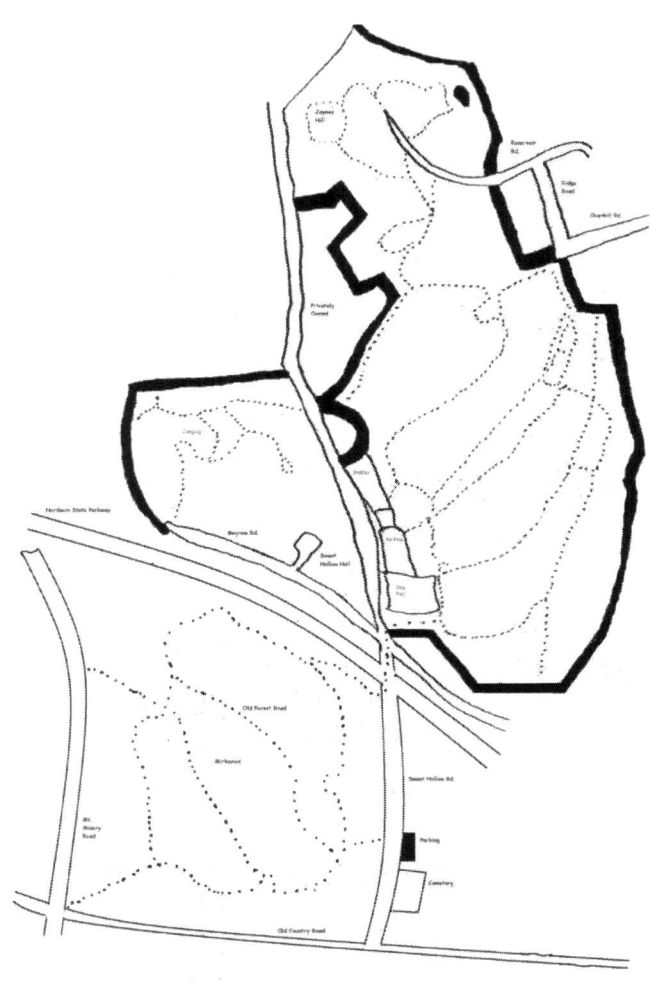

Figure 4 West Hills

JAMAICA BAY WILDLIFE REFUGE

April 22

  I visited this preserve on Earth Day. The clouds drop a little rain. The wind pushes fifty degree air across the bay, and a nor'easter will dump gallons of rain over the next twenty four hours. I want to be home before the rain really starts pouring. As uncomfortable as the rain is, the plants welcome it. Through the winter, and coming into the spring, there hasn't been enough of it. It's been a drier than average year so far. The nor'easter will quickly make up some of the deficit.

  This preserve sits south of JFK airport in the middle of Jamaica Bay. Over the past two hundred years, development drastically changed the bay. Historically, Jamaica Bay had an average depth of between four and five feet. Acres of salt marsh islands poked above the surface of the bay. Between the barrier beach of the Rockaways, and the south shore of Long Island, salt water mixed with freshwater fed by streams. The shallow waters, the blending of salt and fresh water, and tidal marshes all worked together to provide breeding grounds for various fish, and homes for oysters, mussels, along with the shorebirds and larger fish that feed on them. Development, including removing islands, creating island, dredging parts of the bay, paving over and diverting fresh water creeks, changed the habitat, and caused the loss of many species. In addition to the changes brought by rearranging Jamaica Bay, the area has also been polluted and over harvested. Fish, turtles, oysters and mussels were caught here, to be sold in street stands, and gourmet restaurants. Over the past several years, the city and state have been implementing plans to preserve what is left of the bay, and restore the damaged habitats.

The U.S. National Park Service manages the preserve, and requires visitors to obtain a permit before entering the preserve grounds. The knowledgeable rangers spread their enthusiasm for the preserve, answering any questions, and updating visitors with current information with what's on the trails. The National Parks employ great people in all their parks. Their enthusiasm is contagious. The West Pond trail begins immediately outside the visitor center. It is approximately a mile and half around. A longer, loosely connected set of trails circles the East Pond, across Cross Bay Boulevard. Gravel covers the West Pond Trail. You will find a few permissible detours, but it is best to stay on the trial. This habitat is very sensitive to erosion. A number of different shore birds nest here, as do diamond back terrapins. Straying from designated trails puts their nests at risk. Long Island rests in the middle of the Atlantic flyway, the open water and grassland allow for an unobstructed view of the dozens of different species of birds that make their way through here during the year.

After a short walk, the bay is visible on my left. West Pond is on my right. The tide is low, and the wind blowing on the water makes it choppy. Honeysuckle blooms along the side of the trail. Other shrubs include bayberry. In a few weeks, osprey will return to their nests along the bay. Usually you could expect to see boaters and kayakers on the water, but, because of the weather, they all stayed home. Phragmites line the edges of the pond. later this year, Hurricane Sandy will hit, creating a breach, about fifteen feet wide and three or four feet deep, connecting the pond with the bay, and allowing more salt water into the pond. The breach, located a few hundred feet east of the old Terrapin Trail, makes following the trail completely around West Pond impossible.

Interestingly, the park closed the terrapin trail indefinitely, because of erosion from Hurricane Irene which visited here in 2011. Change is the only constant in nature.

The pond provides a brackish mix of salt and fresh water to its inhabitants. An egret wades at the end closer to me, and a flock of ducks congregates at one end of the pond, swimming in unison.

Because of the sandy soil, patches of yucca and colonies of prickly pear cactus grow alongside the beach rose throughout the preserve. Both the yucca and cactus will blossom in late June, at the same time diamond back terrapins climb up on to the beach to lay their eggs. When blooming, yuccas grow clusters of white flowers on stalks, which is why people also call them "Ghosts in the Graveyard". In the nineteenth and early part of the twentieth century, people over hunted the diamond back terrapins. Today, they often get caught in derelict crab traps and die. The turtles spend most of their lives in the bay, and only come on land to dig holes in the sand and lay eggs. During nesting season, diamond backs occasionally cause air traffic delays when they walk out on the tarmac at nearby JFK airport. Through the efforts of conservationists, Their numbers continue to rise, but their long term survival ultimately depend on the health of the bays and salt marshes they call home.

The turtles may not be nesting yet, but the Canadian geese are. At one point, the geese were threatened with extinction, but now, the geese are probably the most common waterfowl in North America. No longer hunted the geese adapt well to life in urban areas. As I walk along the path, I count five geese, in fairly close proximity to one another, sitting protectively on clutches of eggs. They eye me suspiciously as I walk by, and their mates hiss antagonistically. The geese build their nests right on the grass in a fairly open area. Within a month, these mothers will be leading their gaggles of little yellow chicks around the bay.

On the side of the trail, I notice a cherry sapling with a gypsy moth caterpillar nest on the branches. This is the first gypsy moth nest I've seen this season. There will certainly be many more. Invasive pests from Europe, gypsy moths breed faster than birds can eat them. After I make my way around the pond, the rain and wind start to pick up a bit. A wooded area, along one of the side trails has a stand of holly trees. In the upland areas, you'll find birch, holly and cherry scattered about. Willow oaks grow in the more upland area. Willow oaks are named for the long slender leaves that resemble willow leaves. The trail goes back through a shrub area and ends back at the visitor's center.

      Trails on the east side of Cross Bay Boulevard offer plenty for birdwatchers. East Pond is much bigger, but the trails don't follow all the way around the pond. You have to piece together marked trails with fire breaks and a service road. The section of trail between the railroad tracks and the east side of the pond washed out during Hurricane Sandy, making passage impossible. A small section of trail close to the visitor's center has a few bird blinds, and circles a small pond, called Big John's Pond. At the north end, near a gravel road used by the railroad, you will find an extensive birch forest. Hurricane Sandy pushed sand around their bases, hopefully, the changes won't kill them.

Directions:

From the Belt Parkway, take Cross Bay Boulevard South (Exit 17S).
Cross over the Joseph Addabbo -- North Channel Bridge. The entrance is a mile and a half south of the bridge on the right.

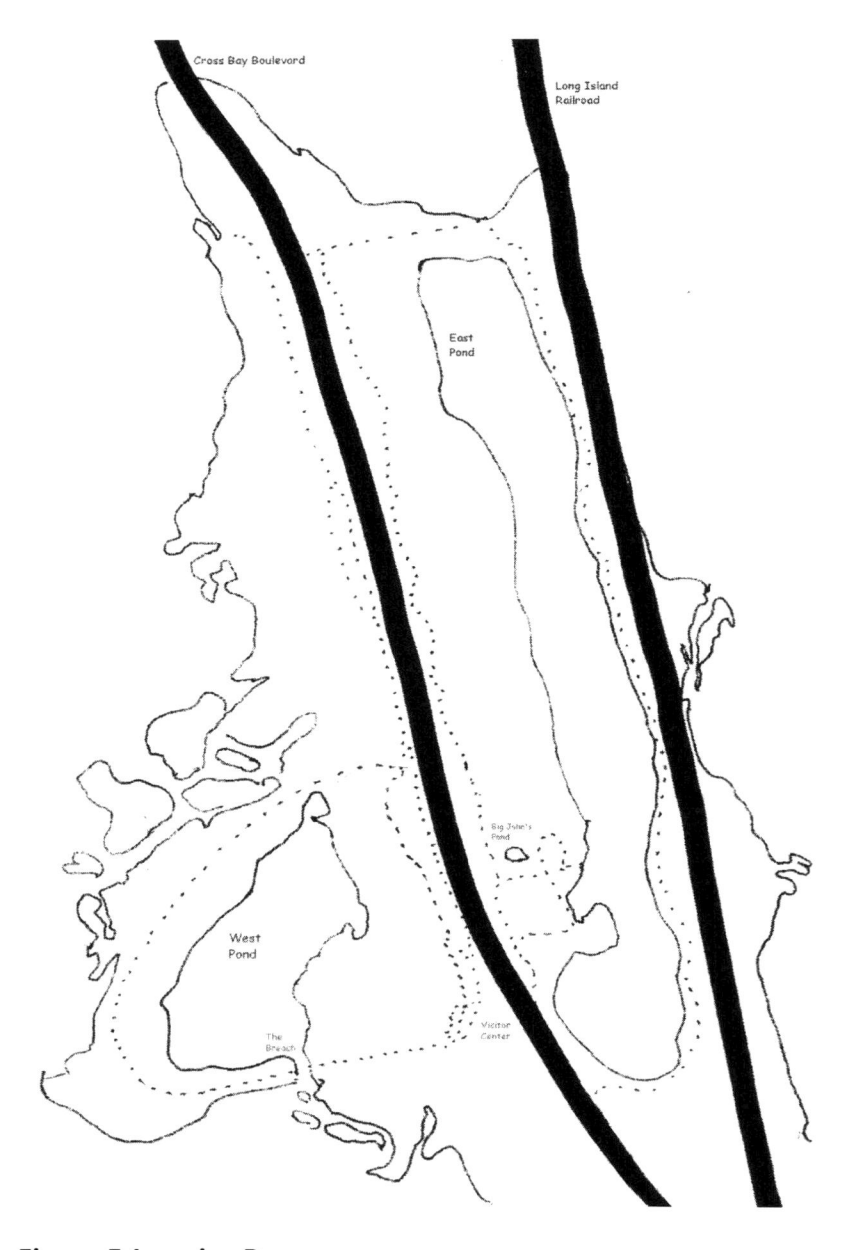

Figure 5 Jamaica Bay

CRANBERRY BOGS

April 28th

Cranberry Bogs preserve offers a quick loop trail, about a mile in length, circling Sweezy's Pond. Hikes through here can be combined with a cedar swamp on the opposite side of County Route 51 and David Sarnoff preserve. From the parking area, a wide trail surrounded by pitch pine leads to Sweezy's Pond. The Woodhull brothers made the pond at the end of the nineteenth century by damming the Little River and flooding its adjoining marsh land. At the pond, a sign points left, indicating the direction of the unmarked trail around the pond. Venturing off the trail leads you deep into mud or water. Looking out over the pond, you will see a shallow grass area on the left side of the pond, and a stand of Atlantic white cedar directly across from where the trail begins. Oak covered with lichens mixes in with the pitch pine. The lichens constitute a combination of fungus and algae living in a symbiotic relationship.

Heading around the pond, a bridge crosses over Little River, a flooded marsh area flowing into the pond. Looking into the water, I see a snapping turtle, slightly over a foot long. Some blue dragonflies fly above. These are the first dragonflies I've seen this season. On the other side of the bridge, an extensive stand of Atlantic white cedar occupies the area closest to the pond. These trees need to grow in saturated soil.

Sphagnum moss grows around their bases. Unlike the sandy soil covering most of Long Island, the sphagnum retains a tremendous amount of water, allowing for thick patches of green on the forest floor. Pine and various oak make up the forest further away from the pond, where the ground remains soft and sandy. Soon, a small foot bridge crosses over a quick rocky brook. Ferns line the side of the brook, and a gargoyle guards the bridge. To the right a large fallen pitch pine opens a space in the canopy. You can see the sand in its roots, and the needles are still green. It has probably been less than a month since it fell.

  A short distance past the fallen pine, the trail splits. The left trail tapers off into the swamp. The main trial on the right continues around the pond. This is where the Woodhull brothers dammed up Little River, creating Sweezy's Pond. The path leads past the cement foundation of the old pump house. Iron wheels rust inside the foundation. Phragmites and a maple sapling grow through the wheels. When this preserve was a cranberry farm, the farmers used water from the pond to flood the bogs on a seasonal basis to aid in the cranberry harvest. The trail follows along a raised sandy area, separating the pond on the right from a maple swamp on the left. The maple swamp fills in the places where cranberries were once grown. This area still floods with enough rainfall. Past the pond, an extensive network of perfectly straight channels left over from the farming operation, now fill with cedar. The techniques used to plant cranberries also accelerated the natural process of filling in the bogs. When growing cranberries, the farmers graded the marsh, and then lined the bottom with sand. Between plantings, they covered the floor of the marsh with more sand, so new plants could be planted.

  The bog itself has not been used to grow cranberries since the 1930's, and has been reverting back to its wild state since. Nature takes back what is hers. Because of the drainage ditches and other modifications made by the Woodhull brothers, sections of the bog have been transitioning to maple and oak forests, and some retain the moss, cedar and other plants more typical of a bog. Left to its own, a bog gradually fills in as dead plant matter piles up and spread out the water. This dead plant matter decomposes very slowly forming peat. Over time, the bog becomes a forest.

As the trail heads up to the beginning, the forest returns to its usual pine and oak composition. The trail around Sweezy's Pond can be covered in much less than an hour, and offers opportunities for bird watching. Various ducks, heron and geese live on the pond, and can be found hiding in the grass at the south end of the pond. In addition the thick cover provided by the cedar offer protection to a variety of song birds.

Directions:

From the L.I.E., take Exit 71 (County Route 94 east) to the traffic circle, and go south on County Route 63.
The entrance to the park is on the west side of route 63 in Riverhead.

Atlantic White Cedar on Sweezy's Pond

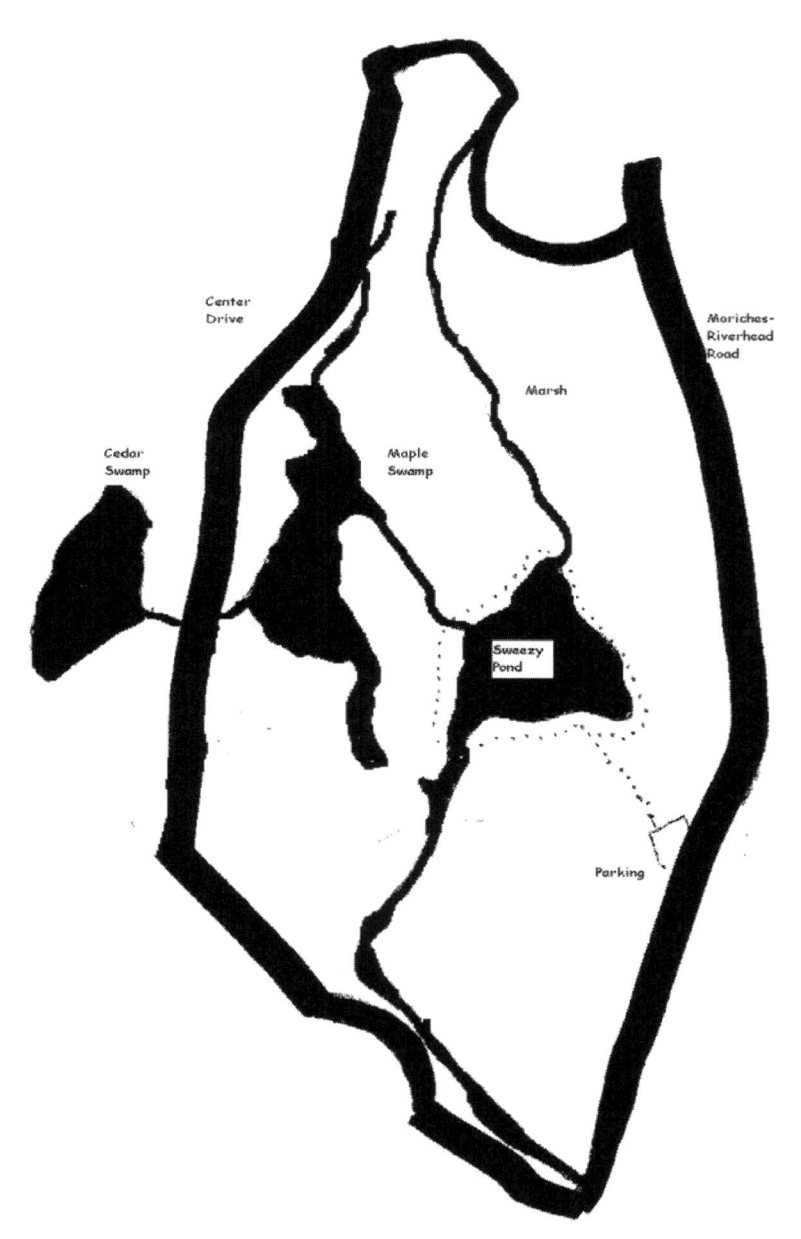

Figure 6 Cranberry Bogs

MAY

Gazebo at King Zog's Mansion

TARGET ROCK NATIONAL WILDLIFE REFUGE

May 1st

  Mayday, Beltane- Older European traditions considered May 1st to be the first day of summer. Today, the temperature is a little shy of forty nine degrees, and rain persists. The adage "April showers bring May flowers", seems reversed this year. It seems like April flowers brought May showers. Target Rock National Wildlife Refuge juts into Huntington Bay at the eastern tip of Lloyd's Neck. The ride along Lloyd Harbor Road leading to Target Rock can be as enjoyable as walking the preserve itself. Target Rock is two miles east of the much larger Caumsett State Park. This preserve left private hands in 1967, and Mother Nature's been taking it back since then.

  Overgrown fields cover a few sections of the preserve, but elsewhere, the habitats go directly from hardwood oak forest to the beach. Because it is early morning on a week day, and because the rain falls forcefully, I expect to be the only human visitor in the preserve today. Two main trails can be hiked, Warbler's Loop and Rocky Beach Trail. Rocky Beach trail is essentially a detour off of Warbler's loop, which leads to the beach. A smaller detour, appropriately called Gardiner's Path, also cuts through an area which used to be the formal gardens of the estate. Combined they cover approximately two miles, and can be walked in about an hour and a half, or a little longer if you take your time. Warbler's loop starts at the edge of a field in the process of gradually growing back in. Thick brambles in the field make great nesting places for various birds, particularly warblers. Because of the weather, the birds all hide today, taking cover in the dense brush.

Where the shrub area ends, a stand of Norway spruce, planted by the preserve's previous owners, rises up. On the left, the Rocky Beach Trail branches off down a hill through an oak forest until it reaches the beach. This morning I hear some rustling in the woods to my right, and see two white tailed deer running deeper into the woods. I must have startled them. They see, hear, and probably smell, me coming long before I have any sense of them. Before the trail reaches the sound, you will find a pond and a duck blind on the right. The duck blind allows visitors to sit quietly and watch the waterfowl in the pond without startling them. Brackish water fills the pond. The water of Huntington Bay floods it with saltwater as the tides rise, and freshwater flows in from upland areas. On the far end of the pond a stand of red cedar reaches upward. Around the edges, cord grass gives way to high tide brush. Another stand of red cedar grows closer to the beach. The cedar is home to a colony of olive hairstreak butterflies. Overlooking the beach, a wooden stand with a viewfinder can be used to view out into the harbor. Seaweed and Irish moss wash along the shore. Shells and driftwood mark the high tide line. The tide slowly recedes.

A red tailed hawk flies into the trees, and a flock of ducks rides the choppy waves in the bay. This beach is home to a colony of bank swallows. The swallows nest in holes they dig into the side of the bluffs. Parts of the beach are roped off to protect the nesting grounds of the piping plover, which lay eggs here during the summer.

Besides the bank swallows, plover, seagulls and other beach birds, target rock hosts a pair of osprey. The couple nests right on the boulder that gives the preserve its name. For people unfamiliar with Target Rock Wildlife Refuge, it got its name, because British naval ships used the giant boulder, which used to be in the bluffs, for target practice. Thanks to the pounding the bluffs took from British ordinance, the giant boulder now sits about fifty feet off shore. Being surrounded by water at all times, it sits completely out of reach of any animal looking to disturb the nest, and right in the middle of the osprey's preferred hunting area. The sound provides a limitless supply of fish, the osprey's favorite food. The nest is right across from the plover nests on the beach, and the bank swallow nests in the bluffs, but since the osprey don't eat bank swallows or plover, the birds can peacefully coexist.

Benjamin Franklin lobbied to have the osprey declared the national bird, instead of the bald eagle. With a wing span that can be almost six feet wide, these are amazing birds to watch hunt. The males and females take turns hunting. If you hang around the beach long enough, you will see one dive for a fish and bring it to the chick.

Ospreys were rare thirty years ago. Today they present one of the best examples of how a species can bounce back because of protection efforts. DDT, an ingredient in pesticides, did a job on the birds by interfering with their ability to make fully calcified eggs. Eggs broke in the nest and their numbers dropped drastically. Since the EPA banned DDT, conservation groups have been placing nesting platforms in estuaries around Long Island, and ospreys have become common again. You can see osprey just about anywhere on either the north or south shores of Long Island. They even nest right on the beach at Gardiner's Island.

I head back up to the trail to Warbler's Loop. Following the trail around, and back to the parking lot, it passes through some grown in gardens and old fields. Even though I wear a hat and raincoat, I'm soaked anyway. I see an elderly couple approach me on the path, the first people I've seen here today. They look drenched also. We smile and say hello. I imagine they are neighbors of the preserve, who walk here every morning rain or shine.

Directions:

From the L.I.E., take Exit 49 (Route 110).
Head North on Route 110 about 7 miles to Route 25A.
Make a left on Route 25A, and head west about a fifth of a mile.
Make a Right on West Neck Road.
Head north about 7 miles, Follow it to the end.
West Neck Road will turn into Lloyds Harbor Road, at the end of Lloyds Harbor Road you will make a left on Target Rock Road, and find the entrance to the preserve.

Osprey Nesting at Target Rock

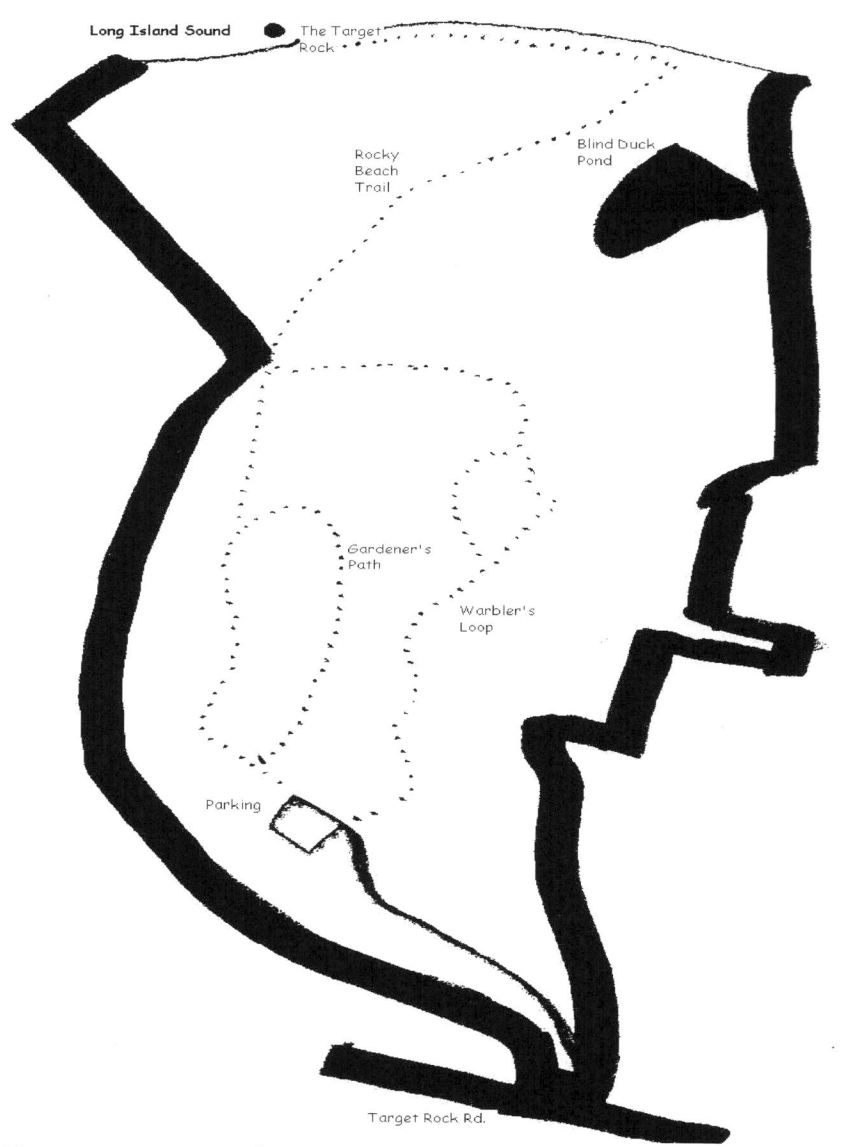

Figure 7 Target Rock

MUTTONTOWN PRESERVE

May 13th

The temperature hovers around the low 70's. With the sun shining, it feels like summer already. This preserve has two entrances. The main entrance, near the nature center can be accessed from route 25A. Closer to the walled garden and King Zog's mansion, the equestrian entrance can be accessed from Route 106. Very popular with horseback riders, Muttontown Preserve incorporates 500 acres of three former estates given to Nassau County in the 1960's. On the grounds, you'll find remnants of the old estates. Many non-native plants, formerly grown on the estate, have since gone wild. At Muttontown Preserve, you can see how quickly nature takes back what belonged to her all along. A number of loosely marked trails weave through the preserve. Numbered and lettered posts can be found along the paths throughout the preserve, but are difficult to follow. The nature center provides maps. The person working at the nature center told me that a Boy Scout troop put the posts in as part of an Eagle project, but that they don't really mean anything.

Because of the varied landscape types, this is a great preserve to visit year round. A moist woodland area with streams and ponds surrounds the area closest to the nature center. Depending on the amount of rainfall we've gotten recently, some of lower areas either get muddy or completely dry up. Typical of wetter areas, the trees in the lower area include maples. Birch and cherry mix in as well. The spring flowers put on quite a show. Most flowers bloom for a few weeks, and we don't see them again for another year. This time of year, a few patches of Virginia bluebell bloom along the ground. A few more patches of Canadian mayflower, also called false lily of the valley hold the mud together. In colonial times, people made a tea from Canadian mayflower, and used it for sore throats. Pink lady's slippers, a type of orchid, also bloom in the preserve this time of year. The ground rolls, gradually rising and getting drier as you head further south in the preserve.

Evergreens populate the west side of the preserve. Most likely, the previous owners planted these. Areas covered by red cedar, give way to white pine. The white pine gives way to a small forest of Norway spruce. Acres of spruce and pine grow gently on the hills. Beneath them an orange bed of dried needles covers the floor. Ivy and various ferns also cover the ground. The white pine and spruce so effectively shade the ground beneath them that on hot days, the air under these trees feels a few degrees cooler than elsewhere in the preserve. The growth of evergreens contrasts the fields and pioneer woodlands on the east side of the preserve, and the wetlands in the northern portion of the preserve.

The County seasonally mows the fields on the east side of the preserve, keeping them as fields, and preventing them from reverting back to forest. Safer than controlled burns, seasonal mowing serves the same purpose. Preserving the fields attracts various types of birds, which rely on the berries from the shrubs and insects for food. The fields can give a great view, particularly during the fall when the leaves on the surrounding trees change color.

Between the fields and the evergreens sits a lower area with several kettle hole ponds. Like the lower areas near the nature center, maples predominate. Passing through here a few years ago during the month of July, I saw a colony of green frogs blending in with the duckweed of one of the ponds. As I walked around the pond to get a better view, they would all jump in the opposite direction, calling out and disturbing the duckweed. As you might expect, the surface of the water in the ponds remains completely still until disturbed by the jumping frogs. A thick mat of decaying leaves covers the bottom.

    The area with the kettle hole ponds ends right about where the back end of the walled garden starts. The garden is one of the few structures remaining from King Zog's estate. So much vegetation covers both the outside and inside of the walled garden that it hides the wall, making it difficult to see in most places. From the entrance to the garden, you won't see the back wall, because of all the trees. The interior of the walled garden provides a classic example of old field succession. During spring and summer, the walled garden is too overgrown to fully explore. Grasses give way to shrubs. Toward the back various trees grow in. Persimmons trees covered in white flowers stand in the middle of the garden.

    Approximately two years ago during late fall, I was able to walk all the way to the back of the walled garden. It took some maneuvering around through the growth back there. I head branches cracking, and leave rustling. It sounded big, and I expected to see another hiker. When I turned and looked, I saw a white tailed deer instead. I took a step toward her, she got a good look at me and she ran. Had I not seen her myself, I would not have expected to see a deer in this preserve, or anywhere this far west on the Island. A year later, I saw two more chasing each other through the spruce.

    Immediately south of the path leading to the walled garden a path leads up a hill through a grove of mountain laurel. The path leads to the ruins of a mansion once owned by King Zog of Albania. King Zog went into exile when Italy invaded Albania at the beginning of the Second World War. After the war, a communist government assumed leadership of Albania. Rumor has it that King Zog bought this estate for $102,800, at a time when Levitt houses sold for just under $8000. King Zog intended to make it his home in exile, but he never actually lived here. Instead, he chose to live in France until his death in 1961. Most of the mansion was torn down, and all that remains is the entrance way to the estate.

    The quickest way to the ruins is up the hill, but the best approach is made by walking east, toward the equestrian entrance, and following another trail south from the parking lot. Going this way allows you to approach the ruins from the front. This is an entrance, so why not start at the beginning. At this end of the preserve, the non-native trees stand out. It's obvious you are strolling what used to be gardens. First you see a concrete building partially underground, and barely visible. With a little imagination, you can picture the living estate in your mind. You can see trees lining the sides, and English ivy growing up the sides of gazebos on either side of a wide stair case. Ivy covers the ground as well. You'll find stone remains of koi pools beneath the ivy. A broken fountain serves as a centerpiece of a crumbling double stairway. Trees grow out of the top of the stairs. Once you get to the top of the double staircase, the ruins end. You can turn around, take in the whole view, and imagine how it once was.

Directions:
From the L.I.E., take Route 106/107 north.
Bear right onto Route 106 when it splits off from Route 107.
The equestrian entrance is on the left side of Route 106.
There is ample parking for non-equestrians.

For the Nature Center entrance:
Follow Route 106 North, until it Reaches Route 25A.
Make a left on Route 25A.
The entrance is on the south side of Route 25A.

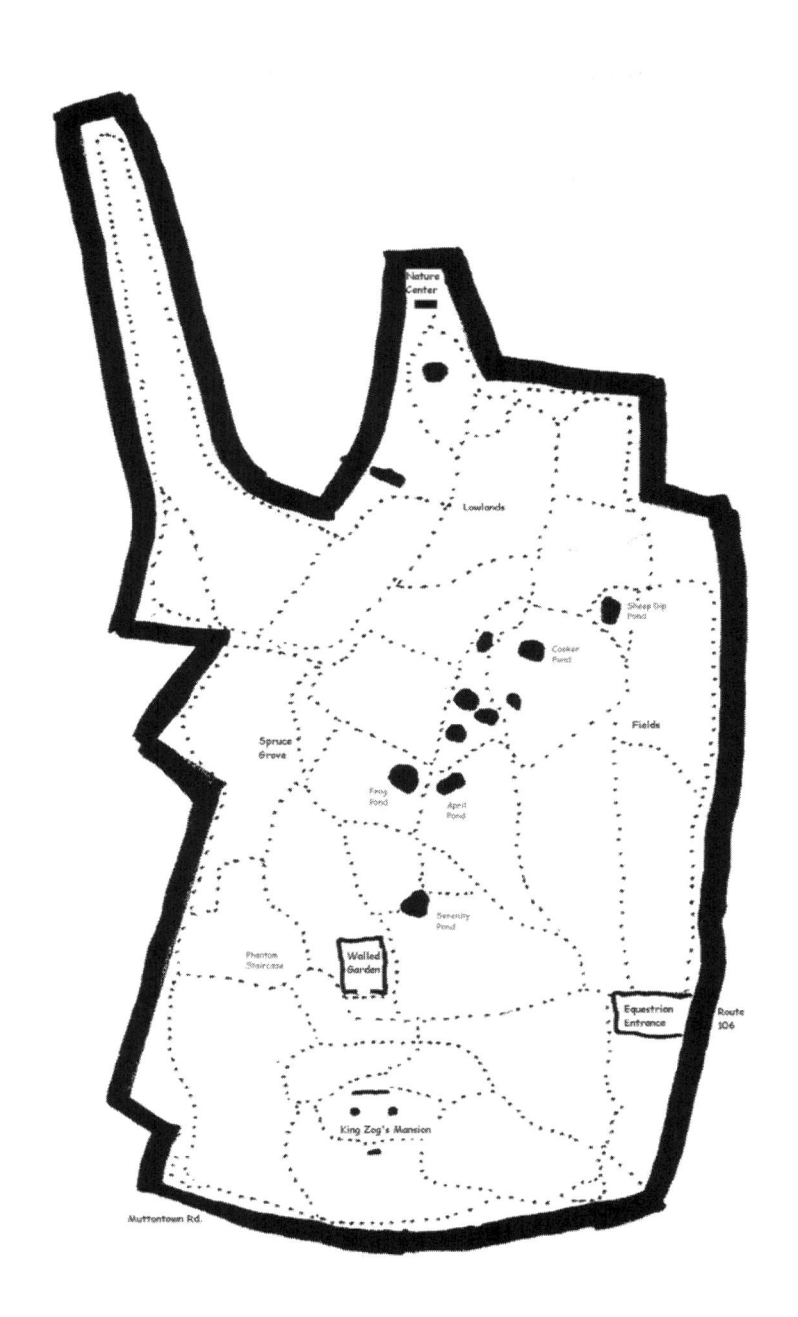

Figure 8 Muttontown Preserve

WERTHEIM NATIONAL WILDLIFE REFUGE

May 19th

Located along the Carman's river in Mastic, and managed by the U.S. Fish and Wildlife Service, Wertheim occupies both sides of the Carman's River immediately before it empties out into the Great South Bay. Like all of the rivers on Long Island, Carman's River slowly mixes salt and fresh water as it gets closer to the bay. Local, State and Federal governments, through various initiatives prevented development along the Carman's River. Thanks to their efforts, visitors can enjoy the most pristine estuary on the Island.

Today is the grand opening of the new headquarters and visitors center for the Long Island National Wildlife Refuge Complex. There are programs and exhibitors, so the park is much more crowded than usual. There's even heavy canoe and kayak traffic on the river. In addition to opening the new building, the rangers also officially open a new trail on the east side of Carman's River, called the "Black Tupelo Trail", which compliments the "White Oak Trail" established on the west side of the river some time ago.

The Black Tupelo Trail takes about an hour and a half to explore, and the White Oak Trail takes slightly longer assuming you walk the long loop. The path connecting the two trails offers excellent views of the river. If feeling energetic, you can walk both. The White Oak Trail has a shorter loop, so, if you're more interested in a casual stroll, you can do half the distance and still enjoy the preserve. As in all the other federally run parks, the rangers do an excellent job maintaining the trails and the preserve. It is impossible to get lost on either trail, or wander off the trail by accident.

At the start of the White Oak Trail, pioneer woods take over an old field. Black cherry and maple predominate, with huckleberry and blueberry filling in the understory. Grassy areas provide habitat suitable for insects, which, in turn, provide food for various birds. On one visit here, I startled an ovenbird. She assumed I was a predator, and drew attention to herself by feigning an injury, and leading me away from her nest. Usually seen and not heard, ovenbirds nest on the ground in a domed oven shape nest. They look similar to thrushes, and are well known for this type of distraction display.

The trail transitions into an oak -pine area, the predominant forest type in the preserve. Pitch pines are a predominant species of pine throughout Suffolk County, and this preserve is part of the extensive Long Island Pine Barrens. Some areas seem to be exclusively pitch pine, while oak populates other areas.

After a while the trail passes a grassland area with a viewing station. Box turtles prefer this area for nesting. Snapping and painted turtles lay their eggs closer to the water, tearing up the landscape during the late spring, and early summer. While the painted and snapping turtles rarely leave the water, you might see a box turtle ambling along on the path. If you are fortunate enough to see one, please let it be.

Once the trail gets to the wetlands, it loops around, and starts its return to the parking area, with the wetlands and river on your right. The wetlands serve as breeding and nesting grounds for a number of different fish and shellfish, as well as snakes, turtles and birds. During the winter you'll find birds from northern climates living on the river. Several viewing stands extend to the edge of the water, providing a clear view of the river and surrounding marsh. While on one of these platforms, I enjoyed the rare spectacle of a mute swan in flight. Frequently seen swimming on nearly every body of water on Long Island, the mute swan rarely flies. Much bigger than a great white heron, the mute swan's wingspan measures between seven and eight feet. The swan is one of the heaviest flying birds, weighing between twenty and twenty-five pounds. Compare that with an osprey, weighing approximately four and a half pounds, with a wingspan just under six feet. As the swan flew overhead, I could hear "voom voom voom", the slow rhythmic hum made by the wings pushing through the air. It looked and sounded like a small aircraft.

  The new Black Tupelo Trail follows the east side of the river, and the adjoining wetlands. Oak and pitch pine predominate, much as they do on the west bank, but you will find some black tupelo trees, if you look for them. You'll see apple galls on some of the younger oak. Identifiable as papery white balls on the branches, they are caused by wasp secretions, and not particularly harmful to the tree. As I walk down the path, I notice a red bellied woodpecker. The woodpecker used to be a southern bird, but in recent years has become much more common in this area. There is also a tufted titmouse, the only species of titmouse residing in the eastern United States.

  The trail continues with the grass area between the trail and the river. It eventually joins up with Indian Landing, a sandy area where kayakers and canoeists can pull their boats out of the water and rest. Until the opening of the Black Tupelo Trail, this landing could only be reached by water craft. Standing here, you have a good view of the river and bay. You can sit on the bench and watch heron flying low over the stretches of cord grass lining the river. After the trail makes a short loop around Indian Landing, it doubles back on itself, and you can follow it back the way you came.

Directions:

From Sunrise Highway, take Exit 58 (William Floyd Parkway).
Head south on William Floyd Parkway, until you reach Montauk Highway.
Make a right on Montauk Highway, and follow it west until you reach Smith's Road.
Make a left on Smith's Road. The preserve entrance and visitor center will be on the right.

An Ovenbird Faking an Injury

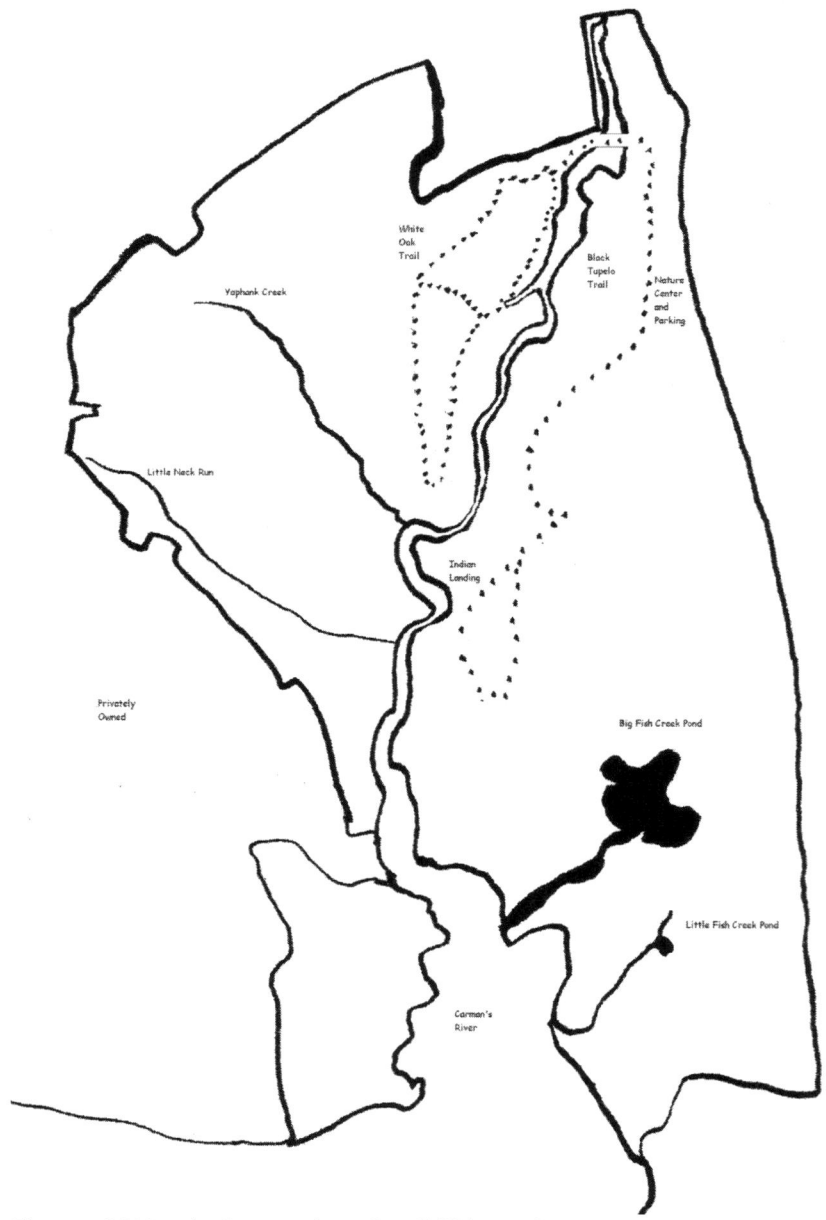

Figure 9 Wertheim National Wildlife Refuge

ORIENT BEACH STATE PARK

May 27th

     Orient point is the absolute end of the north fork of Long Island. For anyone used to the western part of the Island, the north fork offers a completely different vibe. The farm stands alone make the ride out here worthwhile. Add the State Park to that, and you'll have quite a day. Orient Point and Orient Beach State Park are close by one another, but not connected. The point is on county land. For visitors, you'll find a small parking lot where Route 25 comes to an end. From that lot it's a ten minute walk to the point, where the pile of gravel constituting Long Island humbly eases underneath the waves of both the Peconic Bay and The Long Island Sound. It's not exactly a point, because the water level rises and falls with the tides, making it more of a smooth curve. Today, small, gentle waves wash over the end of the Island. Cormorants and seagulls fly over the channel. On the other side of the channel, you'll see Plum Island. There's a very, very nice beach. Terns nest there.

     Orient Beach State Park offers more in terms of hiking, kayaking and beach front. You'll find the park entrance less than a hundred yards from where Route 25 ends. The narrow road from the entrance to the parking area has Gardiners Bay on one side and Hallock's Bay on the other. Small trees and marsh grass grow beneath the osprey platforms on the Hallock's Bay side. Saltwater and surf casters occupy the Gardiner's Bay side. From the parking area you'll find a spot where kayaks can be rented. You'll also find the beach and the park's two nature trails.

     The Roy Latham Trail, a maritime oak forest, begins on the east side of the parking lot. On the west side, another trail extends to Long Beach Point through a maritime red cedar forest. Similar to the barrier beaches, this stretch of sand floods with saltwater during severe storms. Temperatures change quickly, and water drains from the sand as fast as it falls. All of these factors make it a difficult desert like environment for plants to thrive in. Only the heartiest survive. Wind and water erosion constantly re-shape the land.

  The Roy Latham trail offers a quick walk, consisting of a half mile loop through a maritime oak forest. Roy Latham studied plants native to the north shore, and the trail bears his name. Common among the oak here, you'll find blackjack oak, otherwise rare in the northeast. Well adapted for sandy soil, blackjack oak thrives where other trees would not be able to take root. Bees fly around today, but the mosquitoes keep hidden. Undergrowth includes bayberry. Notable for its waxy leaves, it's fairly common on the barrier beaches along with shadbush. Pitch pines and red cedar also take root in the sand. Looking down, the sand contains lots of shells and small pebbles. Beach heather, with its wiry branches and small yellow flowers grow out of the sand. Diamond back terrapins lay their eggs here in June and July, as they do on other beaches around the Island.

  The longer walk is the walk through the cedar forest towards Long Beach Point. The distance between the parking lot and Long Beach Point is about two and a half miles. A sandy path goes through the middle of it, and you can loop around by walking along the shoreline. Truly, this is one of the more impressive hikes on the Island. As you walk down the path, grass grows on either side of the path. On the north side you'll see Hallock's Bay, which is home to oysters, scallops and other mollusks. A brown tide, a type of algae bloom, decimated the scallop population about thirty years ago. Efforts are still being made to restore their numbers. You'll also find several salt water ponds fed by water from Gardiner's Bay. Grasses surround the ponds. Heron and other shorebirds wade in the ponds, similar to the estuaries along the edges of the Great South Bay. Driftwood and broken shells of various creatures fill the spaces between the trees. Whelk, clam and scallop shells are easy to spot. Red cedar grows right out of the sand. They adapt to soil and wind conditions by growing as either a thick shrub or a thin tall tree. The thick shrubby cedars are subjected to more winds, and are spread out for that reason. You'll also find stands of dead stumps where cedar no longer get water from the ground, and dry up. Cedars grow slowly. Trees one foot in diameter are close to one hundred years old. Most of the trees here are much younger than that. Unlike the Atlantic white cedar, which prefer saturated, swampy conditions, the red cedar do well in dry, sandy, soil. They also tolerate constant exposure to salt, surviving for years under conditions which would kill other trees in a few weeks. Hawthorne grows alongside some of the cedar, trying to crowd them out. Growing out of the sand you'll find colonies of prickly pear cactus preparing to bloom within the next few weeks. They put out yellow flowers. Sea lavender, beach pea, and hairy vetch bloom in the sand. Hairy vetch is an awful name for an attractive purple flower responsible for adding nitrogen to the otherwise sparse soil. Shining ladies tresses, with yellow and white flowers blooming in tall clusters, decorate the beach also. Looking over the bay, you'll see Gardiner's Island close by. Walking along the beach gulls, sandpipers and plovers run through the incoming waves, digging for worms and other treats.

    Conservationists erected osprey nesting platforms all along the beach. Several pairs nest here. For the several hours I spent walking along the cedar forest and beach, I watched them fly over the bay, fly over the salt ponds, and dive for fish. I listened to them call out to each other shouting "peep peep peep", and spent the time enjoying their company. This stretch of sand is truly their domain, and I am only a guest.

Directions:

To reach Orient Point, proceed east on Route 25 until it ends.
To reach Orient Beach State Park, proceed east on Route 25. About one hundred yards before it ends, make a right into the entrance.

Beach Pea

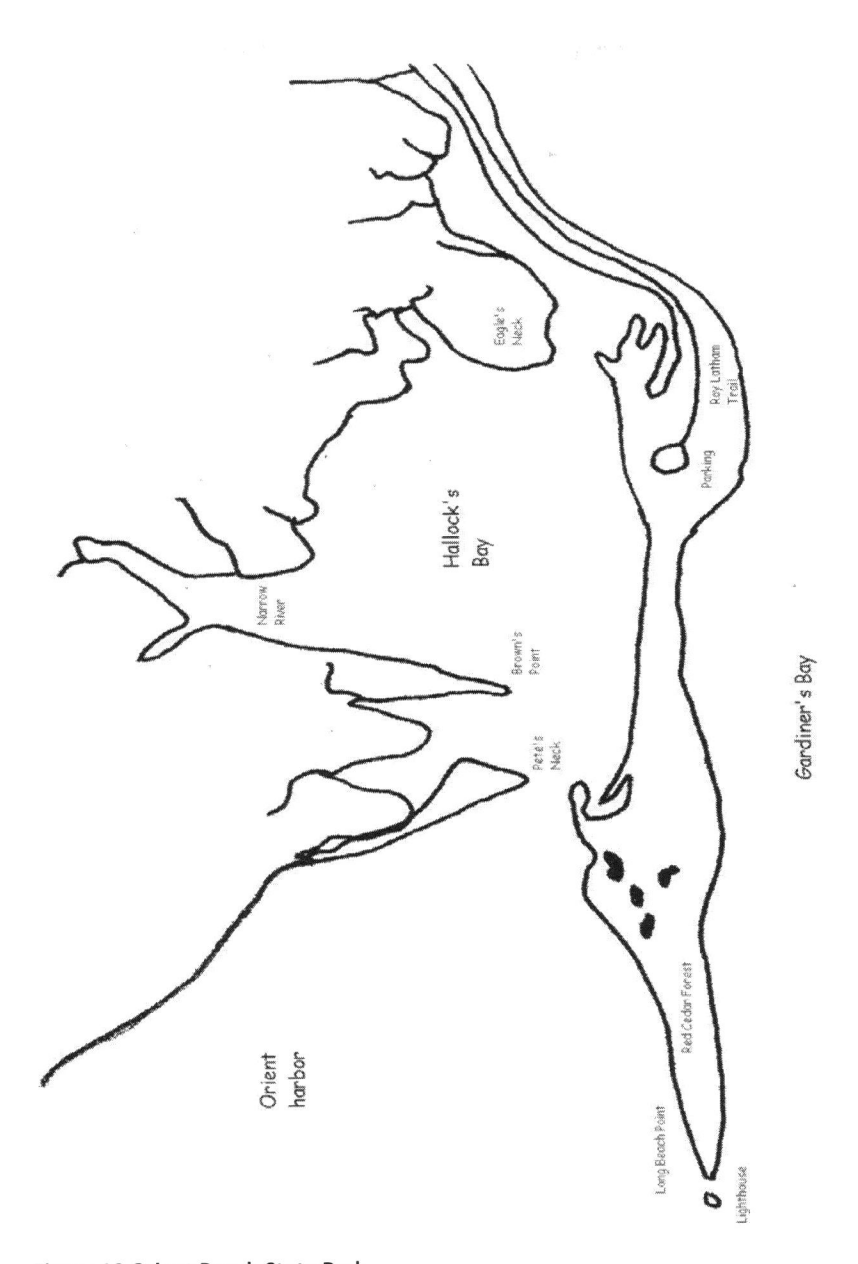

Figure 10 Orient Beach State Park

JUNE

Diamond Back Terrapin on the Move

COLD SPRING HARBOR STATE PARK AND UPLAND FARMS SANCTUARY

June 3rd

The Nassau-Suffolk Greenbelt Trail begins with the hills in Cold Spring Harbor. South of Lawrence Hill Road the greenbelt trail continues through Trail View State Park, Stillwell Preserve, goes over the Northern State Parkway, Under the Long Island Expressway, through Bethpage State Park, over the Southern State Parkway, ultimately ending eighteen miles away at the corner of Ocean Avenue and Merrick Road in Massapequa. You can also start the greenbelt in Massapequa, but it's easier to start with the hills on the North Shore, go across what's left of the Hempstead plains, and finish in the swampy lowlands of Massapequa Preserve.

If you just want to explore the northern section, I suggest combining Cold Spring Harbor State Park and The Nature Conservancy's Uplands Farm Sanctuary. The two preserves sit side by side and provide excellent hiking year round. The entrance for Uplands Farm Sanctuary can be found on Lawrence Hill Road. The two trails combined take about two and a half hours, and cover approximately five miles, with some overlap.

I started in Cold Spring Harbor's parking lot. Earlier in the day, it rained a little. The sun peeks out from the clouds now, but it's humid. Hopefully, the rain will stay away while I hike. Looking out over the harbor, I see the tide is low. The trail starts behind a kiosk on the south end of the parking lot, marked with the greenbelt's white blazes. It immediately goes uphill. Steps cut into the hill make the climb a little less strenuous. The first hill is the worst. The hills get progressively easier as you head south.

If you look on a contour map of the Cold Spring Harbor Preserve, you will see there are really only two hills, but the terrain rolls in such a way that it feels like five hills. Five separate assents stand between the parking lot and Lawrence Hill Road, one mile away. It's not like hiking in the Rockies, or even the Catskills, but it's enough to make even the most seasoned couch potato break a sweat.

    Ivy covers the ground. The trees include maple, with a few cherry mixed in, and a few stately and impressive old oak trees with trunks several feet around. As you walk up the hill, glance over the harbor, and take in the view. A long spit of sand reaches almost entirely across the harbor. The south end of the harbor fades into a marsh; the north opens into the sound. During the fall you can see leaves change on the other side of the harbor, which is also heavily wooded. From this vantage point, you can watch sailboats and shorebirds glide over the water.

    At the base of the second assent, a few small spruce trees mingle with the maple. A chipmunk scurries across the path. Every time I visit this preserve, the resident chipmunks introduce themselves. Mountain laurel grows on the sides of the hills. A long ravine between the second and third assent allows for a bit of rest. You'll find plenty of fallen trees, and very little undergrowth along the trail here. The sky darkens, and I hear thunder west of me. Proceeding through the preserve, the mountain laurel become more and more predominant in the understory, and oak and beech become more and more predominant in the canopy. Besides the hills, the groves of mountain laurel are the most memorable feature of the preserve. This time of year they bloom with large white flowers. The leaves are thick and waxy. The trunks are thin and twisted. The papery bark readily peels off.

    Younger tulip trees start to mix in with the oak closer to Lawrence Hill Road.
Once you cross over Lawrence Hill Road, you leave Cold

Spring Harbor Preserve, and enter the northern edge of Trail View State Park, which connects with Uplands Farm Sanctuary. A barbed wire fence is on your right, and on your left is Uplands Farm Sanctuary. After a short distance, the fence ends, and the trail circles around a ravine.

Eventually, you will find a tulip tree with a double white blaze. If you follow the trail to the right at this point, you will follow along the green belt, and end up in Massapequa. If you go left, and follow the green signs with yellow arrows, you will stay in Uplands Farm. Around this ravine you'll find extensive growths of white pine and spruce, with minimal undergrowth. The towering spruce and pine make the ravine feel much bigger than it actually is. The trail snakes around the ravine, and eventually crosses a road into some old fields which have been growing back in. In a few steps you go from one habitat to a completely different one.

Uplands Farm Preserve used to be a dairy farm. Sandy and acidic might be poor for crops, but it's good for growing grass and grazing livestock. Its previous owner, Mrs. Jane Nichols donated the farm to the Nature Conservancy in 1962. The Nature Conservancy uses the farmhouses and barn today. This preserve is great for observing old field succession. Several trails loop around the old farm, so you can get creative with different routes on different visits. The areas further west are grown in with very dense brush. Sumac and Sassafras are among the more common trees. Cherry and Maple also grow here. On the eastern side of the preserve the Daniel P. Davidson trail loops for about a mile. Most of it circles an area which is predominantly grass and pasture. You'll find a variety of wildflowers which grow well without being shaded by trees. You'll find over forty species of butterflies, attracting as many species of birds. Look for bobolinks, and meadowlarks, as well as bluebirds. The Nature

Conservancy placed nesting boxes around the preserve to help restore their numbers. These birds have become rarer on Long Island, as their habitat has diminished due to development. There are, of course hawks too. The open areas make it easier for them to hunt. A few years ago, while walking through the western part of the preserve, I saw a hawk chase down and grab a smaller bird while both were in flight.

On today's little hike, the skies open up when I reached the Daniel Davidson trail. The rain gods throw lightning bolts in my vicinity, and it occurs to me that the two worst places to be during an electrical storm are in an open field or under a tree. Where do I go? I'm getting drenched, but it's fairly warm out. Getting wet doesn't bother me, but lightning makes me nervous. I'm carrying an aluminum walking stick that I always bring on hikes. I consider ditching it, in the interest of personal safety, but it was given to me by a close friend a few months back. I really like it, it's sturdy, light weight, and retractable. I could hide it somewhere, and come back for it, but with my luck somebody would take it. Even Zeus had to answer to the fates, so, if is my time to get struck by lightning, I figure I'll get struck regardless of whether I'm carrying an aluminum stick or not. I decide to keep my walking stick; it's like a security blanket for when I go hiking. I don't like being without it. Besides, I'm expecting the hills in Cold Spring Harbor to be muddy from the rain. The walking stick will be helpful. I feel lucky that I reached the halfway point before the rain started coming down hard. I walk back in a quick but casual pace. By the time I get back to the hills, the rain has stopped, and the sun is back out. I watch the water run down the mud covered hills, as I carefully walk up them, stick in hand.

Directions:

To Cold Spring Harbor State Park:
From the L.I.E. take Exit 45(Manetto Hill Road).
Make a right onto Woodbury Road.
Make a left onto Harbor Road (Route 108).
The Preserve is on the right side of Harbor Road.

To reach Uplands Farm Sanctuary:
Make a right off of Harbor Road, and onto Lawrence Hill Road. The preserve is on the right.

Chipmunk on a Log

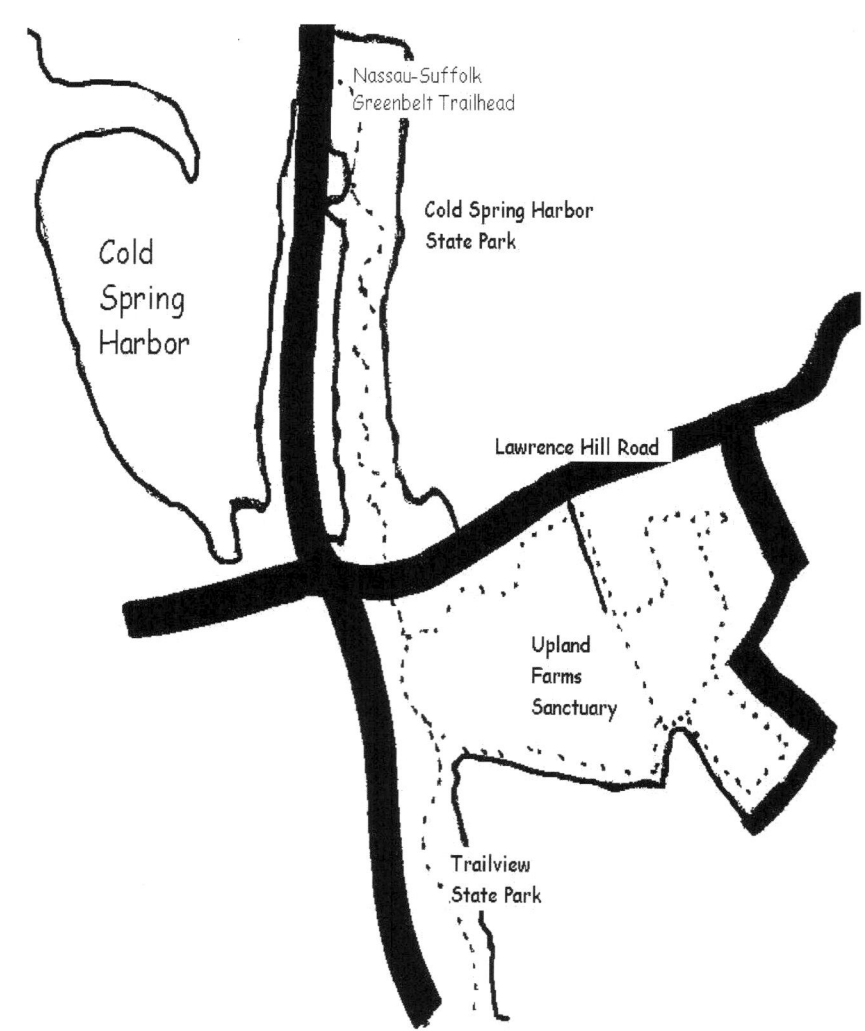

Figure 11 Cold Spring Harbor and Upland Farms Sanctuary

RANDALL POND PRESERVE

June 10th

Two marked trails combine to cover approximately three miles. Near the parking you'll find an informational kiosk providing literature about the pine barrens. The DEC also maintains a hunter check-station during hunting season. Several habitat types can be found. The most prominent habitats include pine barrens, and old fields slowly growing into pioneer woodlands. The DEC periodically mows some of the fields.

The trail starts in the parking lot and proceeds along the west side of Randall Pond, a fairly small, shallow pond, fed by an underground spring. This time of year grasses grow around the north and south ends. A thick layer of duckweed covers the pond surface. Insect larvae swim in the water, and a few blue dragonflies buzz the surface of the pond. Cherry and maple trees reach their branches over the side, their roots holding the banks of the pond. A few wooden fishing stations extend from the water's edge. I am the only hiker in the preserve during my visit. The solitude is comforting, but not nearly as comforting as the smell of the pine, and the cool breeze blowing through the shady places. The trail proceeds north along the west side of the pond.

A short distance after the trail bends away from the pond, it leads into the upland pine forest where a few oak mix in with the pine. A deer watches me from a distance. A number of skittish deer live in the preserve. They keep their distance, and eye me suspiciously. Soon, I reach a clearing in the forest where there is a break in the pine growth. The sun shines in the clearing, it is hot, but not too hot. The air feels dry. Grasses cover the sandy ground. Patches of ferns grow thick in the lower saturated areas.

Oak and a single red cedar line the edges of the clearing. A catbird meows. Catbirds are grey, and can be identified by their black cap, and by their distinctive call, which sounds like a cat. A cherry tree, covered with lichens, grows in the middle of the clearing. The trail continues out of the clearing.

The trail follows along a transition area between the pine forest and a low area thick with shrubs. A pair of cardinals chase each other through the shrubs. Along the side you will find several piles of boulders, most likely placed in their location by a farmer many years ago. The spaces between the rocks make good nests for rodents and small birds. Between the older pine forest and the newer shrub land, the trail follows along a grassy border, which widens and narrows, with the pine on the east side and the shrubs on the west side.

This section of trail hasn't been mowed yet this season. At its lowest, the grass goes up to my knees, at its highest, it reaches slightly above my waist. Before proceeding through the grassy area, I face a decision. Ticks lurk in tall grass. Should I go back the way I came, and call it a day, or should I continue through the grass, knowing it's hopping with ticks. Normally you can minimize the risk of picking up a tick by staying on the marked trails, and out of tall grass, but, in this instance, the marked trail goes straight through the tall grass. I weigh my options. Ticks don't attach themselves immediately, so I'll be able to search myself and take precautions. I've never been to this preserve before, and, for all I know, I may never return. I'm not a huge fan of ticks, but the insect gods put them here for a reason, mainly to provide a steady supply of food for the birds. Like the pretty little songbirds that eat them alive, ticks belong to Mother Nature also. In the interest of making the most of my time here, I place one foot ahead of me, followed by another, and step through the tall grass.

In the grass I find matted down spots where deer

made their beds last night. A pair of deer strolls through grass ahead of me. I keep brushing ticks off myself, and wonder how the deer eat and sleep with these critters through the whole season. I question my sanity at this point. Smelling decomposition, I look to my side and see the remains of a deer quietly returning to the earth. Nobody gives a deer a formal burial, its bones get picked through by scavengers, and the rest disintegrates, becoming the soil.

Eventually, the trail opens up to a grass covered field with a slight upward incline. The maintenance crews mowed trails through the grass here. In the grass a few wildflowers bloom. On the far end, near the top of the hill, an island of trees breaks up the field. I slowly make my way up the hill. Under the trees rests the bleached remains of another deer. This one looks like a hunter left it here during the winter hunt. Ribs, leg bones, vertebrae scatter in the grass, in no particular order. The skull and many other bones are gone. A small piece of hide drapes from the branch of a nearby tree. I tap at it with my walking stick. Sunlight, air, and the passage of time hardened it into place.

I follow the trail through the grass, past a few maintenance buildings and back to the parking lot, where I thoroughly examine my pants and shirt for ticks. By far, this is the worst infestation of ticks I have ever seen. I brush dozens of them off. I'll continue this once I get home. My clothes will go through the washer and dryer. First I drown the little buggers, then I cook them. In the shower, I will examine myself thoroughly, and re-examine myself for the next few days. It takes a while for them to find a spot to dig in and start feeding. Thankfully, none of them attached. Ticks and all, the preserve offers some great hiking.

Directions:

From Sunrise Highway or the L.I.E., Take William Floyd Parkway north.
Make a left on Route 25. Head west a short distance.
Make a right onto Randall Road. The entrance and parking area will be on your left.

A Rabbit

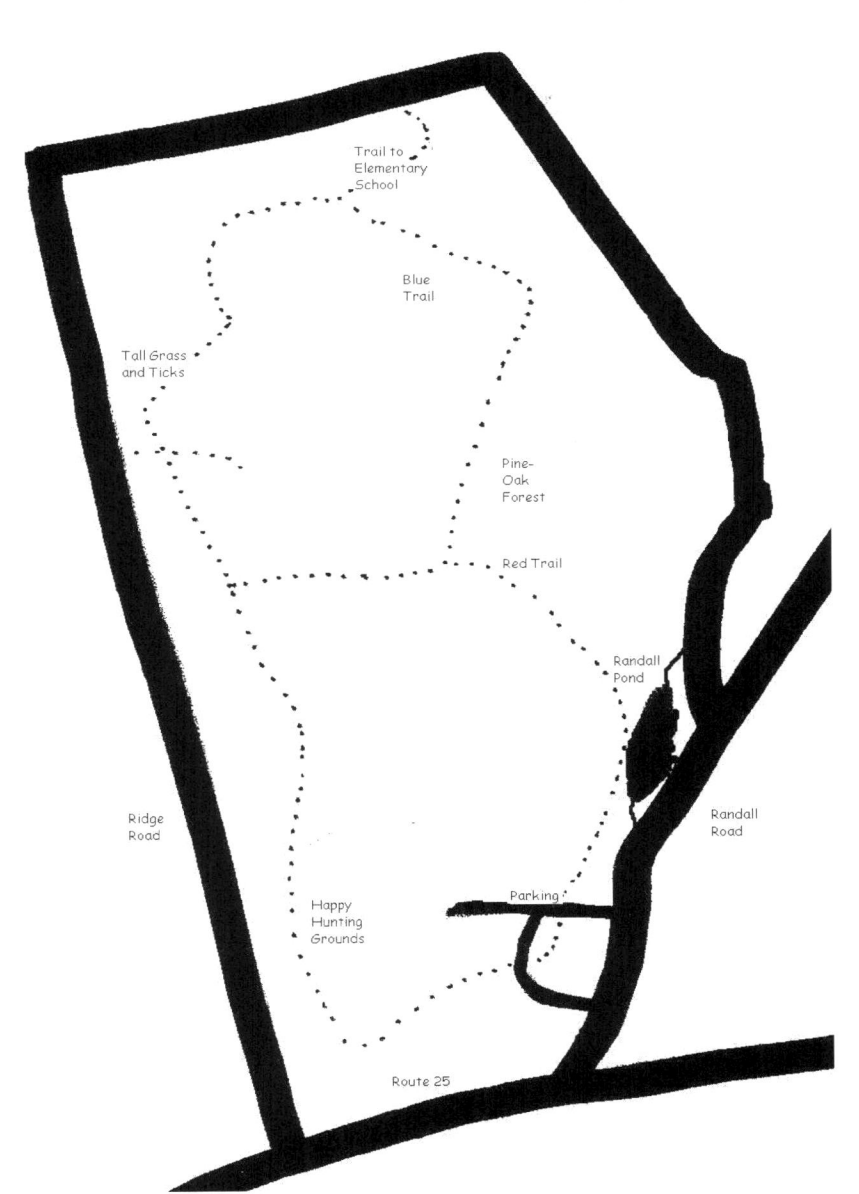

Figure 12 Randall Pond Preserve

MASSAPEQUA PRESERVE

June 20th

The Massapequa River flows from Linden Boulevard to the Bay, passing under Clark Street, Sunrise Highway and Merrick Road. The Nassau-Suffolk Greenbelt starts at the corner of Ocean Avenue and Merrick road in Massapequa. Marked by white blazes, it extends all the way to Cold Spring Harbor on the north shore. A paved bike path extending north to Bethpage State Park also starts at that corner. The lake, sometimes referred to Massapequa Lake, also goes by the name Caroon's lake, named after Richard Caroon, the man who owned the property during the post-war boom in the 1940's. Although named after him, the lake predates Caroon by about a century. David Jones, an early settler of the area, created the lake in 1837, by damming up the existing creek. He raised trout in the lake, and named the island in the middle Mary's Island, after his wife Mary Clinton, daughter of DeWitt Clinton, the former Governor of New York. The lake covers approximately forty acres of land, and history seems to have forgotten what the Jones family called before selling it to Richard Caroon.

    Caroon's Lake, and the pond north of Clark Boulevard both provide great opportunities for bird watching. The past few years a small group of egrets have been congregating on some fallen trees on the north side of Mary's Island. You will also find terns, gulls, geese, swans, and different types of ducks, depending on the time of year. The trees surrounding the lake provide a wonderful view in the fall when the leaves turn.
I grew up a short distance from here, and have been coming here as long as I can remember. I've enjoyed the good fortune of seeing the many subtle changes in the preserve.

I remember where fallen trees once were, which have since returned to the soil. For anybody interested in nature, and appreciating its spirit, there is absolutely no substitute for picking a patch of land, making it your home, and visiting it frequently. You will become tuned to it. You not only see how it changes through the seasons, but also, over course of time. I, fortunately, have been able to see the changes at this preserve for nearly forty years, in all weather, and in all times of the year. The trails flood in heavy rains. The streams flow in generally the same places, but not exactly. Thankfully it is much cleaner now than it was twenty or thirty years ago.

  Today the lake stays relatively quiet, with fewer birds than normal. The egrets are out. A pair of mute swans swim around the edge with their two chicks. They hide their nest on the side of a smaller pond in the swamp immediately north of the lake. Constructed of sticks and mud, the swan's nest measures four feet across. The lake is fairly shallow, between three and four feet deep with a very muddy bottom. Spatterdock, also called cow lily, or pond lily, grows throughout the lake, providing a shady habitat, and food for fish and insects. Some the fish you'll find living in the pond include largemouth bass, pickerel, perch, crappie and carp.

  The pond drains into deeper water south of Merrick Road, until reaching the Great South Bay. One main creek, and two smaller creeks flow from South Farmingdale to Massapequa, fed by both groundwater and storm runoff. Swamps cover sections of the preserve. Several smaller ponds stay hidden off the trails in the area south of Sunrise. Hikers frequently throw fallen trees and branches over the smaller streams, and use these as makeshift bridges to get to some of the less accessible areas. While in the hidden ponds, you need to watch out for alligators, an invasive species. Every few years, alligator sightings get reported to local authorities.

Unfortunately, people illegally keep pet alligators. When they get too big, they let the alligators loose in the preserve where they feed on ducks and geese. Eventually the winter comes and the cold weather kills them. In the preserve, you will find garter snakes, box turtles, snapping turtles, painted turtles, several different types of frogs, wild rabbits, muskrats, and of course squirrels. I personally, have never seen chipmunks in the preserve, which surprises me a little, given the fact that they are fairly common elsewhere on the Island. Of course, the area surrounding the preserve is too populated for any deer to be in the preserve. Because of the several different habitats in the preserve, the plant life is incredibly diverse. It really runs the gamut of the types of trees and wildflowers common on Long Island.

  Several trails lead north, notably a paved bike path and the Nassau-Suffolk Greenbelt, which overlaps the bike path in several places. You can also explore several unmarked paths following the flow of the creek. On a typical day, this preserve, particularly the bike path, gets crowded. Taking the paths less traveled will make all the difference. You will see maple in the swampier areas. Oak and pitch pine populate the drier areas, as they do further east on the Island.

  Brush fires occasionally start south of Sunrise Highway. The past few years, I've been watching young sassafras trees fill in one of the recently burned areas. Sassafras can be easily identified by their asymmetrical leaves. To spot them, remember their leaves resemble mittens, socks and gloves. The mittens have a lobe on one side, the gloves have lobes on both sides, and the socks have no lobes. Several fallen pitch pines on the side of the greenbelt came down during a recent nor'easter, which singled out pine. The storm hit during the month of March, before the deciduous trees pushed out their leaves, so it left those trees standing.

  Once you get to Sunrise Highway, the bike path

passes over the creek. You can sometimes look in the water and see fish or turtles swimming around. North of Sunrise, you will find the Brady Park Reservoir. Engineers built this pond built in the 1880's as part of a reservoir system to supply the City of Brooklyn with water. At the time, Nassau County was part of Queens. Brooklyn used the reservoir system until the 1960's. South Shore communities still rely on it today.

    The bike path quickly goes through the Brady Park section of the preserve. Years ago, visitors could see countless leopard frogs at the bridges during the summer, now you are lucky if you see one. North of Clark Boulevard, you can cross over the Kiwanis fishing bridge and follow unmarked paths, but be prepared for some of them to be impassable depending on the amount of recent rainfall, and the time of the year. The paths tend to be either overgrown with thorns, flooded, or both. If you don't cross over the Kiwanis Fishing Bridge, the bike path follows the flow of the main creek. This time of year wild bergamot, lilies and other flowers line the creek. After a short distance you reach a pond. A wider unpaved path separates from the bike path, going over a culvert. This is where the most recent improvements have been made. The Town and County shored up the banks of the pond and creek, and planted extensively. I was skeptical about the changes at first, but, as they've had time to work their way in, I appreciate more and more how much of an improvement it is. As I pass through today, the sun starts to set, and I can hear bullfrogs. Being the day of the Summer Solstice, we have the most sunlight, but the sun will gradually set earlier and earlier, the days growing shorter and shorter until the Winter Solstice arrives. In Northern Europe, the Summer Solstice is celebrated as Midsummer, with nearly as much enthusiasm as Christmas, which originally commemorated the Winter Solstice.

    Shrubs surround the pond, making it a good home

for a variety of small birds, in addition to ducks, geese and other waterfowl. On the north side of the pond you will find a small colony of prickly pear cactus barely visible in the grass. The preserve offers a lot of options as far as trails are concerned. The paved path runs up the east side of the preserve. A fairly wide path, covered in gravel runs up the west side. The greenbelt, and some side trails go through the middle. The greenbelt is probably the quietest. Although the bike path is always busy, it follows the main creek, so if you're into wildflowers, you can enjoy the different species that bloom at different times of the year. The middle section can be quite swampy or quite dry depending on the season. The preserve ultimately ends at Linden Boulevard, and the greenbelt continues over the Southern State Parkway all the way to Cold Spring Harbor, where I always spot chipmunks.

Directions:

From Route 135, take Merrick Road eastbound.
The preserve will be approximately two miles east, at the intersection of Ocean Avenue and Merrick Road.
You can also park on Sunrise Highway between the Massapequa and Massapequa Park train stations.

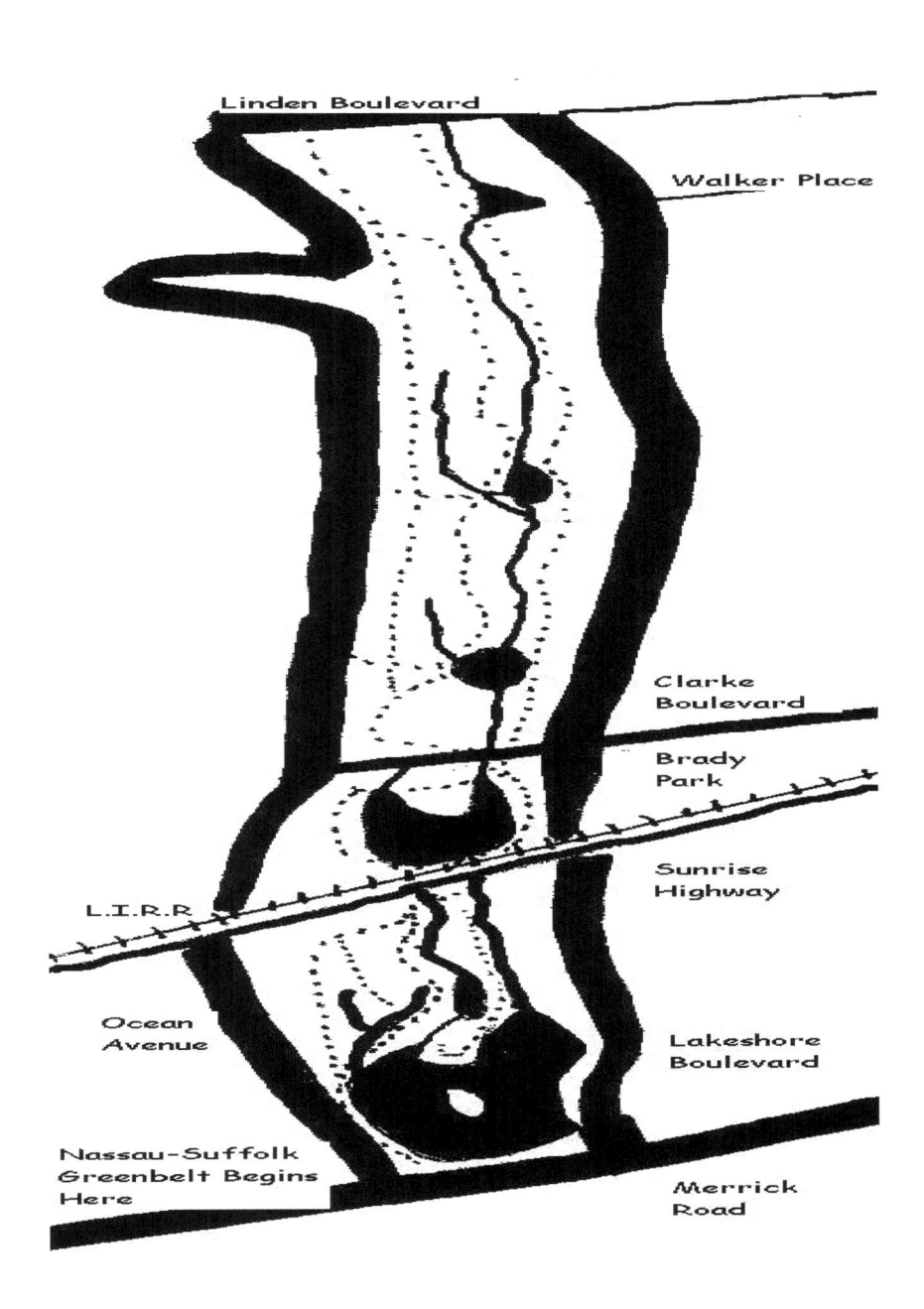

Figure 13 Massapequa Preserve

CALEB SMITH STATE PARK

June 23rd

  This 543 acre preserve surrounds the beginnings of the Nissequogue River. Previously part of the Smith family estate, the Smith family sold the land to the Brooklyn Gun Club in 1888. The Brooklyn Gun Club kept it in essentially the same condition they found it in, and by doing so, saved it from development. New York State acquired the property in 1963, and manages it as a preserve. The Long Island Greenbelt goes through this for a part of its length. Several marked trails circle the preserve, including designated cross country skiing trails that can be enjoyed in the winter. The farmhouse dates back to 1753, and houses a nature museum today. Willow Pond sits across from the farmhouse. The Smith family built Willow Pond in 1795, by damming Whitman Creek, using it to power a gristmill. Today, New York State stocks the pond and streams with trout hatched at Connetquot State Park, and encourages angling on the property. In the pond, you'll find Canadian geese swimming alongside mallards and wood ducks. Looking into the water, you can see various aquatic plants.
  The yellow trail starts behind the nature center. It goes through some field areas which groundskeepers periodically mow. Nesting boxes provide shelter for a variety of warblers and other songbirds attracted to the wild blackberry and raspberry bushes lining the edges of the fields. A bird blind faces a collection of nesting boxes in a cedar stand. You'll also find bat boxes around the fields and throughout the preserve. At dusk, you can watch the bats hunt for insects. Parallel to the field you'll find a trail lined with cedar, oak and maple. Some younger white pines mix in with the hardwoods. The shade offered by these trees has a nice cooling effect on an otherwise hot

day. The scent of pine on the air makes the walk even more relaxing. There is such a thorough mix of trees that it is difficult to pick out a predominant species. The trail crosses over a small stream, and follows along the bottom of a hill. The land rises on the right and the stream and swamp sink below on the left as you head south on this trail.

Fern and vines fill the swamp. Fallen trees covered in moss rest in the mud. The sun is out and the air is warm today, but it rained heavily for the past few days, so the swamp is full, and the water in the stream moves quickly. Stepped trails lead up into the hill areas, consisting of an oak/maple forest, with very light hickory undergrowth. The trail turns left, and a series of three small wooden bridges lead over the streams and through the swamps. Sand covers the stream beds. The eastern most stream moves very slowly, covered with a motionless layer of duckweed. A lone cedar stands on a clump of mud and sand. The stream slowly erodes the mud and sand from under its roots. It leans a little now, but in time gravity will win and pull the tree down.

Nearby, a maple lies in the stream, having lost a fight with moving water and gravity. Back when the Smith family made their home here, beaver filled the streams, often re-directing the flow of the streams with their construction projects. The beavers disappeared through habitat destruction and uncontrolled hunting, so the only mammals left include chipmunks, squirrels, and maybe a muskrat or two.

After going through the swamp, the trail crosses a wider graveled trail. This leads back to Willow Pond and the entrance. A slightly longer, winding trail goes through the wooded areas, and ends closer to the farmhouse where a small gathering of geese honk and waddle across the lawn.

Directions:

From Sunken Meadow Parkway, take the exit for Route 25 (Jericho Turnpike), headed east. The Preserve is less than two miles away on the left side of Route 25.

Wild Raspberries

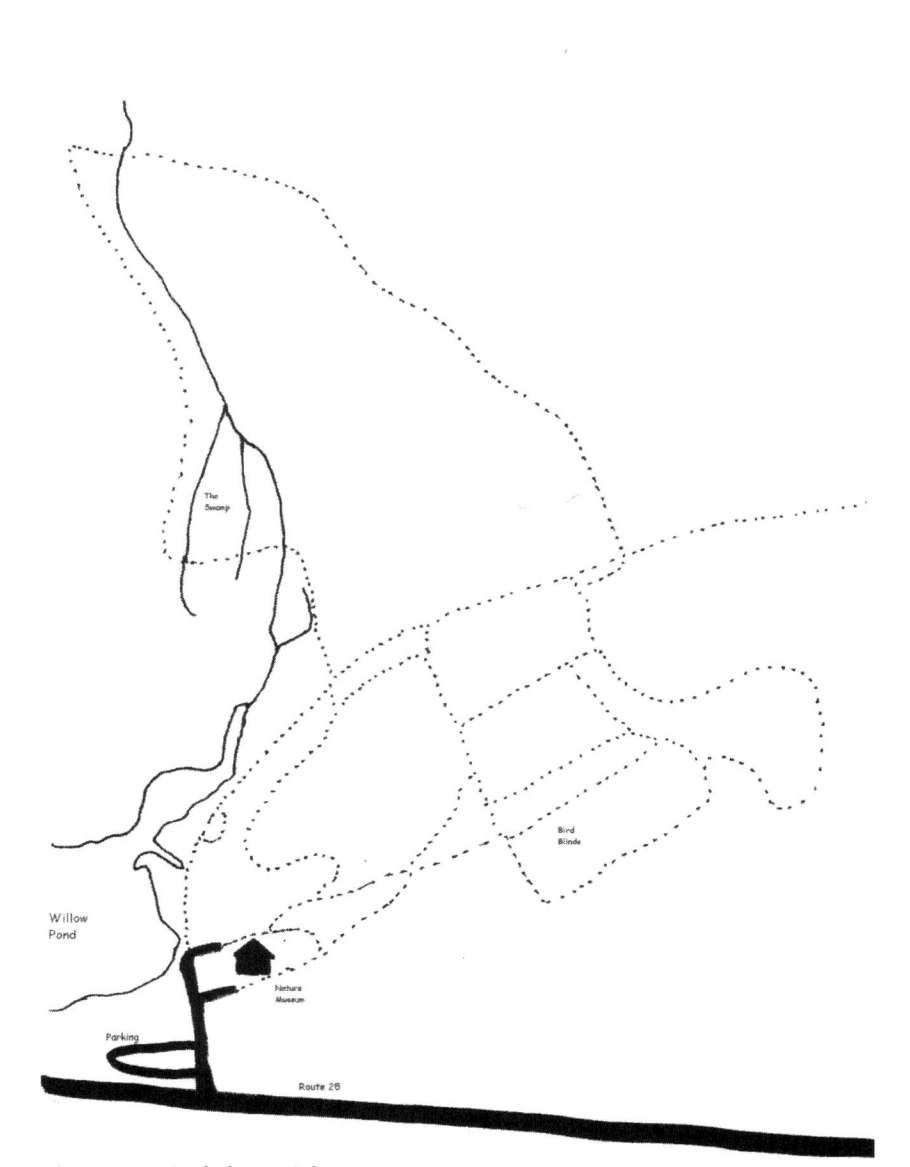

Figure 14 Caleb Smith Preserve

CEDAR POINT

June 30th

      Cedar Point has a campground, hiking trails and a quiet beach on Peconic Bay. The Paumonock path passes through some of the preserve. Today the temperature reaches well into the 90's, perfect for the beach, but a bit rough for hiking. Heat warnings throughout the rest of the country make it rough for everyone. I made sure to bring an extra bottle of water with me on the trail. The sun shines brightly. All around, it feels like a good summer day. The full trail, and a detour to Scoy Pond, adjacent to the park, will take about two and a half hours, and pass through an oak forest, A shoreline habitat, and several smaller ponds.
      Starting behind the park office, the trail goes through an oak/pine forest. Chestnut oak, not to be confused with the American chestnut, predominates. Chestnut oaks thrive in the rough soil common here. The Chestnut oak gets its name, because it looks similar to the American chestnut. The long oval leaves look almost identical, the notable difference is that the teeth on the edges of the American chestnut come to a sharp point. The barks of the trees differ also, in that the chestnut oak's bark looks a little rougher. The trail proceeds through some briar patches, and reaches an observation platform on top of the bluffs. From the observation point you can view most of Peconic Bay, including Gardiner's Island, Shelter Island, Orient Point and Plum Island. Take a few moments and quietly contemplate the seagulls, their place in the universe, the slow advance and retreat of the glaciers, the waves, not just rippling through the water, but rippling in the gradual movement of the sand on the beach. Contemplate whatever else comes to mind.
      After your moment of Zen, you can follow the trail as it proceeds along the top of the bluffs parallel to the

shoreline. Eventually the trail reaches a woods road where you can choose to go through the camping area, or past the cedar pond, and along the beach.

Choosing to go along the beach, you first pass a shrub area with beach plum, bayberry, and, of course, cedar. The spit of sand is Cedar Point. At the end sits a lighthouse. The original lighthouse was built in 1839, but the lighthouse standing there now was built in 1868. At the time the lighthouse was built, Cedar Point was Cedar Island, and not connected to the rest of the South Fork. The 1938 hurricane, also known as the Long Island Express, created the spit of sand now connecting the lighthouse to the South Fork. This same storm created the Shinnecock Inlet, and made several other notable alterations to the South Shore of Long Island. The effects of storms are all part of the natural process of erosion constantly changing the shoreline. Rangers roped off the central part of the spit of sand leading to the lighthouse. Plover nest and breed there, and beach grass grows in the sand. You can walk along the tidal area. The waves are gentle, and the plover and sandpipers keep a safe distance.

Rocks cover the beach area south of the sandbar. With the tide fairly low, you can see mussels and clams clinging to the rocks. Irish moss and some other sea plants wash up on the beach. One of the edible wonders of the shoreline, Irish moss can be identified by its reddish purple color and parsley like shape. It contains carageenan, a substance used as a thickener in many common foods, including ice cream. In parts of Ireland and Scotland, people boil it in milk and flavor it with cinnamon, vanilla and whiskey. Homebrewers also use it when boiling the wort, because it attracts proteins and other solids, making a clearer batch of beer. The beach eventually leads to where Alewife Brook empties into the Peconic. You can also walk off the beach and into the picnic and camp area, following the main road to the entrance, and the start of the second trail.

The second trail proceeds through wetlands, following about a third of the way around Alewife Pond. This is where the Paumonock Path goes through Cedar Point Park. Shortly after you follow this path out of the park, you reach Scoy's Pond. Once I'm away from the beach, and near the pond, I quickly realize that the mosquitoes are out and they are hungry. Reeds surround the pond. Several duck blinds, used for hunting during duck season, can be used to set up a camera and get a good view of the pond. I see the first of several deer, a seven pointer. The trail proceeds south, and out of the preserve. Once out of the preserve, a few more deer show themselves. From the swampy low areas on the west side of the trail you can hear bullfrogs. The trail leads through a pine area, and in a short time crosses over a stream, reaching Scoy's Pond.

In February 2007 hikers found a beaver lodge on Scoy's Pond. Beavers haven't been seen on Long Island since the 1700's. Although they prefer fresh water, Beavers are exceptional swimmers. The beaver in question probably made its way over from Connecticut. Beavers have been seen in recent years on Plum Island. Their construction projects have been found in fresh water ponds as recently as February of 2012, although the more recent constructions may be the Scoy Pond beaver. Try as I might, I can't find any signs of beaver. I retrace my steps past Alewife Pond and back to Cedar Point.

Directions:

From Sunrise Highway, head north on Stephen Hand Path in Easthampton.
Make a left on Old Northwest Road.
Make a right on Northwest Road.
Make a left on Alewife Brook Road.
Make a right into the preserve on Cedar Point Road.

Beach Rose

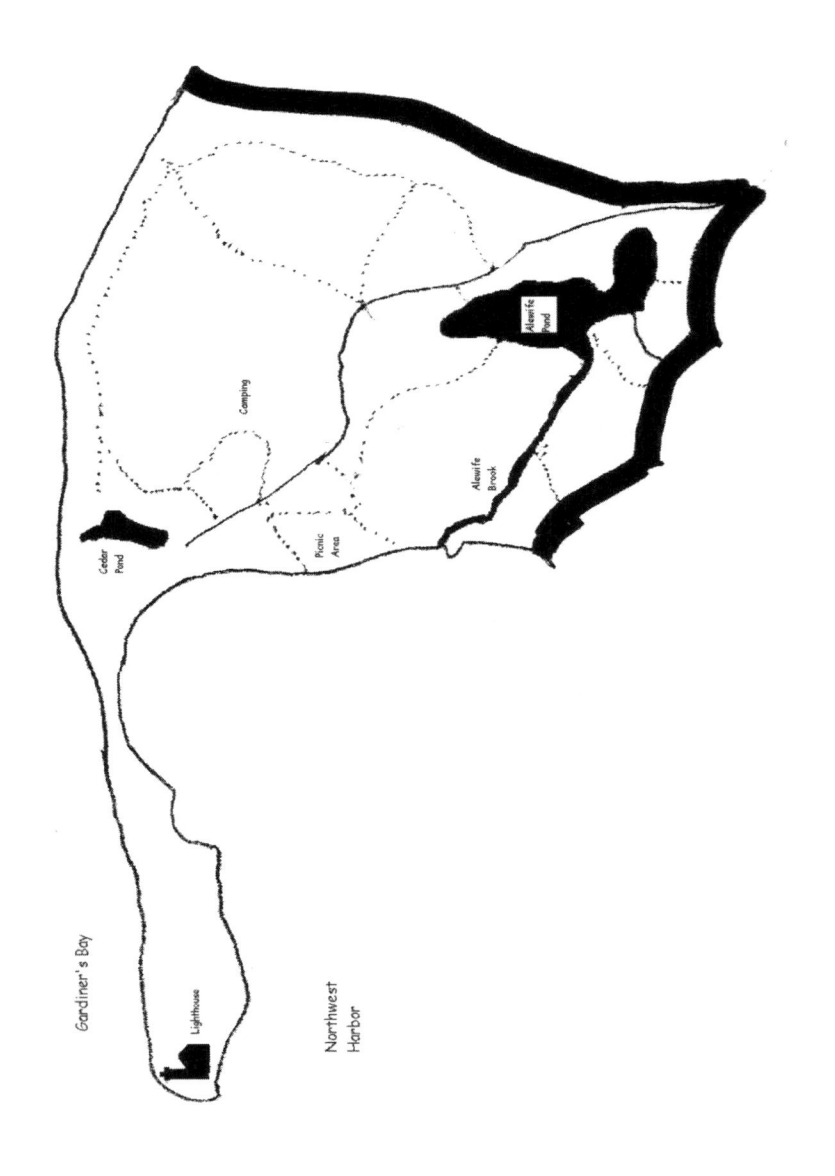

Figure 15 Cedar Point

JULY

Prickly Pear Cactus In Bloom

OCEANSIDE MARINE NATURE STUDY AREA

July 7th

On the edge of The Great South Bay, this little 52 acre salt marsh offers the best bird watching on the South Shore. Bring a pair of binoculars, or, even better, bring a camera and tripod. The Town of Hempstead manages the study area which includes an interpretive center, providing detailed resources for people interested in local ecology. Inside the nature center visitors can post their bird observations on whiteboards. Monitors show live images from cameras focused on the preserve's osprey, peregrine falcon, and tree swallow nests. These cameras allow visitors to get up close and personal to these animals without actually disturbing them. The trail goes around a manmade pond on the south end of the preserve, and through a sample sand dune created on the western side of the preserve. These trails include boardwalks which safely bring you over the salt marsh, protecting you from it, and more importantly, it from you. You definitely want to take it very slow and easy. Several benches provide an opportunity to sit and take in your surroundings, enjoying a view of the bay. Pick a bench, and watch the various birds do what they do. Hunt, fish, swim, fly, preen, lurk in the marsh grass, pick through the mud, or simply chase each other. On this visit, I was able to spot numerous gulls of different varieties, snowy egrets, great white herons, Canadian geese, various ducks, red winged blackbirds, catbirds, yellowthroats, terns, and tree swallows.

A glossy ibis, much less common than most of the other birds, waded in one of the channels. The glossy ibis can be identified by its curved bill and iridescent wings. Ornithologists believe the ibis arrived in North America from Africa in the 19th century. A great white heron allowed me to get within three or four feet of her and take some pictures. As if aware of the camera, she fixed up her feathers and posed coyly. She didn't get spooked, and didn't seem the slightest bit nervous with me around. I watched a cormorant grab a fish from the water and suck it down. I also watched a clapper rail land and then probe for food along the edge of the pond.

The real stars of the preserve are the osprey. This summer a whole family, consisting of a mating pair and two chicks, lives on the platform. One week into July, and the chicks approach the size of their parents. Most field guides refer to birds this age as immature, but they seem to be behaving in a respectful and responsible manner. On the path approaching the platform, a wooden bridge separates the bay from the manmade pond. On its handrail, one of the young osprey and a snowy egret look each other up and down scoping each other out. They knew I was there. The adult at the nest kept calling out warnings. I didn't get much closer than seventy five yards or so. Osprey won't attack people, but feel stressed when people get near their nest. I didn't feel any pressing need to follow the trail all the way around the pond, so I turned around and enjoyed the rest of the preserve.

Besides looking up at the birds, you can also look down at the tidal pools and shallow streams cutting through the cord grass. Most of the preserves in this book provide different experiences at different times of the year, depending on the season. Depending on the tides, the Nature Study Area provides different experiences at different times of the day. Looking in the water, you will see mussels, killies, and fiddler crabs. At extreme low tides, you can see the mussels piled up around the grass roots, and orderly piles of sand left behind by the fiddler crabs. The salt marshes that mark the edges of the island provide a breeding ground for many different types of fish and invertebrates. The grasses give them a place to hide from predators. Additionally, the calmer water makes it easier for many types of plankton and algae to thrive and start a cycle where decomposing matter which doesn't get washed away allows for more evolved plant life to develop. The success, or failure of the algae and other plant life, has repercussions all the way up the food chain. Algae and plankton feed the insect larvae. The insect larvae feed the fish and invertebrates, which in turn feed bigger fish and invertebrates, all of which wind up on our dinner table. The larvae that don't get eaten my fish turn into insects which are fed upon by various birds.

    The grasses on the marsh also tell a story. Three dominant types of grasses make up the salt marsh, salt marsh cord grass, salt meadow cord grass and giant reeds. The salt marsh cord grass is taller, than the salt meadow cord grass, and grows right in the water. It can get up to five feet tall. Saltwater floods it; submerging its roots twice daily. The salt meadow cord grass stands about two feet high growing in thick clumps. Mother Nature designed it to tolerate frequent flooding during extremely high tides, instead of daily year round flooding. The giant reeds, or phragmites, grow further up land where it floods only occasionally. You can tell how frequently different parts of the marsh are inundated with water by the type of grass that predominates. Ecologists consider the taller salt marsh cord grass an engineering species, because it grows in first, starting a cycle. It develops a soil, and builds up a land mass, allowing the salt meadow cord grass, and eventually other plants to work their way into an environment. It is in this manner that the island slowly uses its salt marshes to push its boundaries south.

Directions:

From Sunrise Highway:
Take Milburn Avenue South.
Make a right on Atlantic Avenue.
Make a Left on Waukena Avenue.
Make a left on Park Avenue (at this point, signs lead in the direction of the Nature Center.)
3rd left on Golf Drive
Golf Drive banks left becoming Bunker Drive.
Cut right onto Slice Drive.
The preserve is closed on Sundays.

Herons in the Grass

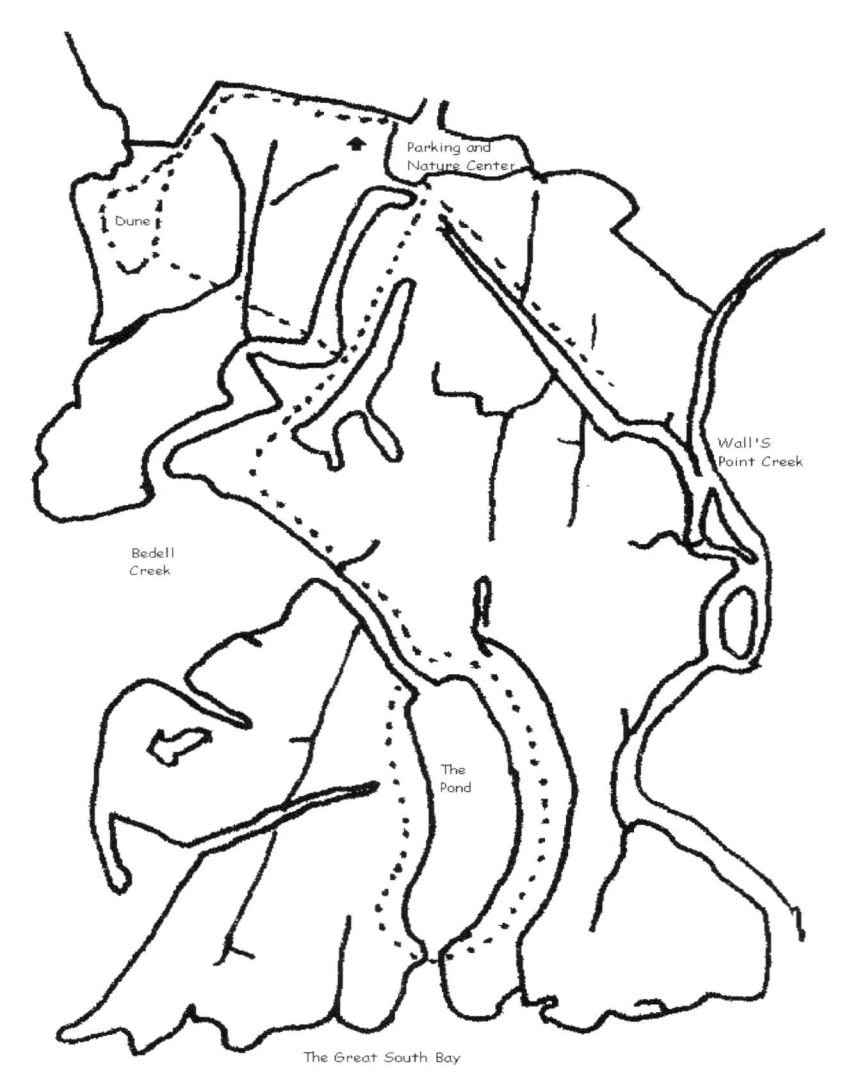

Figure 16 Oceanside Marine Nature Study Area

SUNKEN MEADOW STATE PARK

July 14th

Immediately west of the mouth of the Nissequogue River, Sunken Meadow State Park encompasses three miles of beach along the Long Island Sound. The park covers nearly 1300 acres, but a significant portion of that is dedicated to a golf course, and picnic areas. If you happen to be at Sunken Meadow for a picnic, make it a point to walk along the beach, the bluffs or both. Immediately east of parking lot number three, a salt pond and marsh can be found tucked between the bluffs on the south side, and the beach on the north. It extends all the way to where the Nissequogue River empties into the sound. The pond and surrounding salt marsh area constitute the outflow of Sunken Meadow Creek, which starts further west in the park. You can walk east along the beach, and circle back around on the north side of the pond. Plover, sandpipers, and other shorebirds nest on the beach.

You can also walk a loop, following the south side of the pond to Nissequogue River State Park, go up the bluffs via stairs, and return to Sunken Meadow State Park along the top side of the bluffs. The hike covers less than two and a half miles. On the day I visited this spot, it was sunny and the temperature made it into the eighties, a robust summer day. During the summer, an ice cream truck can be found at the Nissequogue River parking lot, about halfway through the hike. Hopefully, it will be there today, and I can stop for an Italian ice. The contrast of the beach area and wooded bluffs make this a special hike. As I started on the hike, a young man, finishing his hike with his small children looked at me and commented on the wildlife.

On the west end of the pond, where the trail starts, a

stand of sumac trees grow above some shorter bayberry bushes. You'll also find a designated kayak launching site on the west end of the pond. The water in the pond is much more tranquil than the water at the mouth of the Nissequogue, making it a great spot for some relaxed kayaking.

  Patches of aster and thistle bloom on the sides of the trail, along with various other wildflowers. Cord grass marks the edges of the pond. You can see how low the tide is by the dried mud on the stalks of cord grass. In the wet sand where the tide retreated, a few fiddler crabs pop in and out of their holes. Staring out over the pond, you can take in the view of the bluffs and the beach, with the pond in the middle. In the distance on the sand bar, a patch of sparsely leaved sumac stand out as the tallest trees, growing alongside red cedar, pitch pine and other shrubs typical on a sand bar. A thin patch of sand and rocks forms a berm, separating the west side of the pond from the rest of Sunken Meadow Creek. A row of trees blocks an easy view to the creek area, but as I poke my head through, I see seven double crested cormorants perched on a large rock in the creek. Cormorants are fairly large shore birds, identifiable by their grey and black bodies and their bright orange beaks.

  The trail turns to the left and proceeds along the bottom of the bluffs. The bluffs go straight up. Moss, oak, and other plants cling to the sides of the bluffs. Some of the trees have roots exposed through the gradual, but constant erosion of the bluffs. Some trees have already fallen. One tree, which looks like it fell during the winter, lays across the trail with its roots completely exposed.

  At the base of the bluffs, thickets of salt spray rose grow. Common on Long Island, salt spray rose emigrated from Asia. They are sometimes referred to as beach tomato. The bright orange fruits look like small tomatoes, and grow alongside the plant's pink and white flowers.

Looking out over the pond, you can watch herons and other shore birds take off and land on the calm surface of the water. As I walk a little further, I find a huge mud area, covered in sea lettuce, deposited with the dropping tide. A colony of fiddler crabs, their numbers easily in the hundreds run along the edge of the pond. Watching these adorable little critters pop in and out of their holes and scurry along the sand excites me. They move, almost in unison, like a school of fish when I walk toward them. Seeing me as a threat, a few of the bolder ones wave their claws in a display of intimidation, as if to say, "Yo! 'sup?".

The males have one claw considerably larger than the other, accounting for about a third of his body weight. Juveniles and females, on the other hand, have two smaller claws, both used for eating. They use the smaller claw for eating the detritus in the sand and mud. The little balls of sand the crabs leave at the opening of their holes are made from the sand left over, after they sift for food, similar to a plate of shells and bones left over after certain primates eat all the flesh. Their burrowing and constant sifting through the sand aerates the soil. Statistically, about twenty five percent of the crabs are left clawed, compared to about ten percent of the human population being left handed. The claws regenerate if knocked off. In fact, nature designs them to come off easily. If caught, under a rock or other debris, crabs will snap off their own leg, so they can live to fight another day.

The larger claw is for display and sparring. When juvenile males hit fiddler crab puberty, their combat claw grows, and they get more aggressive. Although unusual, some males hit puberty and develop two giant fighting claws. They look badass, but, without a small claw, they are forced to eat by plowing their face through the mud. They don't make the tidy little sand balls the more dignified crabs make after a meal.

Being tough little critters, it makes sense that, their favorite sport is boxing. The fighting isn't just ritualistic, and it's not as simple as a competition over the ladies. Like humans, the crabs fight over territory. They compete over prime locations for burrow digging. It's not so much the guy with the bigger claw that attracts the ladies, but the guy who can build and defend the best bachelor pad. The crabs find the best accommodations in the intertidal area. Males commonly instigate fights by pulling opponents out of their holes, challenging other crabs to a duel. After digging their burrows, the males wave their claws to attract the attention of the ladies. Once a female selects the male with the most appealing hole in the ground, they have a quickie, and the inseminated female lives in the burrow with her developing eggs, until they hatch. It takes about two weeks for the larvae to develop and swim free in the water. During that time, the affectionate male keeps his lady cool and moist by covering her with a loving blanket of wet sand.

At the east end of the pond, where it empties into the Nisseqougue River, the water moves notably faster, and larger pebbles can be found in the stream bed. Several sand bars break up the shallow water. Extensive mussel shoals cover the beds of the shallows. The mussels clump together, and pile on top of one another to such an extent that you can't see the sand. Although tempting, harvesting mussels here is illegal.

At Nissequogue River State Park, where the Nissequogue River empties into the sound, the river, starting about eight and a half miles inland, is subject to drastic tidal changes. The tide rises and falls approximately seven feet here. When people kayak or canoe the Nissequogue River, they coordinate their trips with the tide, either riding the tide in, or riding it out. If you don't have your own kayak, several companies rent them, and offer guided tours. The best way to see, and truly appreciate this tiny little river and its salt marshes is on a kayak or in a canoe.

    Once you're at Nissequogue River State Park, You will have to ascend a small flight of stairs and cross a parking lot to get to the top of the bluffs at this point. The ice cream truck waits in the parking lot for me. I grab an Italian ice, lemon flavored, and rest for a few minutes taking in the sound and the sand bars before I go along the top of the bluffs.

    White blazes mark the Long Island Greenbelt Trail at the top of the bluffs, follow them west. Following the white blazes south along the river will bring you through Arthur Kunz Preserve, Caleb Smith Preserve, Blydenburgh Preserve, Lakeland, Connetquot State Park, and so on, until you reach Heckscher State Park, thirty one miles away on the south shore. You don't want to make a wrong turn here.

    As you leave the parking lot, some smaller red cedar trees line the trail. The woods consist predominantly of oak, although cherry and beach are well represented. A few pitch pine can be found, which become the predominant tree further south and east. As you go west along the trail, you can take in the view of the salt marsh and sound from a number of different vantage points. As you walk along the trail, be aware of the poison ivy lining the sides of the trail. You can also find some large glacial erratics which make good places to stop and rest. In one area several tree falls block the trail, attracting catbrier, wild raspberries and other vines. The trail goes up and down a few small hills, and ultimately reaches the picnic area. You can get back to the parking area by following a gravel road, and crossing a wooden bridge with scenic views of Sunken Meadow Creek.

Directions:

Sunken Meadow State Park can be reached by following the Sunken Meadow State Parkway all the way north. The parkway ends at the park entrance.

Fiddler Crab

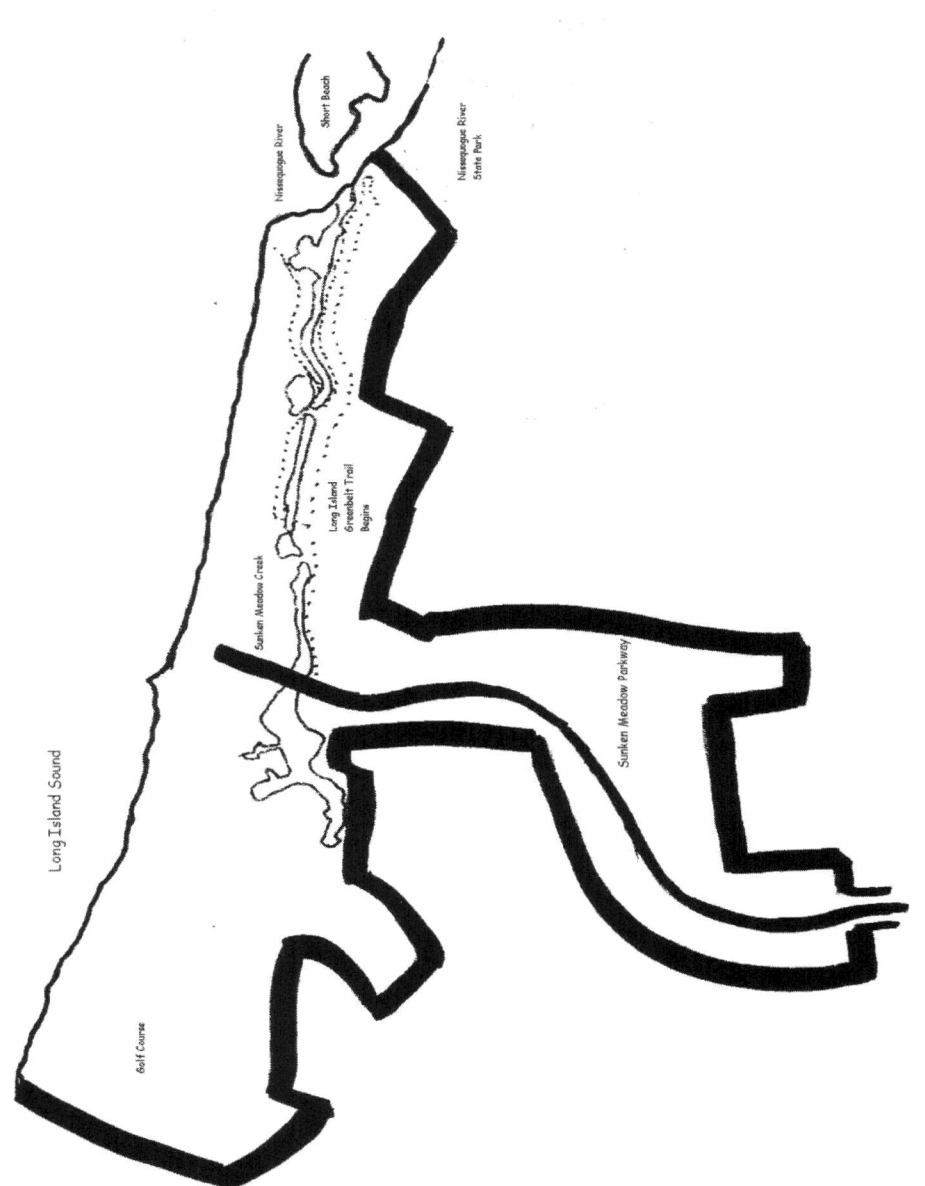

Figure 17 Sunken Meadow

AVALON AND EAST FARM PRESERVES

July 22nd

The two adjoining privately owned preserves are located in Stony Brook, across from the historic gristmill. Combined, they make up approximately 140 acres. The Paul Simons Foundation maintains Avalon. His family and friends established the foundation and Avalon to celebrate the life of Paul Simons, a fellow traveler, who, like anyone reading this book, loved and valued nature. The Nature Conservancy maintains East Farm Preserve. Both organizations rely on donations to continue the good work they do. Designed by a landscape architect, the preserves feel structured, and lack a real wild, "Mother Nature is in control" vibe to it. The preserves offer visitors a pleasant and relaxing walk, the longest trail being a two and a half mile loop. You'll find several shorter trails as well, all very well marked and easy to follow. It's a popular location, and when the weather cooperates, can be a little crowded.

A pond and adjoining wetlands graces the entrance. A boardwalk through the wetlands allows visitors access to the rest of the preserve. Approximately two feet deep, and home to an assortment of ducks and geese, the pond occupies several acres at the base of a hill. Duckweed covers the quieter corners of the pond. Maple and other trees shade the boardwalk. Purple milkweed lines the trail. At the end of the boardwalk, the trail proceeds up the side of a hill, passes a small pond, reaching a labyrinth and a sculpture at the top of the hill. As I walk along this trail, I notice huckleberries, and I notice bees pollinating honeysuckle. Once you reach the labyrinth, you can take a few moments and walk it in quiet contemplation. Past the labyrinth, monarch butterflies search the wood sorrel, aster and purple coneflower for nectar.

After the flowers, the trail goes through an area planted with rhododendron. A common native plant, rhododendron appears similar to mountain laurel, another common native plant. Both shrubs have white flowers, although rhododendron flowers can vary to pink or purple. Mountain laurels grow bigger, and have a papery bark, similar to cedar. Rhododendron bark contains more ridges, they also bloom later in the spring than the mountain laurel. The thick leaves of both provide shelter for smaller birds and animals all year round.

Past the rhododendron, the trail leaves the garden and enters the preserve part of Avalon connected to East Farm Preserve. The path takes you through some beech trees, and slowly brings you up a hill. On the edge of the woods, a large glacial erratic attracts kids of all ages, silently begging to be climbed on, it offers a good place to sit and rest.

From here, you can walk around the field and enjoy the wild flowers. At this point in the summer, purple coneflower, a type of daisy, blooms, alongside black-eyed Susans and whorled rosinweed. These are yellow flowers with a yellow center, looking similar to black-eyed Susans, but without the black eye. Neither the coneflower nor the rosinweed comes from Long Island. Queen Anne's lace and field thistle, common throughout the Island, also bloom. Butterfly weed, also known as orange milkweed shows its small clusters of bright orange flowers. I even found foxglove, identifiable by its drooping purple flower. Like most of Long Island's other inhabitants, foxglove arrived from Europe. The plant is used to make digitalis, a common heart medication.

Touch-me-nots also started blooming, and will continue blooming into early fall, covering large areas wherever they grow. Their flowers are orange and trumpet shaped, with brighter orange spots. The name is ironic, because the flower provides relief for poison ivy. It would make more sense to call poison ivy "touch-me-not", and come up with a different name for the "touch-me-not".

The remains of wild raspberries cling to the sides of the trail, already picked through by various birds. A favorite food for birds, deer, and any animal capable of reaching them, the wild raspberries disappear as soon as the flowers turn to fruit. I can hear a hawk, but can't see it. Field areas like this offer ideal hunting spots for birds of prey. Rabbits and chipmunks can easily be seen from the sky. In the tall grasses, islands of pioneer trees, such as sumac and juniper stand out. Red cedar also grow here. The designers strategically placed a few stone circles, allowing guests a few moments of rest or meditation before they continue their walk back through the forested areas.

Directions:

From the L.I.E. Take Nicholls Road North (Exit 62).
Follow Nicholls Road until it ends at Route 25A.
Make a Left.
Follow Route 25A. After a mile and half, bear right onto Main Street.
Make a left on Harbor Road.
The entrance is on the left side of Harbor Road.

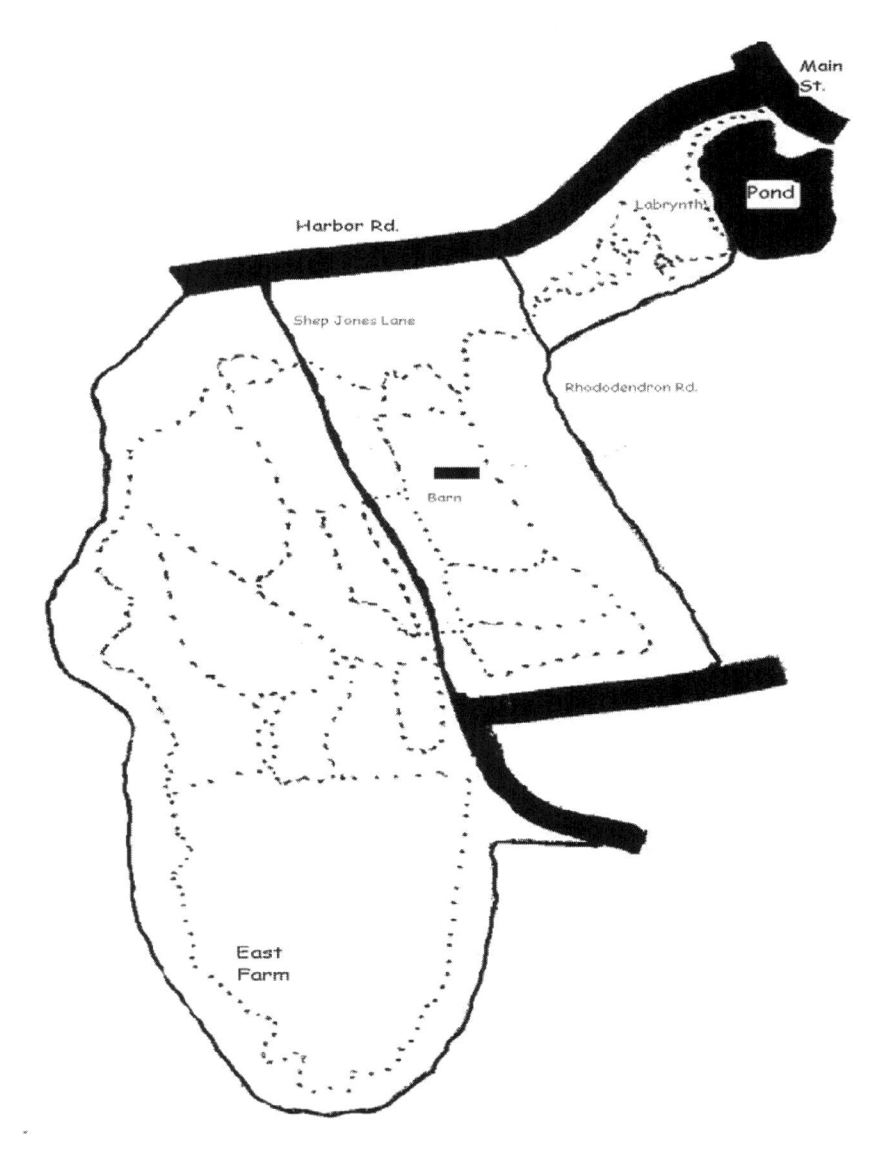

Figure 18 Avalon and East Farm Preserve

AUGUST

Chicory

STILLWELL WOODS

August 1st

  Stillwell Woods offers 270 acres of hilly terrain to explore. The main trial starts at the edge of the athletic fields. Volunteers keep it marked with yellow blazes. Stillwell Woods connects to Trail View Preserve, a narrow seven and a half mile park surrounding the Nassau-Suffolk Greenbelt Trail. The portion of the Nassau-Suffolk Greenbelt trail passing through this area can be identified by white blazes. If you want to expand your hike, without doing the whole Nassau-Suffolk Greenbelt, you can also park your car at the Trail View parking lot on Jericho Turnpike, about a mile south of Stillwell Woods.

  The preserve also includes the busiest mountain bike trails on the Island. It's a stretch to call the sport mountain biking if it is being done on Long Island. Sand hill biking would be a much more appropriate. Although it's never a good idea to feed wildlife, you can bring a few cans of Mountain Dew for the mountain bikers.

  The hiking trails go up and down sandy hills, and aren't as well marked as the preserve's mountain bike trails. No matter how hard you try to stay on the designated hiking trails, it becomes real easy to find yourself on the mountain bike trails. If hiking the whole Nassau-Suffolk greenbelt trail, be meticulous about following the white blazes. Stillwell Woods is the only spot on the Nassau-Suffolk greenbelt you are likely to get lost. Countless unmarked side trails can be fun to explore, but they have a tendency to keep you in the park for longer than you intend to stay.

  It rained earlier today, but the rain did nothing to help the humidity. Clouds color the sky orange. The dusk hours bring out clouds of gnats. It looks like it's been months since the county's made any effort to clear some of the trails. On the edges of the trail, pioneer trees, including sumac and cherry line up. A few of the sumac display bright orange leaves this time of year. The sumac's distinctive red seed clusters are out, and have been for a few weeks. Grape vines climb the sides of the trees, grabbing on to whatever they can for support. In bloom you'll find red clover, Queen Anne's lace, and pink wild bean.

    Eventually the overgrown area gives way, and the forest takes over. In the northwest corner of the preserve a fairly substantial growth of white pine can be found. Past the white pine, a maple and oak forest takes over, with oak predominating. All types of oak common on Long Island can be found here, scrub oak, big leaf oak, white oak, black oak, scarlet oak. On the sides of the trails, chestnut oak grows alongside the surviving American chestnut. In the winter, when the leaves are down, you can stand on some of the elevated areas get a really good perspective on the lay of the land, and the depth of some of the ravines. In some areas, you can find old farmer's fields transitioning back to woodlands. Juniper, cedar and cherry slowly take over. A few quaking aspen mix in these areas. Quaking aspen get their name, because when the wind blows through their leaves, their leaves flutter, showing their light and silvery undersides.

    The large field serves as the centerpiece of the preserve. The county mows it on a seasonal basis. The mowing functions as safe replacement for brush fires. The field needs a seasonal purge to keep it from being grown in by shrubs and trees. Naturally, periodic brush fires replenish the soil and preserve the grassland habitat. In the interest of safety, the field is mowed instead, and the natural decomposition of the grasses replenishes the soil. A trail circles the field. As you walk around the field, you can easily see the distinction between grassland and old field growth. On the more grown in side, you'll find catbrier, cherry and juniper. On the field side you'll find various grasses, with a selection of wildflowers changing, depending on the time of year.

Last year, I visited in the early fall. The grass stood close to three feet high, and crickets kept jumping ahead of me. As I went around the trail, they jumped from one stalk of grass to the next, shaking the grass. I felt like I was slowly chasing a wave of crickets. Red tailed hawks frequently fly above the field, looking for rabbits hiding in the grass. Songbirds rely on the field, attracted by the crickets and other insects living in the grass. Besides attracting birds, the field also attracts people who fly kites and gliders. Clubs meet here to fly their contraptions, so as you hike around the edge of the field, you can enjoy their hobby as well. On the southeast end of the field an Amur honeysuckle tree, in full bloom, guards the entrance back into the forest. This particular species emigrated from Asia, and offers visitors sweet tasting white flowers.

The trail splits at the honeysuckle tree. You can follow it around the field, and back to the parking area, or you can follow it further into the woods. The forest in the south east corner of the preserve consists almost completely of red cedar. Oak populate the west side. The Long Island Railroad marks the southern boundary of the preserve. The whole southern end of the preserve dips downhill. At the base of the hill, you'll find a small stream, occasionally dried up, cutting into the sand. On the east side, the greenbelt trail brings you down a hill, through a stand of bamboo and under the tracks. Beyond the tracks, Trail View State Park continues, leading to Bethpage State Park, and ultimately Massapequa Preserve.

On the west side, unmarked trails follow along the edges of the ravine. Catbrier covers the ground, and oak covers the canopy. Further west, mounds of rocks run in long straight lines. No doubt, farmers placed them here to mark the boundaries of now forgotten fields. These become more noticeable when hiking in the winter, when the undergrowth doesn't cover them. You can't help but speculate as to how long ago farmers placed them there, and how long they will remain there before the catbrier, and oak trees pull them apart.

Directions:

From Route 135, Proceed East on Jericho Turnpike (Route 25). Make a left on South Woods Road.
The preserve is a mile north on the east side of the road. Look for soccer fields and a parking lot.

Amur Honeysuckle

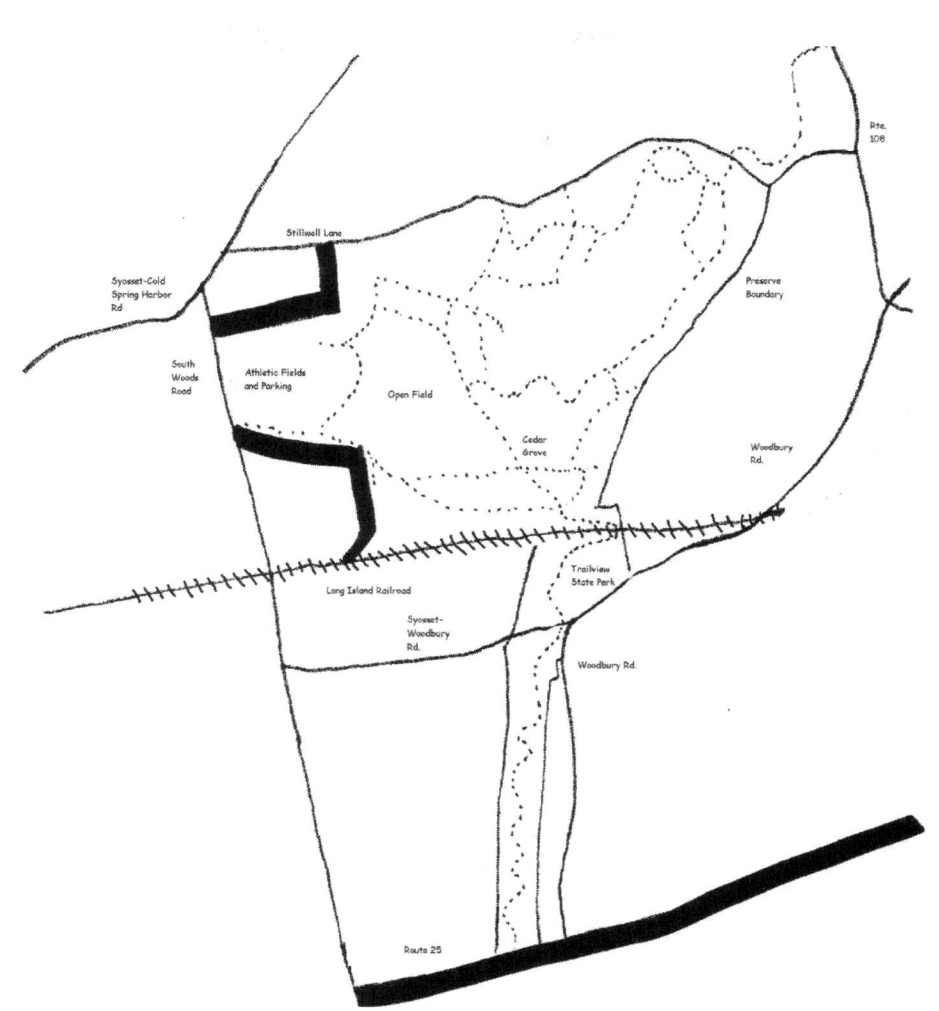

Figure 19 Stillwell Woods

CAUMSETT STATE PARK

August 5th

Prior to European settlement, The Maneticock Indians called the area Caumsett, which means "place by a sharp rock". One can only speculate that the sharp rock they referred to was the same "Target Rock" used by British sailors to test their cannons. The park encompasses 1600 acres, big enough to discover something new on each visit. There are buildings of historic significance, a stable and extensive bridle paths, as well as paved paths for bicycling or jogging. For nature enthusiasts, such as us, the preserve includes a diverse range of habitats. In one day you can walk through fields of wildflowers, investigate a tidal marsh, visit the beach, and explore fairly unique oak-hickory, and oak-poplar forests, containing pockets of old growth.

It rained overnight and early this morning, leaving the air hot and humid. Thunderstorms will roll in later in the afternoon. Starting from the parking lot, you can go north towards the sound by following a trail on the west side of the old dairy farm. The trail goes through some pasture areas which the grounds crews mow seasonally, allowing them to grow back with a variety of wildflowers. On this visit, black-eyed Susans bloom alongside chicory, also called "blue daisy". Chicory flowers look pale bluish purple, with petals radiating like aster. Very common on the sides of the parkways, chicory blooms throughout the summer. It has a number of uses, one of which is as a substitute for coffee. Historically, the roots, which have a bitter taste, were dried, ground, and added to coffee. You'll also find bee-balm, also known as Oswego tea. Its lavender flowers always look a little rough for the wear. Dried and ground, Native Americans used it as a seasoning. It possesses antiseptic qualities, and was used to treat sore throats. Thymol, an active ingredient in mouthwash comes from this plant.

In one of the trees, a mockingbird, alerted to my presence, attempts to sound a warning. Fortunately he doesn't try to fly at me and attack. Known for very aggressive behavior, mocking birds attack people they consider a threat. Capable of recognizing and remembering a human face, they will attack you if you return. Flying across the field, near the trees, a large flock of swallows moves like a cloud in the wind. Alongside the trail, between the forest and the field, a living fence grows, made up of catbrier, grapes and wild raspberries draped around sumac and sassafras. Birds picked through the sweetest berries. Grapes, just coming into fruition, will most likely be picked away within a few weeks. Small and sour, the wild grapes don't taste as good as supermarket grapes. Naturally attracted to grapes, yeast, a white powder, grows on their skins. When picking and eating any type of wild fruit, be careful when identifying the plant. Also, be sure to wash it thoroughly. Fungus sometimes grows on the surface of the fruit, similar to the coating of yeast on a grape, which can cause an allergic reaction.

The "living fence" forms a boundary between the field and the forest and provides a home to birds and rabbits. On the other side of the living fence, an oak forest grows. Just before I move out of the field area, I notice a doe cautiously standing at the tree line.

Once past the trees, a forest of oak and tulip tree opens up. I notice a younger tulip tree, at least twenty feet tall. The leaves are big in proportion to the rest of the tree, like a puppy's paws, and the tree will certainly grow into them. The trunk is about as big around as a coffee cup. The bark feels very smooth, but you can see where furrows and ridges will develop as the tree grows. Under the right conditions, these can live several hundred years. As they grow, tulip trees shoot straight up. Their trunks get thicker as they get older.

As you walk along this trail, the lower area is on your left, and the more upland areas are on your right. The lowland areas eventually form a stream, which develops into a salt marsh. You'll find a small trail where the main trail turns, where you can go down and get to the edge of the salt marsh for a closer look. Ninety acres of salt marsh stretch out in front of you. An island covered with oak rises in the middle of the marsh. The tide sits fairly low right now, and the sun reflects off the dark muddy bottom. In the few pools of water where marsh grass isn't growing, you can see the movement of insects walking on the still surface. When the tide comes up, the flats get inundated, creating a lot of movement in the water. Close by, a pair of adult herons and one of their chicks wades through the mud. I go back up to the main trail following it north, towards the beach.

Immediately before the sound, on the left side of the parking lot you'll find my personal favorite spot in Caumsett. Behind a gate, between the salt marsh and the beach, a raised spit of sand extends between one half and three quarters of a mile towards a harbor. You can walk out on it along a narrow path that runs the whole length of it. The gate is there to keep cars and other vehicles off the sand. As I reached the gate, two blue heron fly from the salt marsh towards the sound. The plants are typical of a dune. You'll find lots of red cedar and juniper, and pokeweed, with its flowers turning into fruits. Growing from the sand, you'll also find beach rose, with both their flowers and their fruits out, goldenrod, golden heather growing under bayberry, with its small light blue berries. As you go a little further out, you'll find quite a bit of blueberry, with all their fruits, ready to be picked. Look out for poison ivy in the shrub area along the sides of the path. After a short walk, you will reach a dilapidated board walk. Built in the 1920's it leads to the cove where a previous owner kept his yacht. It looks rickety, but the boards are thick. I hope I am right in my assumption that the boards are too thick to break, and that the dried out and rotting ones are noticeable. If I fall through, it's only a two foot drop into a patch of poison ivy — not a big deal. Poison ivy also lines either side of the boardwalk. I need to watch my step, and not touch anything. The board walk continues for several hundred feet. At the end of the boardwalk, the trail goes back to sand, and I reach the reward which makes the walk out here worth it. The reward is not the dried fox turd in the sand, although some naturalists would find such an item fascinating. The reward is the cactus colony. Nobody ever comes out here. On your left, you can take in the whole salt marsh. On your right, you'll find an extensive growth of cedar, so thick you can't see the beach or the sand, although the waves are close enough to hear and smell. Underneath the cedar, blueberries and other shrubs, you'll find the most extensive colony of prickly pear cactus on the island, and hardly anybody knows about it. Sand dunes drain quickly, and have much in common with deserts. Prickly pears thrive here, growing like grass on a lawn. The trail continues with the cacti and the cedar and the salt marsh until it reaches another rickety boardwalk area, which is more of a deck, and a small cove. Cormorants swim on the surface of the water. A sun showers passes through for a few minutes, cooling things down. I turn back around, finding a trail leading through the cedar and blueberry to the beach. I walk along the beach for a while. The wind makes the water on the sound choppy. You can see how thick and hazy the air is as you look down the beach towards the bluffs. A rock crab crawls where the waves hit the beach. As I walk down the beach, a few semipalmated plovers keep a consistent fifteen feet or so in front of me. Eventually they fly off, and a sandpiper leads me the rest of the way down the beach.

I get back to where stairs lead up to the road. Going up them, I follow the road up a hill. It is a bit of a strenuous climb. I welcome the cool shade offered by the oak. Going off the sides of this road, you'll find a number of smaller trails providing great views of the sound, or leading into amazing pockets of old growth oak. The people who lived here over the past several hundred years didn't cut everything down. You'll also find old fields grown in, and some hidden fields which are kept mowed by the ground crews. The alternating forest and field feels like a maze. When this was an estate, the owner liked to hunt pheasant, and had parts of the grounds arranged this way to make the hunts more challenging. It's anybody's guess as to whether they intended to confuse the hunters or the birds. You can still find feral pheasants descended from the pheasants that survived the hunts.

Eventually, you reach the more developed area of the park. On the far east side, a building with a rolling lawn looks over a freshwater pond. It's a great view. Ospreys have been nesting here the past few years. You can watch them hunt over the water. The paved path will take you past some of the historic buildings, and past equestrian areas and stables, and back to the parking lot. You'll even find a grove of white pine tucked away on one of the side trails.

Directions:

From the L.I.E. Take Exit 49 (Route 110).
Head North on Route 110 about 7 miles to Route 25A.
Make a left on Route 25A, Head West about a fifth of a mile.
Make a Right on West Neck Road.
Head north about 7 miles, Follow it to the end.
West Neck Road will turn into Lloyds Harbor Road.
The entrance to the preserve is on the left side of the road.

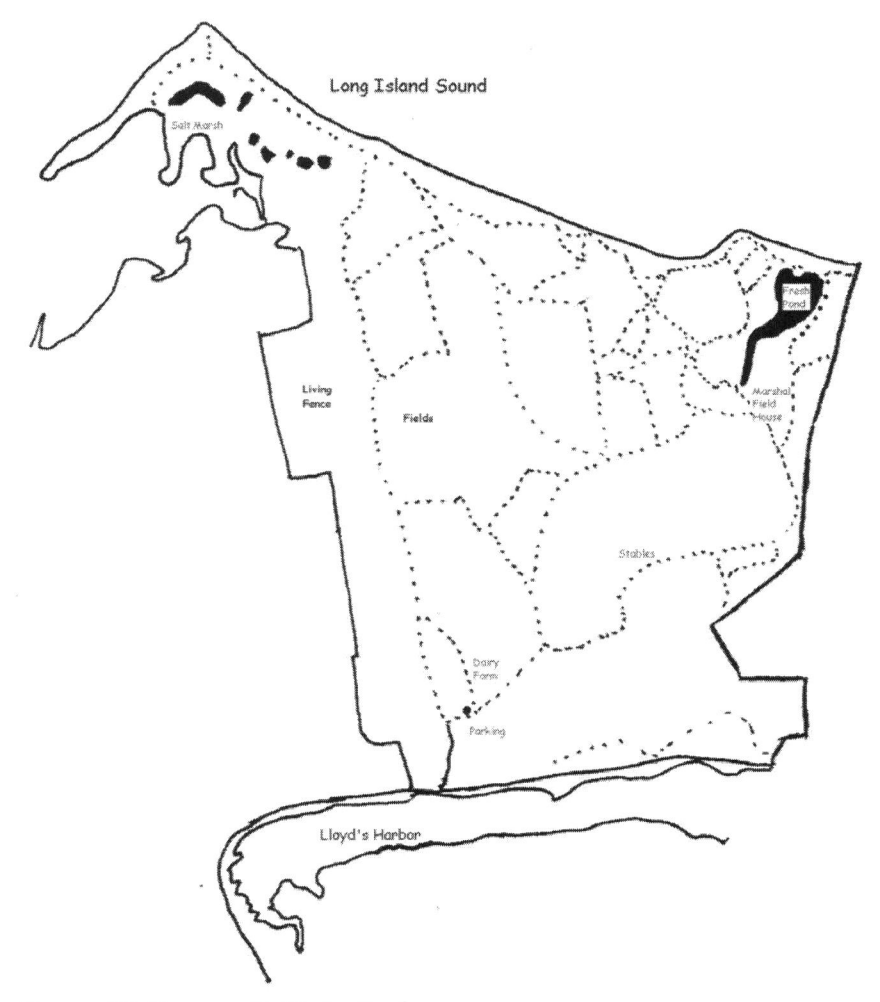

Figure 20 Caumsett State Park

SUNKEN FOREST

August 15th

Every Long Islander must visit Fire Island's Sunken Forest at least once. You can reach this globally rare maritime holly forest by ferry from Sailor's Haven, or you can walk over from Cherry Grove by following a paved path through the dunes connecting it with Sailor's Haven. If you start at Sailor's Haven, the trail extends for a mile and a half, most of it along boardwalks, built to protect the sensitive dunes. The oldest holly trees in this forest are about two hundred years old. When holly grows as a tree, instead of a shrub, the trunk takes on a gnarled appearance. The sunken forest is not just a local environmental treasure, but a globally rare habitat. You'll find very few forests like it in the world.

On the day I visited the Sunken Forest, it rained heavily in the morning. While waiting for the ferry, I watched thunder and lightning roll through. I saw a few lightning strikes hit the Island. Weather reports indicated the storm would let up by the afternoon. By the time the ferry docked at Cherry Grove, the rain tapered off, and the sun peeked out during my hike. Mother Nature gave me a wink and a few hours of clear skies. At the start of the trail, I took a good look at the ocean. The storm strengthened the crashing waves. Except for a few diehard beachgoers, the beach was empty. Darker clouds moved eastward, taking the thunder with them. While hiking, I watched the sky, knowing more thunder storms would be rolling through from the west.

Starting at Cherry Grove, I followed the paved path through the swale behind the primary dune. Before I reached the entrance to the Sunken Forest, the clouds completely gave way. The sun shone, as it can shine only on a beach. I broke a pleasant sweat as I walked behind the dunes. Even with consistent rain, the dunes might as well be a desert. Even this far from the ocean, salt spray hangs in the air. Catbrier, bayberry, blueberry, and beach plum form thickets, while beach grass and heather grab a tenuous hold in the sand. These provide food for the birds and deer that live here. I see an oriel, a catbird and a pair of cardinals. Fox roam through here also, but can be quite elusive. The taller trees you'll find include juniper, cedar, and, of course, holly. Some stretches of sand can only support beach heather. Stands of pitch pine, some of them dwarfed, grow in the swale also. Sections of the path give a view of the bay. Today, the waters of the bay look choppy, but appear serene compared to the ocean. Erosion slowly pulls the cedars and other trees right into the bay. Waves slowly dig at the sand under the roots. At most about six inches of top soil cover the island. When Hurricane Sandy arrives later this year, salt water will inundate the Island, washing away or killing much of the vegetation in a narrow section between Sailor's Haven and Cherry Grove, and eroding a few sections of the paved path into the bay. The flooding from salt water will kill the pitch pine that the waves don't tear up, leaving orange needles on the trees. Natural erosive forces gradually move Fire Island westward and northward toward Long Island, changing it constantly.

    Patches of sand on the calmer bay side have a reddish color coming from the garnet mixed in with quartz. Quartz makes up 98% of the sand on the beach, making Long Island's barrier beaches among the most beautiful in the world. The garnet tends to accumulate and be more noticeable on the north side of Fire Island. You can find similar accumulations of garnet on the beaches at Montauk and elsewhere on Long Island.

    The entrance to the forest brings to mind the darker

parts of fairy tales, suddenly getting colder as soon as you walk in. It takes a few moments for your eyes to adjust to the shade, but the cooler air instantly refreshes you. Besides the holly, sassafras and cherry trees make up most of the trees in the forest. The deer feed off of both the holly and the cherry trees, but the cherry trees, with a shorter life span, tolerate it better. The deer population makes it difficult for new hollies to sprout, and replenish the older growth. The forest sits behind a secondary dune, growing in the remnants of an inlet which once flowed between this dune and the ocean. The primary dune rises closest to the ocean. Because of the salt spray and wind, it is nearly impossible for plants to grow on the part of the dune facing the ocean. This secondary dune protects the forest from the ocean. Unlike the dune area, the holly forest has a fair amount of top soil, allowing for different plants.

   The boardwalk passes by several freshwater ponds populated with ferns and topped with duckweed. Moss forms on the roots of the trees lining the ponds. The fresh water rises up from an aquifer located under Fire Island. Catbrier and cattails grow around one of the ponds. All that is needed to complete the scene is a catbird, and that would be, to quote Julie Newmar, purrrfect.

   In one of the other low boggy spots, a small sourgum tree, also known as black tupelo, gives the first hint of autumn, its leaves already turning red. Eventually the boardwalk leads to a large deck where you can rest. Several ancient hollies grow through holes cut out of the boards. Unfortunately, people feel compelled to gouge their initials in these very old trees. The way relationships go, I doubt Phil and Corine are still together, but their names will remain carved in the side of the tree for years to come. At this point, you can follow a boardwalk back to the swale, or you can follow another boardwalk through a small salt marsh area overlooking the bay. If you do both, visit the salt marsh first, and then walk back to Sailor's Haven on the path between the dunes.

The salt marsh isn't as well developed as the marshes across the bay. You'll find phragmites, salt meadow cord grass, and in the areas closer to the bay, salt marsh cord grass. In mid-August, several whitish pink swamp mallows bloom on the side of the boardwalk.

Going back up through the forest, the boardwalk ends at a high spot at the top of the back dune. You can get a good view at the swale area between the dunes. You can see greener tops of the hollies. Stands of pitch pine and cedar also scatter between the dunes. The effects of the wind, sand and salt can be seen in the shapes of the trees. A few dead pitch pines still stand in the soil with orange needles and pine cones attached, either victims of lightning strikes, or shifting groundwater. You can also see the ocean extend toward the horizon beyond the primary dune.

Walking down the steps toward the trail leading between the dunes, I see three white tailed deer, a buck, a doe and a spotted fawn. The island is heavily populated with deer, so the deer on Fire Island always look a bit scruffy. As I move closer to the deer, I startle them, and they, in turn, startle a rabbit. The only visible birds are seagulls. The sky to the south and west darkens and thunder rumbles. The air turned hazy and yellow, a noticeable contrast with the cooler air under the canopy of the Holly Forest. I head back through the dunes before the rain returns.

Directions:

Take a ferry to either Sailor's Haven or Cherry Grove. If you have your own boat, there is a marina at Sailor's Haven where you can dock your boat.

Figure 21 Sunken Forest

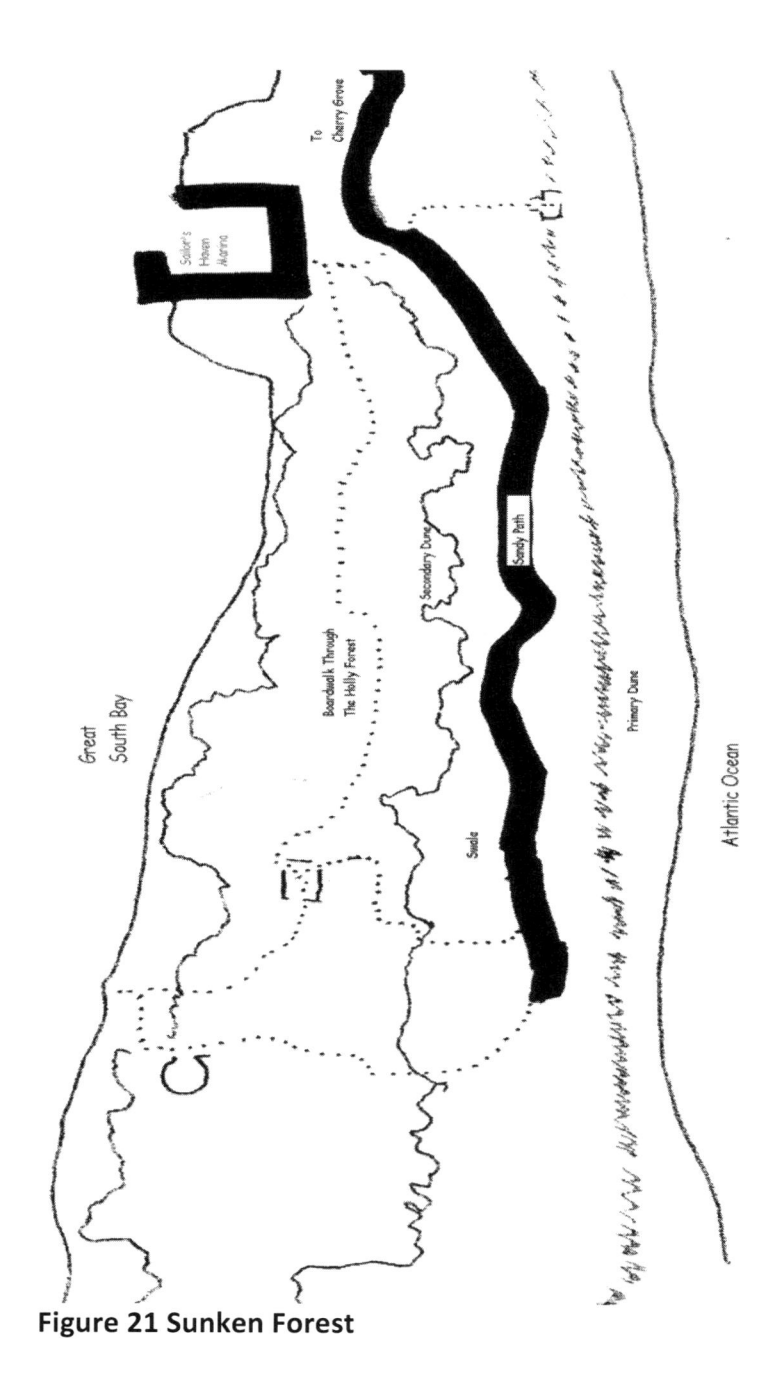

WILDWOOD STATE PARK

August 20th

 Known as a popular camping destination, Wildwood is also great for day hikes and beach going. The park covers 600 acres along the sound. You can visit the beach, the woods, or both. Camping allows you to take your time and enjoy the stars over the nighttime beach. This weekend, I camped at Wildwood, and severe thunder and lightning storms drenched the campground on the first night. By the following afternoon, the sky cleared and the air warmed up.
 The beach at Wildwood tends to be more rocky than sandy. Cormorants and gulls congregate on algae covered boulders along the shoreline. The boulders, made of gneiss, were broken off of outcroppings approximately ten miles or so north of here in the middle of what is now Long Island Sound. The water on the sound is usually calm, today being no exception. Beach bums trying to enjoy the last days of summer crowd the beach. When less crowded by people, ducks and other shorebirds swim in the water. During the winter you can walk the beach and hang with the various waterfowl which migrate here from northern latitudes.
 Above the bluffs, I watch two red tailed hawks circle. The bluffs rise about 160 feet above the beach at their highest point. Made of sand and clay, they are fragile. Poison ivy clings to the sides. A few small juniper shrubs take root in the sand alongside blueberry and rose bushes. The forest ends abruptly at the edge of the bluffs, often less than fifty yards from the water. The waves don't crash, sending salt spray into the air. The plants don't need as much protection from the dunes, as they do on the South Shore. The biggest threat to their existence comes from

people who don't realize the amount of harm they bring. As tempting as they are to climb and explore, the bluffs are easily eroded by the thousands of people who visit this beach during the summer. At the eastern end of the beach a small creek and tidal marsh empty into the sound.

    The forest starts immediately at the top of the bluff, and the land behind it slopes down gradually. Primarily, the forest consists of oak and beech, with significant amount of hickory and maple mixed in. The hiking trails are easy to follow, providing options for different length hikes. The Yellow Trail is the longest loop at 3.8 miles. The other loops divide the Yellow Trail into smaller segments. The smallest marked trail is the red loop at 1.8 miles. You also have the choice of making longer hikes by crisscrossing the trails, or by combining the beach and forest areas. On the trails closest to the edge of the bluffs, you can peek out over the sound. A few unmarked trails can be found and enjoyed by people who like to get a little lost and explore a big area like this. While back there, I accidentally startled a mother deer and her fawn.

    The beech trees took a beating from last night's lightning. You could see scorch marks. The dried leaves immediately next to the trees were also charred and grey. In the movies, when lightning strikes a tree, the tree practically explodes, but in real life, it only leaves a burn. Lightening can damage some trees to such an extent that they die off. In a few days, the leaves will get blown around a little, and the mark from the lightning strikes will barely be visible. For some reason I don't understand, I only see scorch marks on the beech trees.

    Red cedars populate an extensive section on the east side of the preserve. Further east still, an old field area slowly transitions back into a forest area. A line of white oak and spruce, clearly planted at some point in the distant past marks the south boundary of the preserve.

    The trail ends in the campground area. With the

undergrowth kept cleared, the campground shows how the retreating glaciers arranged the landscape many years ago. Boulders, more scientifically referred to as glacial erratics, remain scattered around. Besides depositing boulders, the glacier deposited chunks of ice. After the ice chunks melted, they left recesses in the ground called kettle holes.

   In late August, summer slows down, and autumn starts creeping in. The raspberries next to my campsite have been picked clean by birds. The hickories drop their nuts with frustratingly good aim. Through binoculars, a friend and I watched a young squirrel climb to the furthest extent of the swaying branches of a hickory tree grabbing for a nut to eat. The claws on a squirrel's feet are like talons, designed for digging into and gripping the sides of a tree, allowing them move nimbly through the canopy. I also noticed crows starting to gather; that's the real sign of autumn's arrival. Crows don't always migrate. During fall and winter, they roost together when food becomes scarce. I watched a small group chase each other around, playfully making their way from branch to branch through the trees. Crows are very intelligent animals, capable of not only using tools, but making them as well. Younger crows also find objects and play with them, similar to the way younger people. They communicate with each other by variations in their calls, making their foraging easier, and warning each other of prospective dangers. Some cultures regard crows as being symbolic of change and death, making them appropriate messages to signal the coming of fall.

Directions:

From The L.I.E., take Exit 68 (William Floyd Parkway).
Take William Floyd Parkway North.
At Route 25A, make a right (Proceed East).
Make a left on Randall Road.

Make a Right on North Country Road.
Bear left onto Wading River Road.
Wading River Road ends at the park entrance.

Rock Crab and Sea Lettuce

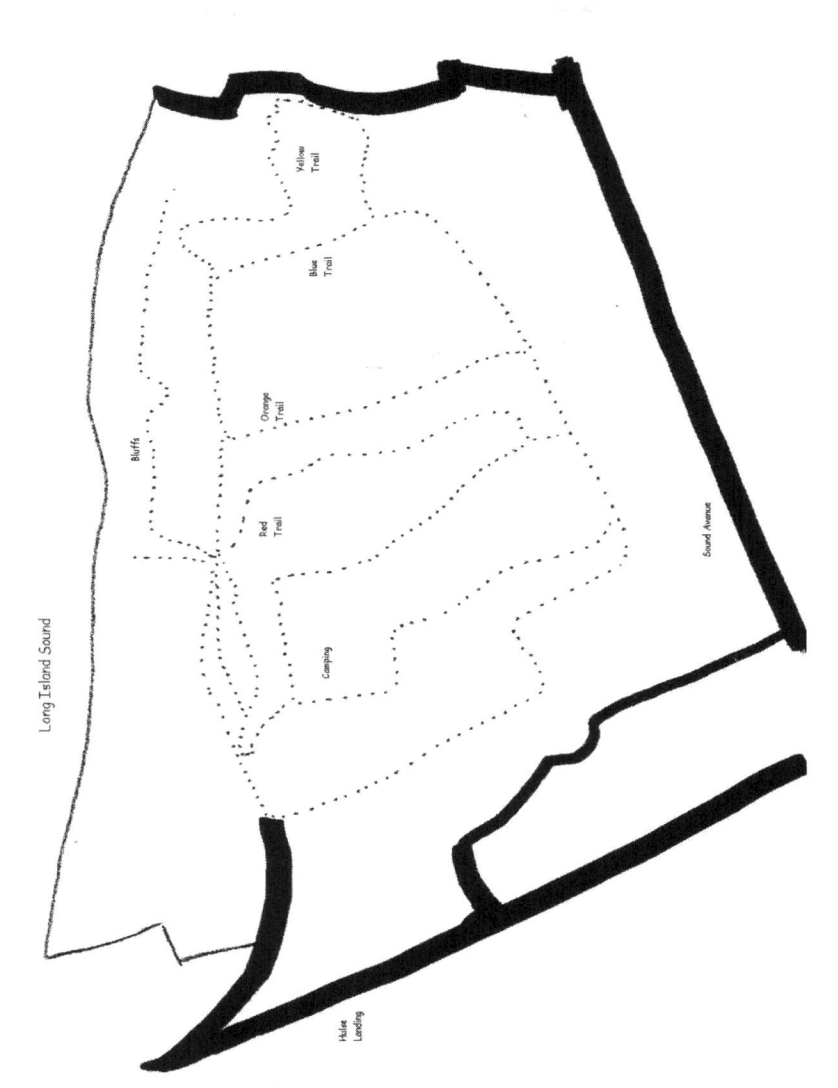

Figure 22 Wildwood State Park

MANORVILLE HILLS

August 25th

Manorville Hills offers 6,000 acres of roadless land. In it you will find some of the most isolated spots on Long Island. It remains one of the few places on the island where you can hike, and not be within hearing distance of a major highway or train line. The trails feel like they go on forever. Bring a compass and a map. The landscape and trails can be confusing. You can easily get turned around and lose track of where you are. Primarily a pine and oak forest, the hills are comprised of the Ronkonkoma Moraine. It is a "knob and kettle" terrain, which means that when the Wisconsin Glacier receded 20,000 years ago, it left chunks of ice embedded in sand. These melted, leaving depressions and sand piles along the bigger moraine. The glacier left a few sizable erratics to rest here also. Approximately ten miles of the Paumanok Path wind through here. Hikers marked several loop trails which can be followed. The longest, the Orange Trail, forms an eight mile loop. In addition to marked trails, you can explore countless unmarked trails.

The skies are clear, and the temperature is in the seventies. The parking area can be found at the end of a gravel path, surrounded with various grasses. A Maryland golden aster blooms in the sand on the edge of the parking lot, as does a patch of Pennsylvania smartweed. The cherry tree near the entrance starts to turn color. Underneath the cherry tree a white oak sapling gets ready for fall, its leaves a deep dark shade of green. In the parking lot, the county posts a map of some of the trails. The trails can be a little confusing to follow at the beginning. A bridle path, a mountain bike trail and the hiking trails all start and intersect at various points here. To make matters a little more confusing, the yellow trail, which leads to the orange trail, is marked with white blazes where it overlaps with the Paumanok path.

Initially, the trails go through some lowlands areas, with fern and catbrier covering most of the ground. A few spice bush show themselves as well. The tree canopy provides a fair amount of shade, complimenting the occasional cool breeze. Here the forest is predominantly oak, with a fair amount of pitch pine mixed in. Some of the pine trees are huge, and probably quite old. A pitch pine can live up to 200 years, but it is difficult to estimate the age of a tree without cutting it down. On the side of the path a few patches of telegraph weed prepare to disperse their seeds to the wind. The flowers turn to seed heads, similar to a dandelion. Each seed has its own parachute to carry it with the wind. Telegraph weed is a type of aster native to California. They do well in sandy soil, and, apparently, found their way to Long Island.

The lowlands give way to some old fields growing in, slowly being reclaimed by Mother Nature. The grass in the fields is a golden brown color. Juniper and cedar mark the edges of the field. Immediately after the field, a grove of fairly young white pine, the remnants of an abandoned tree farm, grow close together. Planted uniformly in rows, the white pines stand less than twenty feet high.

Underneath them an aromatic bed of needles covers the ground. Dead branches rest on the needles. Like pitch pine, white pine self-prune. The branches at the bottom naturally lose their leaves and drop off as the tree grows. The competition for sunlight in the grove is cut throat, no holds barred, and on such a long time scale, you barely notice it. The casualties of this slow conflict litter the floor of the pine grove, decaying back into the soil.

Once you move past the field and the pine grove, the pine-oak forest begins with the orange trail. The contours of the land become much more obvious. Some of the taller elevations go above 200 feet, not nearly as high as West Hills, but still a formidable mountain range compared the rest of the Island's terrain. Thankfully, the trails are cut in such a way, that the rises and falls of the moraine feel gradual.   Once you're into the pine barren areas, there is much less variation in scenery. As you look around it feels vast. Standing on the side of one of the hills, I see a red tailed hawk swoop down through the trees, close enough to appreciate its size. Pine needles and oak leaves cover the sandy soil. Lichens cling to the sides of oak trees. Moss grows in clumps around the bases of the trees. On this visit, I see a fowler's toad, common throughout the pine barens, sitting on the floor. As I move in to get a closer look he stares at me, not the least bit frightened.   Beneath some of the fallen branches you may find tiger salamanders.

   Wildflowers put on their show between spring and summer. Once summer ends and fall begins, nature's stage belongs to the fungi. You'll find a little more moisture in the soil, a little more debris on the ground, a little less sunlight, and the temperatures are just right. Mushrooms begin to put on their colorful displays. With the lighter undergrowth here, the mushrooms demand attention. Walking through, I see some white coral.   Continuing with the nautical theme, a red mushroom known as a shellfish scented rasulla pokes through the pine needles. A mushroom by any other name would probably smell sweeter. I also find some orange chanterelles. They are bright orange and easily noticeable as they emerge through some oak leaves. Mushroom names can be really colorful. Alone on the forest floor is a bleeding agaricus, a greyish brown mushroom that turns red once you cut it open. Residing in a rotten stump is an old man of the woods, a mushroom that looks like a burned marshmallow, but tastes like a portobello. The mushroom has a fluffy white appearance with carbon black spots on its surface.

Moving through the woods, I keep running into spider webs. There are more insects this time of year, so it follows that there would be more spiders casting their nets looking for prey. Spiders aren't concerned about the business and goings on of people, and rebuild their nests as quickly as I stumble into them.

Chiggers always present a problem in late summer and early fall. These little mites live in the leaf litter, alongside the mushrooms and toads. On this hike, they swarmed me. The only other time I was ever swarmed by chiggers was about this time of year five years ago. They feed off of animal flesh, and are small enough to crawl through the fabric of your socks and pants. Not having wings, they swarm around your ankles and legs, leaving hundreds of bites. You can feel them bite immediately, and they itch more than any other insect bite I've experienced. As soon as you feel them, the best thing to do is to walk a few yards from where you are standing, take off your shoes and socks, and start brushing them off. They tend to cling a little. You will find more in the fibers of your socks, so it's best not to put your socks back on. The chiggers don't transmit diseases, but an attack by a swarm of chiggers can be about as much fun as a rash from poison ivy. Your legs will feel like they are on fire. Use a little extra bug repellant around your ankles, and remember to re-apply it after you've been hiking for a few hours. An ounce of prevention beats having to walk five miles back to your car with chigger bites covering your ankles.

Directions:

From Sunrise Highway, take exit 62 north on C.R.111 the county park sign will be on your right.

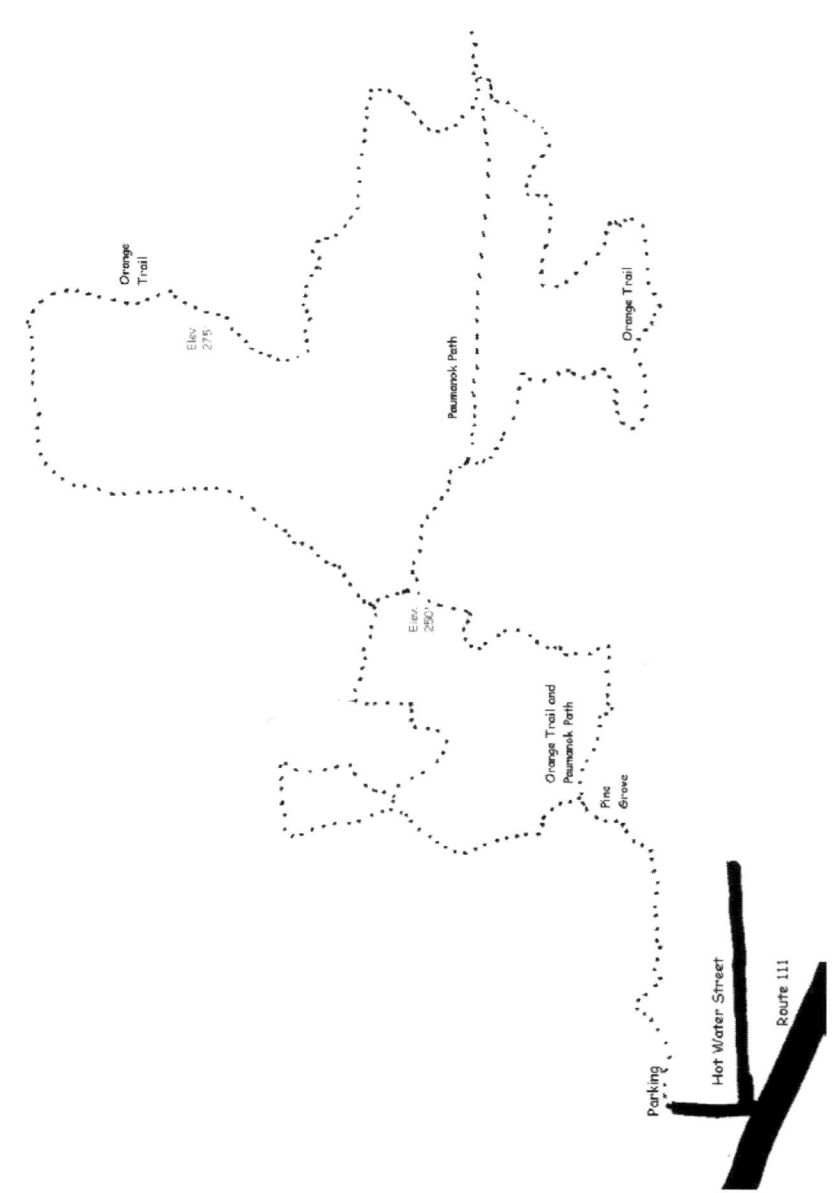

Figure 23 Manorville Hills

SEPTEMBER

Indian Pipe

MARINE PARK
SALT MARSH NATURE CENTER

September 1st

    The Salt Marsh Nature Center is one of a handful of preserves within New York City. It protects the southern end of Gerritsen Creek in Brooklyn, occupying 798 acres of salt marsh on the western edge of Jamaica Bay. While Long Island was created over 20,000 years ago by glacial deposits, the bay, and barrier beaches developed much more recently. Jamaica Bay began formed 5000 years ago when ocean currents deposited sand on what is now Coney Island and the Rockaways. Prior to urban development, Gerritsen Creek extended twice as far inland as it does today. Developers converted the freshwater portion above Avenue U into an underground storm drain. Like many other creeks on the Island, it is tidal, in that salt water flows in and out with the tide, mixing with the fresh water flowing in from further north. The creek is named for Wolfert Gerretsen, a Dutch settler who built a grist mill on the creek. The mill burned down in the 1930s, but its pilings, covered in barnacles and algae, still peak above the water at low tide.

    The city made commendable efforts over the past few years to restore it, as best as possible, to its original condition. On the day I visit here, the trail on the east side of the preserve is closed, so they can continue those efforts. It will re-open in a few months. They've been removing garbage, and invasive species, particularly phragmites, which are still prevalent on the west bank of Gerretsen Creek. The city's also been reintroducing native plant species, and allowing natural conditions that encourage native animals, particularly mussels and various birds to increase in number.

The west bank of the creek flows less than 200 yards from a busy Brooklyn neighborhood. It's not a place where you can completely escape the urban environment. Its reminders are frequent in the debris washed up on the side of the creek, and in the noise from the nearby streets. It is, fortunately, a place that reminds the visitor that nature is much stronger than we can imagine. She can do just fine in spite of our efforts to pave her out of existence. Shorebirds, oblivious to what the Cyclones are doing, enjoy the sun and shellfish. Fish fill the creek, crabs walk on the sand. Plants take root anywhere they can. The tide comes in and goes out, as it has for thousands of years, and as it will for thousands more, city or no city. It's not a monument to what used to be. Instead it's a reflection of how things are in nature today.

Near the Information Center, volunteers tend gardens featuring various native plants. A few black locust trees provide shade. A group of birdwatchers take pictures of a green heron standing in the grasses on the edge of the creek. A gate closes off the upland portion of the preserve. The phragmites have been cleared out, and the land stands barren, except for some grasses coming up. As I walked past the information center, I asked one of the park rangers about the restoration, he told me that the east side would be open in several months. Next spring, the east trail will be surrounded by grasses, and wildflowers, including purple coneflower, coreopsis and butterfly weed. The upland trail offers a much different perspective of the creek than the trail following the bank on the west side. Gravel covers the trails. Overlooking the creek, you'll find a bench at the edge of a spiral where you can sit and contemplate the churning currents of the ever expanding universe.

The ranger also told me that back in June, he was on the west side of the creek late one night, and witnessed hundreds of horseshoe crabs mating under the light of the full moon. As he put it, they were having a party on the beach, carrying on and feasting on mussels.

Horseshoe crabs have been celebrating the summer moons with a good old fashioned romp on the beach for 450 million years. To put that into perspective, 450 million years ago, all animal life lived in the water, and the only plants to be found clinging to the edges of Pangaea consisted of algae, and moss. Horseshoe crabs enjoyed the status of being one of the more evolved life forms on the planet.

During late spring and early summer, horseshoe crabs spawn on all of the quieter beaches around the island, waiting for high tides to crawl onto the beach during the new and full moons. With horseshoe crabs, the ladies grow bigger than men. When laying eggs, they dig into the sand, almost burying themselves completely. The guys cling to their backs, waiting for her to let loose. Like many other animals, fertilization occurs externally. She'll deposit anywhere between 16,000 and 65,000 eggs. I imagine it feels good for both of them, and neither one expects a phone call the following day. Three weeks later, the larvae moult for the first time. The larvae serve as a protein and nutrient rich superfood for many animals. Their copper based blood gives them a greenish tinge, and a distinctive flavor. Assuming they avoid being eaten by one of the many predators relying on eggs, larvae or young crabs for food, a horseshoe crab can live up to forty years. During winter, the green blooded hobgoblins hang out along the continental shelf, eating whatever they see with their nine eyes, or whatever they can shove into their jawless mouths. If aliens ever visited the earth, they might resemble horseshoe crabs.

As I walk down the west edge of the creek, I watch the tide going out. The lower tide gives off a sulfuric smell. Great white herons swim and fly alongside mallards and gulls. A yellow crowned night heron wades near the pilings of the old grist mill on the north end, where

Gerretsen Creek emerges from a culvert. A few cormorants rest on the water. On the sand I find washed up blue claw crabs. Fiddler crabs scurry through the algae on the mussel beds. The fiddlers leave little balls of sand after they siphon the muck for food. These will be smoothed back into the rest of the sand when the tide comes up. The shorter marsh grass quickly gives way to larger phragmites. Small groundsel trees and sea lavender bushes grow between the grass and phragmites.

People harvest mussels from the banks, but various contaminants make the mussels dangerous to eat. Mussels and other shellfish filter out and break down toxins in the water. Elsewhere in the city, oysters are being reintroduced for the purpose of cleaning out pollutants. Until the end of the 19th century, New York was known for its oysters, which have since largely disappeared, because of over harvesting and habitat destruction. The extensive dredging that's gone on in Jamaica Bay and elsewhere destroyed their nesting areas.

A little further up the bank, cherry and sumac become prevalent. Some of the sumac trees have white seeds, instead of the usual red seeds. Elderberry bushes also grow. Their dark purple berries give off a distinctive, sometimes unpleasant odor, and are used to flavor a number of different desserts and liquors, including sambuca. If not picked at the correct time, or prepared correctly, the berries can be toxic.

A few beach rose still bloom, although most of their fruits have dried up. Hog peanuts also bloom. Also starting to bloom this late in the season are purple morning glories, and blue Asiatic dayflowers. This time of year, the ends of the phragmites turn reddish brown. Poison ivy changes from deep green to deep red. All in all, there are fewer flowers and fruit. Eventually the trail alongside the creek becomes too grown in to follow any further, and I head back to the entrance to the preserve.

Directions:

From Belt Parkway, take Exit 11N (Flatbush Avenue).
Head north on Flatbush Avenue.
Turn left on Avenue U.
The Nature Center is on the Left side of Avenue U.

Figure 24 Shorebirds on the old pilings

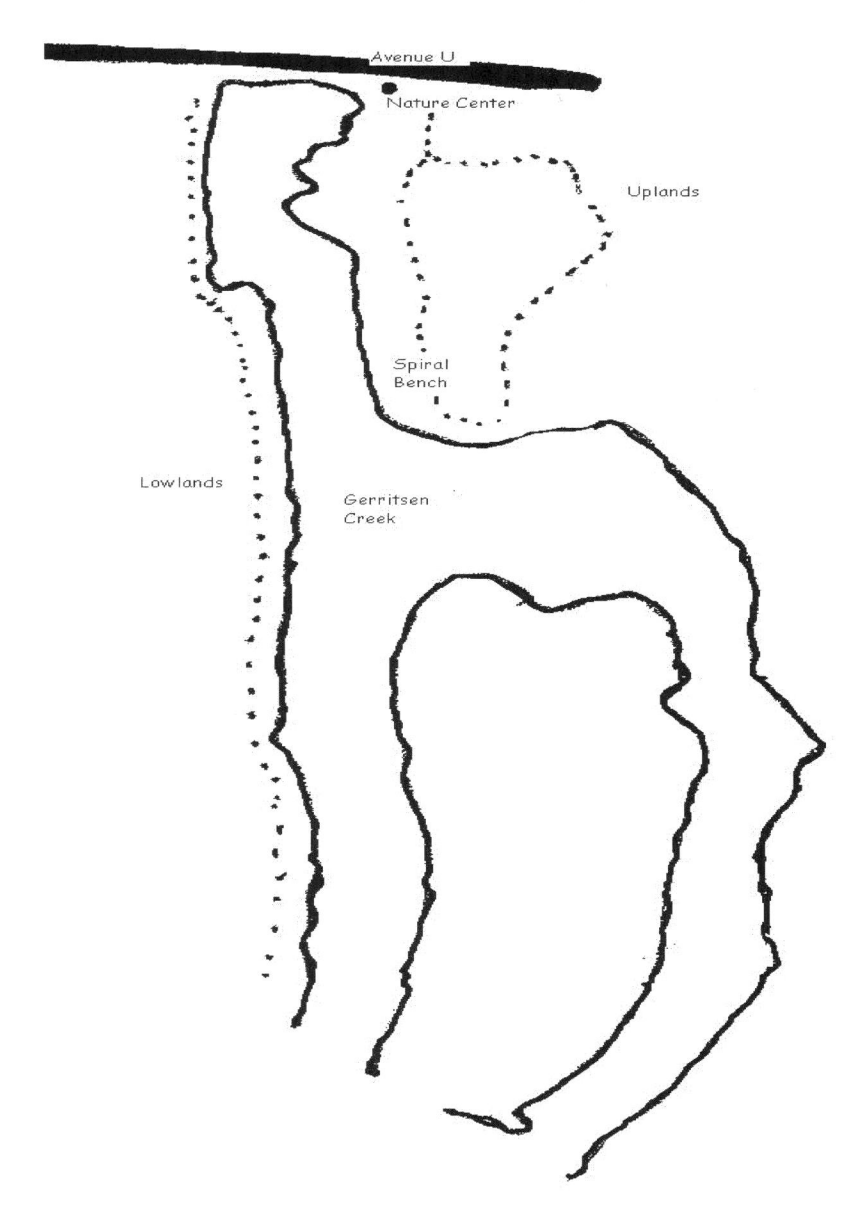

Figure 25 Marine Park Salt Marsh Nature Center

TIFFANY CREEK

September 9th

Nassau County maintains this 230 acre preserve in conjunction with the Nature Conservancy. Several marked trails wind through the preserve. A kiosk in the parking lot, located on the west side of Sandy Hill Road, provides an enlarged map of the trails. Approximately forty five acres can be explored on the west side of Sandy Creek Road, and the remainder of the preserve can be explored on the east side. Nature provides clear skies with temperatures in the seventies today. The sunny weather follows several days of heavy wind and rain. Tornados even formed in Brooklyn and Queens yesterday. The preserve covers forested areas, old fields in the process of growing back, and some hilly upland areas as well.

Following the blue trail, west of Sandy Creek road, Virginia creeper and English ivy cover the ground thickly. White wood aster also grows in spots. Raspberries grow also, but in September, there fruit is long gone. Land sits fairly low on the west side of the preserve, and closer to the water table, so various ferns inhabit the muddier areas off to the sides of the trail. Maple and oak, particularly white oak, predominate. You'll also find a fair amount of beach lining the paths. Tulip trees are also present, most of them young. Further along the trail, a twisted grove of mountain laurel provides an understory. These stay green after the leaves fall off the other trees in the preserve. Also in the understory, a few scraggly American chestnut trees hold on to their place in the forest. You can spot these by their oval leaves with pointy, saw like, teeth around the edges. American chestnut trees once competed with oak, filling most of the forests on the east coast, but due to disease, they rarely live more than thirty years.

The trail comes back around to the parking lot. At the edge of the lot, I find a small patch of Asiatic dayflowers, and follow the trail past an old field, completely grown in with touch-me-nots. Their orange trumpet shaped flowers grow as a thick, shrub like, vine. Going briefly back into the woods, red cedars grow between the oak. Whorled aster form white patches on the forest floor.

The trail tracks alongside Sandy Hill Road for a short distance, until it crosses over the road into a heavily grown in field area. Trails are mowed through it. It's best to watch out for poison ivy here. For the most part, the field has developed past being mainly grass to being shrubs, vines and small trees. On the sides of the mowed path, bees work over the touch-me-nots and golden rod. Rosebushes line the paths, but are finished blooming for the year. A few young cherry trees stand in the middle of the field, alongside sumac. The more grown in area of the field gives way to tall grass. In the grassier area, you can easily see how sandy the soil is, and watch grasshoppers jump from blade to blade. Few deer come this far west, so ticks aren't a problem, like they are further east. A few remaining chicory also grow through the grass. As you get to the end of the field, the trail splits off. You can continue around the field, or you can head into the woods.

Once in the woods and out of the sun, the air feels cooler. A large sycamore, unique in these woods, and probably planted years ago, rests on the side of the trail, its leaves already yellow. These are among the first trees to turn colors. Mountain laurels make up a large part of the understory. On the east side, the contours become more varied without being hilly. The taller trees in this section of the preserve consist of mainly oak, beech and some old growth tulip trees. A few of the tulip tree leaves already turn yellow, and begin to fall. The rest have not caught up yet. You can hear the beech dropping their nuts through the leaves. A black and white warbler makes its way up the side of an oak tree.

Tiffany Creek flows through the main ravine. Essentially a muddy patch, marked with ferns and moss, the creek grows into a puddle and then into a slow moving brook. Eventually, the creek opens up into a quiet one acre pond, called Held Pond, at the north corner of the preserve. A pair of mallards swim though the duckweed. A large beech tree lays fallen in the pond, its leave still green and alive, although slowly yellowing with the rest of the beech this time of year. Immediately next to the pond stand a number of ancient tulip trees, with trunks between four and five feet in diameter. Shallow with a muddy bottom and a film on the surface, the pond marks the edge of the preserve, beyond the pond sits private property. It is believed that settlers constructed the pond during colonial times, but nature took it back long ago. I hear a dog barking angrily from one of the nearby properties, warning me not to cross into his domain. I return the way I came in.

Directions:

From Route 135, take Exit 14W (Jericho Turnpike).
Head west on Jericho Turnpike.
Turn Right onto Jackson Avenue. Proceed north.
Bear right onto Berry Hill Road
Bear right onto Sandy Hill Road.
The preserve entrance and parking are on the left.

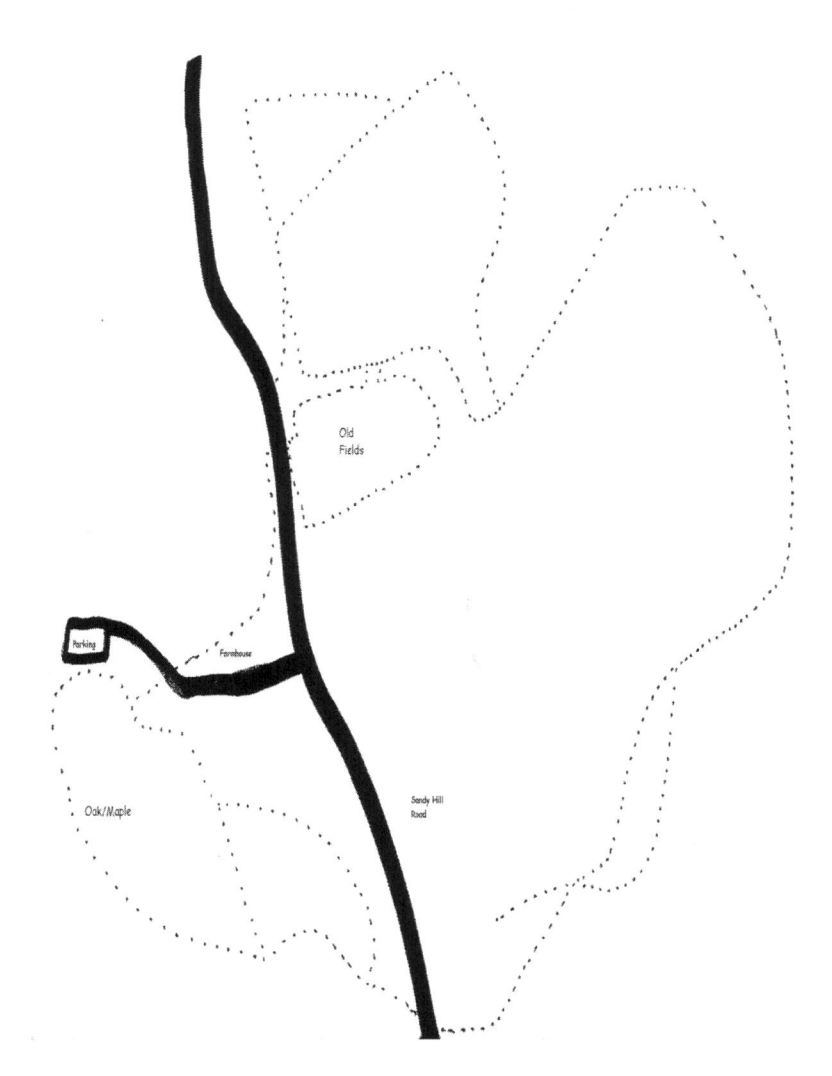

Figure 26 Tiffany Creek

OTIS PIKE NATIONAL WILDERNESS AREA

September 15th

Seventy degrees and clear skies stretch out to the horizon, this last official weekend of summer I visit Otis Pike Wilderness area, occupying nine miles of the Fire Island National Seashore, between Smith's Point and Watch Hill. Camping is permitted at Watch Hill, and recommended if you want to enjoy the quietest beach on the south shore. When writing this book, I camped here six weeks before Hurricane Sandy carved an inlet a mile and a half from Smith's Point beach. The inlet created by Hurricane Sandy connects the ocean to the bay, and occurred in the Old Inlet area. An appropriate name for the inlet might be New Old Inlet. After the formation of the inlet, rangers suspended camping on the portions of the beach east of the inlet. When I visited Otis Pike six weeks before Sandy, I headed west along the beach, past the crowded parts of Smith's Point beach, past the nude beach, to where it was just me, the shorebirds, and an occasional deer. Even on the warmest and sunniest weekends, you can find solitude on this stretch of beach.

Few beaches on the south shore are truly empty and free of distractions, especially during the summer, but Otis Pike happens to be one of them. When you visit, I suggest taking off your shoes and walking along the water's edge. Let the waves wash up around you. Walk at a slow measured pace. There is no real destination or reason to hurry. The beach extends for miles, so you can stay in the moment, mezmerized by the water, the wind and the sand beneath your feet. Coordinate your breaths with your steps. Breathe in when your right foot moves forward, and exhale when your left foot moves your forward. As you exhale, let go of any tension in your body. Smile a little. Stretch your feet and toes out completely, enjoy the movement of the wet sand under your soles, and enjoy the waves washing over your feet. Focus on your steps and contemplate your connection to the earth, the sun, the wind and the ocean. Take in the movement of the clouds, and the shapes of the waves. Contemplate your connection to the here and now. You can't stop the waves or count the grains of sand on the beach. If you visit the ocean, you will understand your relationship with the divine, and know humility.

This late in the season, the osprey left for their winter homes further south, and rangers put away barriers protecting the piping plover nests for the winter. A sign near the ranger station announced that a total of fifteen piping plover chicks fledged on this beach this season. As I walked along the beach, I saw a few piping plover foraging for tiny crustaceans and worms, along with a small mixed group of shorebirds, including semipalmated plover and a few sanderlings. The feast prepares them for their flight south. Although different species, the birds routinely join together for protection and companionship. The semipalmated plover are much more common than the piping plover. The sanderling, a bird similar to a plover, breeds north of the Arctic Circle during the summer, and visits Long Island on its migration. Washed up on the beach you'll find lots of debris, some of it natural, and some of it man made. Among the driftwood, seaweed and whelk eggs, I found a refrigerator door, a rusty can of Engine Brite, and, oddly, an unbroken fluorescent light bulb.

I found a clear spot behind the dunes in the Old Inlet area and set up my tent. Behind the beach area, the dunes rise up, and behind the dunes, the swale grows thick with grass, shrubs, and poison ivy. Ticks lurk in the grass. The leaves on the poison ivy recently turned bright red. This coloring attracts birds to its berries. I've seen much more poison ivy around the island over the past several years than I'm used to seeing. Looking across the back dunes, you can see parts of the island only several hundred yards wide. In some areas pitch pine and cedar grow in isolated stands. White tailed deer forage through bayberry and groundsel trees. In most places, the sand can only support heather and beach grass. Behind the dunes you'll find a few freshwater ponds lined with phragmites. Near the Old Inlet area, a small boathouse and dock, connected to a boardwalk leads from the ocean to the bay. It will be washed away by Hurricane Sandy. As I walked along it, I saw a flock of monarch butterflies hovering over a thicket of groundsel. Monarchs are known for their migrations, but no individual butterfly makes the whole migration. Individuals typically live about two months. They lay eggs and die during the migration, and the next generation completes the migration. How they know where to fly to remains a mystery science has yet to explain.

 Once the sun sets, the Milky Way stretches across the sky surrounded by stars. Without light pollution, the stars reveal their secrets. I visit on the night of a new moon and clear skies. Mars shines bright red above a black ocean. I hear only the wind and waves. It humbles me to think that the spot where I set up camp, will be washed away in six weeks.

 New Old Inlet is one of several breaches that occurred during Hurricane Sandy, but it's the only one that will remain open. The Inlet separated the area to its east from the rest of Fire Island. As the name Old Inlet suggests, an inlet existed in that location in the past. The previous inlet closed up in the 1820s, after being open for about sixty years. Chances are the New Old Inlet will eventually close, but it's anybody's guess as to when that might be. The opening and closing of inlets, and constant re-arrangement of the barrier beaches is part of nature's continual evolution of the natural world. Nature corrects herself, continually moving toward equilibrium.

 Immediately after the storm, the breach measured

108 feet wide on the ocean side, 276 feet wide on the bay side, and 900 feet in length. Ocean waves continue to widen the inlet. By July of 2013, the inlet measured 1407 feet wide on the ocean side, 505 feet wide long the bay, and 1447 feet in length, about a third of the size of Moriches Inlet further east. Politicians and scientists debate whether the inlet should be closed. Politicians fear that the inlet will make the South Shore of Long Island more susceptible to flooding during storms, and scientists hope that the inlet will benefit plant, fish and shellfish populations in the bay.

Nearly a year later, I visited the New Old Inlet. Humbled by the drastic change, I watched ocean waves roll through, breaking as they entered the bay. I walked along the new sandy beach from the Atlantic Ocean to the Great South Bay and back. With the opening of the inlet, positive impacts can already be seen in the bay. Fishermen report seeing more flounder and fluke. Shallow sandbars on the bay side of the inlet provide a habitat for shellfish. One the east side of the bay, algae blooms have been minimal. With the inlet open, the bay becomes cleaner and healthier from the exchange of ocean and bay water. Perhaps nature's most qualified to decide whether to close New Old Inlet, or keep it open.

Directions:

From Sunrise Highway, take exit 58 (William Floyd Parkway).
Head south on William Floyd Parkway, until it ends at Smith's Point Beach.
The ranger station is on the west side of the parking lot.

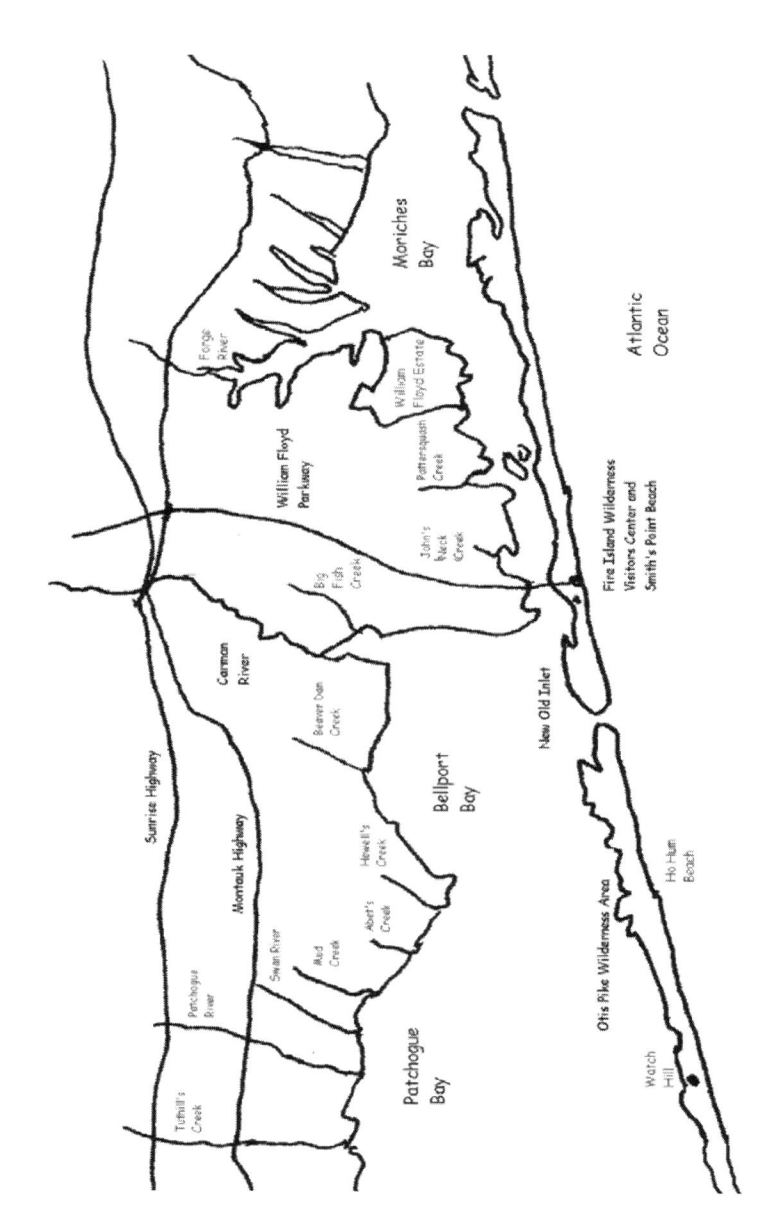

Figure 27 Otis Pike National Wilderness Area and the Great South Bay

BLYDENBURGH PRESERVE

September 22nd

Today is the Autumnal Equinox. Stump Pond is one of the best places on Long Island to enjoy the fall foliage. In a few weeks the colors will fully emerge. Today the sun shines. The air is a crisp fifty degrees. When spring returns six months from now, fifty degrees will feel warm. The Blydenburgh family created Stump Pond in the early 19th century by damming the Nissequogue River at the northwest corner of the pond, where the mill house stands today. They flooded one hundred acres of forest to a depth of eight feet. Locals named the pond Stump Pond, because when the Blydenburghs cleared the original chestnut and oak forest that grew here, they left the stumps in the ground, which took years to fully decompose and return to the earth. Blydenburgh Park consists of nearly 630 acres, bordering Caleb Smith State Park to the north and Bill Richard's Town Park to the southeast. You'll find a considerable amount of open space in Smithtown, tucked between the various developments. Several trails go through Blydenburgh Park, linking it with the adjoining spaces. The blue trail circles around the pond. Any time I've hiked it, it's taken between four and five hours to complete.

Starting at the parking lot near the entrance on Veteran's Memorial Highway, the forest consists primarily of white pine, but with a good mix of oak and maple well represented. On the south side of the trail young thin tulip trees reach skyward. The trail follows along the swampy edges of the pond. Along the sides of the trail, white wood aster and goldenrod still flower. Touch-me-nots bloom in the lower places, their orange flowers, looking a little tired, quietly trumpet the departure of warmer weather. I reach the dock on the pond in about twenty minutes. During the summer, the county rents boats to visitors. I walk to the edge of the dock, and take a few pictures of the ducks and the foliage. Reds and oranges start coming in in a few places. A small flock of ducks lands on the water. I check the time, and notice it is exactly 10:49 am, the exact minute fall begins this year. What a strange synchronous moment. I couldn't have timed it that way if I tried.

    I continue around the pond. I still have a long way to go. Between the path and the water, a nannyberry tree, one of the early color changers, shows its dark purple leaves. Close to the water, hemlock blooms. Their branchy white flowers look similar to Queen Anne's lace or water parsnip. I notice a few isolated American chestnut saplings, and think of the Blydenburghs clearing the forest to make this pond two hundred years ago. The woods they knew two hundred years ago looked much different from the woods we know today. In addition to being populated with healthy, full sized, chestnut trees, the oak and other trees around them would have been several hundred years old. It was a virgin forest. On the pond today a convoy of mute swans swims out to the center. When the Blydenburgh's created this pond, the swan's ancestors were still in Europe.

    A few dogwood trees also grow on the water's edge. Their leaves turn from green to orange, and their famous flowers are long gone. Black tupelo and red maple also sink their roots at the edges of the pond. At the north east corner of the pond, where one leg of the Nissequogue flows in, marsh grasses and phragmites grow thick, providing cover for the ducks and other waterfowl. At this end of the pond, a flock of Canadian geese congregate, around some fallen trees. Sitting on one of the fallen trees I spot a double crested cormorant. Normally these birds stay in small groups close to the bays, but here he is, all alone in Stump Pond. As I round the north east corner, I notice winterberry, a deciduous species of holly, near a stream coming from under the road. At about this point, the blazes turn from blue to white. On the north side of the pond, you can follow the trail up hill, and through some open grass areas, or you can say closer to the pond. The two trails will eventually merge back together, once you get near the mill house. The trails are fairly wide and sandy on this side of the pond. A few large puddles remain on the trail. I notice a frog in one of them, and watch a blue jay bathe in another. On this side, a few cedars can be seen among the pitch pine, as can chokecherry which offer fruit to birds preparing to fly south.

    One of the more interesting flowers blooming today was the northern fog fruit. The flower is almost egg shaped, and quite distinctive for that reason. Ducks eat the seeds. The extensive root systems provided by this plant help to create a very stable soil.

    When you get to the dam and mill, you'll find only one spot where the water flows through until it reaches the sound. This is the best place to view the whole pond. The pond is shaped sort of like the letter L, with two branches. In most spots around the pond it is difficult to see both branches of the pond, but near the mill you can easily see both, getting an idea of the size of the pond. The shape seems so natural. Creating it must have been quite an undertaking. Without cranes, bulldozers or other modern equipment, they had to rely on horses and oxen to move the sandy soil.

    Further up, the trail splits off, you can continue directly south, or cross over a small bridge, and continue south on the opposite side of the stream, closer to the edge of the pond. Calling it a bridge is an overstatement, it's really just a few planks placed across the water. Sand filled in beneath it, and water rushes over it at a depth of about two inches. Plants and grasses fill the stream, creating a bog. After crossing the bridge, the trail goes directly up a hill, cutting deep into the sandy soil. Mosses grow in the sides of the trail. This trail goes north, leading to the tip of a small peninsula, and then returns south, following the pond through some hilly areas. At the tip of the peninsula, almost like a marker, stands a big old white pine. A few smaller white pines also mix in with the oak and beech trees. At the water's edge, I look up and notice a red tailed hawk. I also notice a northern pintail duck paddling through the water. Further south, American chestnut become common, their spiky nuts scattered on the ground. You'll find plenty of tree falls on this side of the pond, and some of the dead trees, covered with different types of fungus, dissolve into the soil. You'll also find the beginnings of a grove of white pine. Most of the white pines are fairly young, shorter than twenty feet in height.

  The trail returns to low areas, near where streams start to feed into the pond. A boardwalk goes through a section of swamp. Black tupelo and maple, well suited to wet soils, are again common trees. Closer to the south end of the preserve, a bridge goes over a small shallow stream, and the trail leads past the maintenance buildings, returning to the parking lot. I look at the time; it is almost five hours after I started.

Directions:

Follow the Northern State Parkway east, until it ends, changing into Veteran's Memorial Highway (Route 347/454).
The park is on the north side of Veteran's Memorial Highway, shortly before route 347 splits off from Route 454.
From the L.I.E. take Exit 57 (Veteran's Memorial Highway).
Travel north. The preserve will be on the right side.

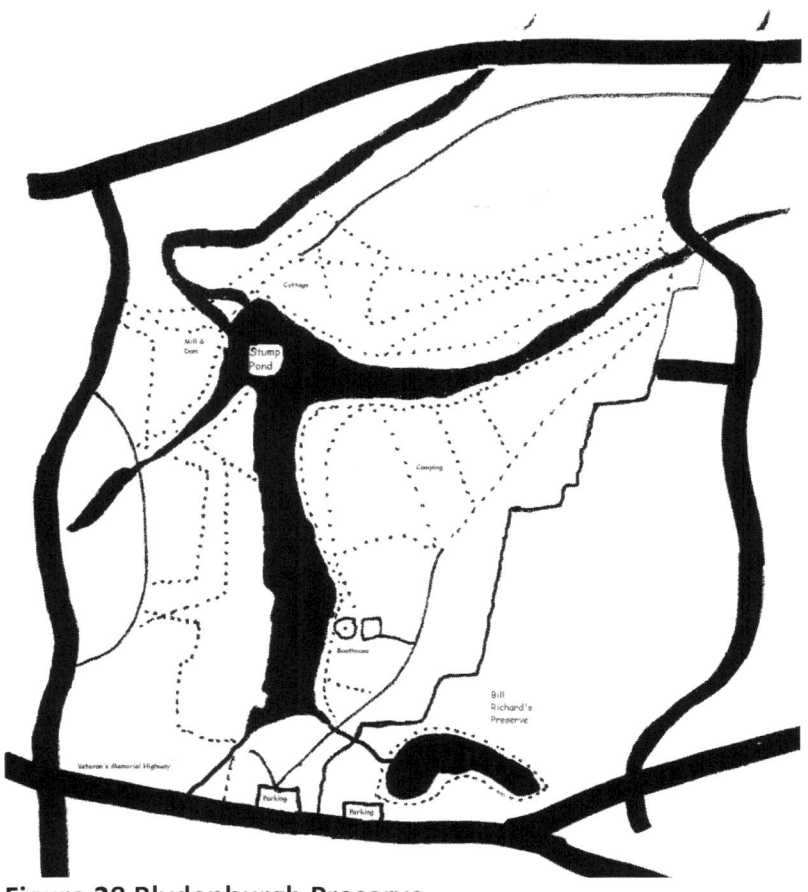

Figure 28 Blydenburgh Preserve

HUBBARD COUNTY PARK

September 29th

  Hubbard County Park sits between Hubbard Creek and Mill Creek in Flanders, a short distance from the locally famous Big Duck. A number of trails can be found in the preserve. The main trails include the Black Owl Trail, a five mile loop incorporating part of Sears-Bellows Preserve, and a section of the Paumanuck Path, a much longer trail extending from Rocky Point to Montauk. Eventually the trails lead up to Flanders Bay and the Ghost Forest. Parking can be found on the side of Red Creek Road. Look for the metal gate at the entrance of the preserve, and proceed north. You will pass the Black Duck Lodge and ultimately reach Flanders Bay and the Ghost Forest. You can also follow the trails south of Red Creek Road, and these will lead you through Sears-Bellows Preserve and parkland owned by the Town of Southampton. If you camp in Sears-Bellows, you can very easily incorporate this hike into a much larger hike, making the most of your visit to the south fork. This morning the weather is cool and slightly rainy. Autumn starts to settle in. Oak and maple still hold onto their green leaves, although the shades are much darker, as they tend to be before they change. On the ground, catbrier's colors shift to yellow, and the Virginia creeper colors ooze into orange. In a few weeks both plants will disappear until spring. Thistle and chicory, being hearty plants, still bloom. A downy woodpecker, the kind without the red head, clings to the side of a tree poking for some bugs to eat.

  Closest to Red Creek Road, the forest consists of mainly pitch pine and oak, as it is south of the road. As you proceed north on the trail, you eventually pass the Black Duck Lodge. Built by E.F. Hutton, the white building came into the county's possession along with the rest of E.F. Hutton's personal hunting grounds which make up the preserve today. Past the lodge, the trail leads through some old field areas, slowly growing in with pitch pine, but still very grassy. For the most part, ticks become dormant this time of year, but you should still be cautious. The few stragglers hunger for a blood meal. The thinly spaced pine closer to Flanders Bay gives the forest an open feel.

 Right before the trail opens up into the salt marsh, a sign warns that, for the protection of the nesting osprey, the trail remains closed to hikers between April 15th and August 15th. Since it's late September, I can walk out on the salt marsh. A wall of groundsel marks the edge between the marsh and the forest. Typical on higher areas of a marsh, the groundsel's white flowers, eventually open up and scatter seeds on the wind, similar to the way its distant cousin, the dandelion, does. This time of year, the leaves have yellow spots, as they start to turn. Sweet bay magnolia can also be found, although not flowering.

 The trail continues across the sandy tidal area, which extends for acres. Perhaps because of the slight breeze, the marsh remains relatively insect free, except for the occasional mosquito. An osprey platform stands empty in the middle of the marsh. Deer tracks in the sand lead to an elevated mound of sand, called a hammock, in the distance. Less prone to flooding than the lower lying marsh, it supports a grove of cedar and pitch pine on the edge of the bay. Before proceeding out into the tidal area you must take a few moments and enjoy the view. This time of year a lot of red and orange mixes in with the green and yellow. The green and yellow comes from the salt hay and cord grass. The red and orange comes from the glasswort changing to its fall colors. An edible, and tasty marsh plant, some people call glasswort pickleweed, because of its briny flavor.

The marsh area floods constantly, so the plants adapt well to the salty conditions. On the areas to the left and right of the trail several inches of water saturate the plant roots. Looking on the ground, you can see mussel and molted horseshoe crab shells. Several small channels and ponds divide the marsh area. The creeks flowing into the bay are fresh water, providing a brackish mix of fresh and salt waters, similar to the marshes on the Great South Bay, although on a much smaller scale.

Eventually, the trail reaches the hammock of sand and the south edge of Flanders Bay. Patches of goldenrod above the grasses give a little color. Prickly pear cacti grow in the sand. Pitch pine and red cedar create a thin canopy. The plants hold the sand together, keeping the hammock from completely eroding into the bay. Along the edge, the erosion is obvious from the visible roots and trees falling into the bay, the waves gently washing the sand from beneath them. The tide is slightly up. At lower tides, the Ghost Forest becomes visible. The Ghost Forest is made of the stumps that remain of a forest of Atlantic white cedar which once grew in what is now the south end of Flanders Bay, where the sea slowly reclaimed the forest.

The remains of a brick and stone fireplace are the only structure you'll find in the grove. As I examine it, I imagine E.F. Hutton and friends gathered around a fire, looking out over the bay on an autumn night a century ago, everyone listening intently to Mr. Hutton's words. Pondering this, I startle the deer who's tracks lead me here. The deer sprints back to the sandy trail, eyeing me suspiciously once she gets a safe distance away.

Tidal pools form in the sand adjacent to the cedar and pine grove. In the pools small fish swim and a few fiddler crabs crawl along the bottom. Water submerges most of the grass around the edges. Returning to the hammock, I hear a chirping, rattling call, and see a silhouette of a bird flying in an erratic pattern and returning to the trees. As I get closer, I realize it is a belted king fisher. These aren't nearly as common as egrets or other shorebirds, so seeing one is a rare treat. It has a white belly and slate blue wings. The feathers on its head form a mohawk. As I get closer, I watch him. He puts on quite a show. Unlike a hawk who circles slowly and methodically looking for his prey, the kingfisher calls out, flies in erratic patterns, and returns to the trees. Perhaps he is trying to scare me off, and mark his territory. Watching him for a while, I notice a method to his madness. Eventually he dives and snatches a fish from the water. Kingfishers nest on the ground by burrowing into the sand, similar to bank swallows. The raised hammock offers an ideal place to nest, because it lies immediately next to a bay filled with fish, but still above the parts of the marsh that flood. The trees also provide a good vantage point to look out over both the bay and the ponds and streams. After watching the kingfisher in amazement, I make my way back across the marsh and return to my car.

Directions:

From Sunrise Highway, take Exit 65 north.
Follow Route 24 north. Make a left onto Red Creek Road. A metal gate marks the entrance to the park. You can park on Red Creek Road.

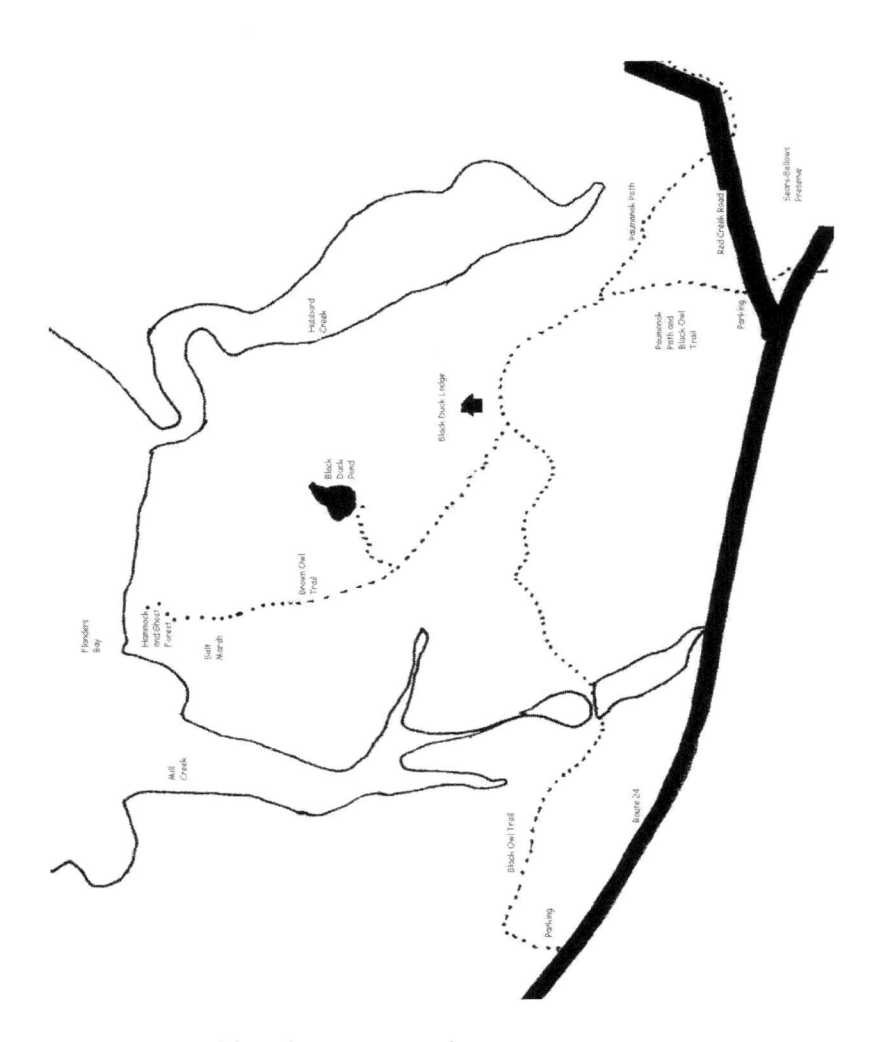

Figure 29 Hubbard County Park

OCTOBER

Turkey Tail

UDALL'S COVE

October 7th

New York City offers very little in the way of open and natural spaces. The City even converted an abandoned elevated train line to park space to bring a little more green into its resident's lives. The few wild spaces left tend to be filled with trash and weeds. Most city dwellers can't see the natural world beyond the concrete, unless they look for it. Of course, from a wider perspective, the whole city and its residents are as much a part of the natural world as the harbor, the salt marshes and patches of trees tucked away here and there throughout the five boroughs. Most people just won't see it, even when they're surrounded by it. The crowds, the cars, the runoff and trash continue to be an imposition on the immediate world around them, creating a new environment, drastically different from the west end of Long Island as it was, even as recently as the end of the nineteenth century.

In Douglas Manor, near the Queens/Nassau border, Gabler's Creek feeds Udall's Cove, an inlet tucked away in a corner of Little Neck Bay, itself an inlet tucked away in a corner of the Long Island Sound. The cove sits in a ravine, and freshwater flows into the salt mash by way of Gabler's Creek. At the edge of the cove you'll find Virginia Point. Udall's cove came into the public's hands in 1989, after twenty years of hard work by some individuals in the community who, recognizing its beauty and understanding its importance, fought to protect it from industrial development. Aurora Pond, in the middle of the preserve, is named after Aurora Gareiss, the woman who led a small group of residents and advocated for the protection of the cove. They petitioned the city to purchase the property from developers and set it aside as a preserve.

The preserve encompasses a long and irregularly shaped forty-one acres. It provides a reminder of what this area may have looked like over a century ago. A small trail allows visitors an opportunity to explore the preserve. Densely grown in, and muddy in spots, makeshift wooden walkways make the muddy parts of the trail a little easier to cross. This late in the year, the touch-me-nots look like they've been touched a little too much. Phragmites grow thick alongside Gabler's Creek and Aurora Pond.

In early October, the arrowwood's purple and pale blue berries offer a nourishing meal to migrating birds. Stands of sumac and cherry show their fall colors. On the dead branches of a cherry tree, I see a type of woodpecker, known as yellow shafted flicker. The flicker can be identified by its brown back and red head. A few beach roses bloom closer to Little Neck Bay.

Along with the phragmites, groundsels line the water's edge. The stream sits still, covered in a thin film. A cloud of mosquitoes hangs in the air. Low tide allows you to see the fresh water of Gabler's Creek wind through the mudflats. The dried mud caked to the bottom of the cord grass, gives a clue as to how deep the water gets when the saltwater tide flows in. I watch several heron pick through the greenish mud of the creek bottom. The humidity leaves a haze over the bay, and promises rain within the hour.

The open salt marsh at the end of Gabler's Creek attracts birds that avoid the rest of Queens. It is as if they don't realize they live in the middle of an urban area. It's just another salt marsh, albeit a salt marsh with a little more trash on the bottom. The crabs and mussels still make a living here. Fish still breed here, feeding on the mosquito and other larvae in the creek. Heron and other waterfowl go about their business, oblivious to the heavily developed urban area surrounding them.

The whole area can be explored in less than an

hour, but I'm sure few people in the neighborhood make the effort to stop by. It's doubtful that more than a handful of the 1.6 million people living across the bridge, in that other part of the city have even heard of Udall's Cove. In Queens and Brooklyn, developers squeezed most of the natural streams and creeks into cement culverts underground. Thanks to Aurora Gareiss and her friends, Gabler's Creek still flows freely into Udall's Cove as it has for thousands of years, and as it will continue to be for thousands more.

Directions:

From the L.I.E., take the Exit for Little Neck Parkway. Head north on Little Neck Parkway until it ends at 255th Street.
Parking is available on the street.

Gabler's Creek at Low Tide

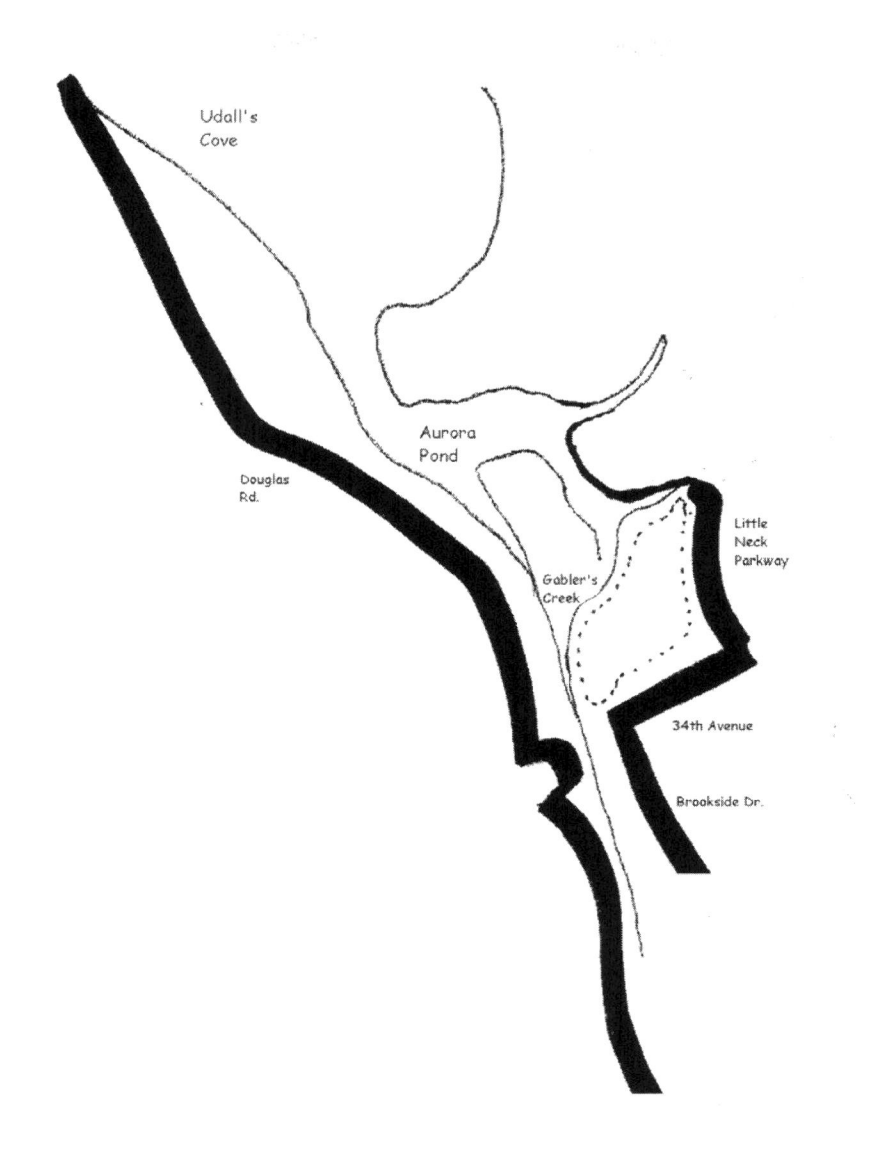

Figure 30 Udall's Cove

ROBERT CUSHMAN COUNTY PRESERVE

October 13th

Robert Cushman preserve is one section of several connected areas south of Wading River in the Manorville area which can be hiked. It connects with Brookhaven State Park in the North, via the yellow blazed Brookhaven Path. The Paumonouck path, marked in white blazes, also passes through the preserve. In addition to the marked paths, many unmarked paths can be found and explored. Bring a map and compass, or, if you prefer newer technology, a handheld GPS will lead you back to your car. The county opens it to hunters during the appropriate season, please treat them with respect. This area can be accessed in several places. One of the easier spots to start is a small parking area on the south side of Route 25, a little west of Wading River-Schultz Road.

Close to twenty shallow ponds can be found in the preserve, with names like Woodchopper's Pond, Peasy's Pond, Zeek's Pond, Cryan Pond, Linus Pond, Sandy Pond, Big Sandy Pond, Fox Pond...You get the idea. These are all incredibly rare coastal plains ponds, formed by the glacial outwash of the last ice age. These are all fed by runoff, instead of groundwater, so during drier times, the ponds consist of nothing more than wet sand, although they can be between two or three feet deep during rainy periods. The water feeds into the Peconic River, and ultimately into the Peconic Bay. The ponds serve as a home to one of the more diverse selections of plants and wildflowers to be found on the island. You'll find several species of rare or endangered plants reliant on the ponds. During warmer months you will find white fringed orchid, water lilies, and a host of other flowers. You will also find several types of bladderwort and several different species of sundew. The nutrient poor sand forces these plants to trap and eat insects in order to survive. During the summer, the ponds offer plenty to eat. On this visit, several of the ponds formed an extensive open patch of wet sand. Grass and even small shrubs grow above the sphagnum. Even the deeper ponds remain fairly shallow, less than a foot deep, covered with yellow and orange lily pads, and other floating vegetation. Phragmites grow around the edges. I notice a raised patch of mud, on which several turtles sun themselves, no doubt aware that winter is just around the corner.

    The preserve occupies the northern part of the pine barrens. Pitch pine and oak abound. Some of the oak leaves were halfway between green and yellow. Bright orange sweetgum leaves contrasted nicely against the mostly green pine trees. Along one of the paths, I find several enormous wasp nests several feet in diameter.

    In April of this year, wildfires consumed the areas in the south and east of the preserve. Acres of dead and blackened trees can be found in the preserve, burned in the recent fire. Wild fires are part of the natural course of death and rebirth in the pine barrens. The state conservation agencies engage in controlled burns to allow the natural processes to take course, without damaging private property. Occasionally, particularly under dry and windy conditions, wild fires start. Between fires, fuel in the form of dead trees and branches accumulates on the forest floor. Pitch pines self-prune as they grow, dropping dead branches to the ground, adding to the available fuel. In addition, trees die, or get knocked down by wind, over the course of time. In years following hurricanes and nor'easters, greater dead fall on the ground translates into a greater chance of a severe wild fire. The pitch pines adapt well to forest fires, and rely on an occasional burn to let their seeds germinate. Their pine cones can stay attached to the branches for twenty years or more, and only open when exposed to heat. The fires are a necessary part of their reproductive cycle. Their bark is fairly fire resistant, but a severe enough fire will still destroy the trees, as they did here.

In the area east of Grassy Pond, acres of dead pine trees, charred black, stand tall, patiently waiting for the next storm to push them to the ground. Back in April, all the vegetation on the ground completely burned as far as you could see. It looked like Mordor. Nature recovers quickly. The burned trees replenish sandy and poor soil with nutrients allowing for healthier new growth. Within a few weeks of the fire, thick grass covers the forest floor underneath the burned trees. During the summer, it grew bright green, contrasting with the black trees. Now that autumn is well along, the grass fades to a dry yellowish brown. In a few places oak saplings grow out of burnt stumps. Fire doesn't reach below the ground. Oaks survive forest fires by regenerating from their roots. Many of the blackened pitch pines, not thoroughly damaged by the fire, sent out new shoots along their sides. As time goes on, the effects of the fire will slowly become less and less noticeable.

Directions:

Parking is east of William Floyd Parkway, on the south side of Route 25.

Figure 31 Robert Cushman Preserve

MASHOMACK PRESERVE

October 20th

Located between the two forks, Mashomack Preserve takes up a third of Shelter Island. The Nature Conservancy owns it and manages it through donations from visitors. The 2000 acres and ten miles of coastline making up Mashomack Preserve was nearly sold to developers twice since the 1920s. Fortunately The Nature Conservancy and residents of Shelter Island recognized its importance and rescued the land in the preserve. The preserve remains one of the more pristine preserves on Long Island. It includes salt marshes, meadows, oak forest, pine forest, several ponds and a rare pine swamp. Used as a natural laboratory, the Nature Conservancy and biologists use the land to study local plants and animals. Since The Nature Conservancy purchased the land in 1980, they recorded over 200 different species of birds, including 79 nesting species. Many rare species of plant can also be found in the preserve.

Five marked hiking trails and a sixth designated kayak/canoe "trail" highlight the diversity of the preserve. The hiking trails range from one mile to ten miles, and intersect in several places, making them fairly easy to combine. As much land as the trails cover, significant parts of the preserver remain off limits to visitors. These sections of the preserve completely belong to Mother Nature. Prohibiting access allows sensitive ecological communities to develop with minimal human interference, benefiting all plant and animal life in Peconic Bay. The preserve's wetlands serve as breeding grounds for crabs and shellfish, particularly bay scallops. The wetlands also provide one of the better osprey nesting areas.

On this day, the weather gods bless me with fairly

warm weather, considering it's the end of October. The day started off foggy and overcast, but the sun emerged. This will be one of the last days like this until spring comes around again. Blessings, like good weather, come and go. The darker, colder, deader times of late fall and winter follow closely behind today's warm air and sunshine. The day I walk through this preserve, an unnamed tropical wave moves across the Caribbean. In a few days it will form into Hurricane Sandy, bringing floods to the south shore and re-shaping the barrier beaches. Immediately following Hurricane Sandy, a nor'easter will drop the first snow of the season, and remind all Long Islanders that we remain at nature's mercy.

  The trails start out in the pine swamp area. The swamp consists of white pine and a variety of other plants rooted on floating mats of sphagnum moss. The swamp is a relic of an older time, geologically speaking. Samples of the mats revealed that they are composed of organic material which has been accumulating for nearly 4000 years. The presence of white pine is a throwback to a time when the island was cooler, and more suitable for white pine. Over the course of the past several thousand years, pitch pine has been gradually edging out white pine. If the mats which make up the floor of the swamp are 4000 years old, bear in mind that Shelter Island itself is between ten and twenty thousand years old.

  Venturing past the swamp, you'll come to a coastal salt marsh named Miss Annie's Creek. Like other salt marshes, it serves as a breeding area for shellfish and a nursery for the many different types of fish that make their home in the larger Peconic Bay. The terrain of Shelter Island is a little hilly, in much the same way the north shore of Long Island can be hilly in places. In the area where the yellow, blue and green trails meet, a meadow opens up. This area used to be farmed by the same Annie whom the creek is named after. The Nature Conservancy lets it remain an open field. This time of year the fall colors shine their best. Bright red sumacs, orange-red oak leaves, green pines, yellow sassafras, all can be seen in patches, and along the edges of the field. A red tailed hawk flies up above, looking for a meal in the meadow. Following the green trail takes you closer to the shore first, while the blue trail leads you into the interior of the preserve, along Gardiners Bay and eventually back to the green trail.

Oak and beech make up the interior of the preserve. All of the oak species present on other parts of Long Island can be found here. Nature rounded up the usual suspects - red oak, scarlet oak, white oak, black oak chestnut oak - and placed them here in a well-mixed forest. Several kettle holes can be seen as you walk through the preserve. On my hike, I saw a hermit thrush, one of the last birds to migrate south in the fall. A flock of crows followed me for a while, suspicious of my presence. Most visitors don't venture onto the blue trail. People generally go as far as the yellow trail, or, if they are a little more robust they visit the green trail, but the blue trail remained empty, except for the chipmunks and other animals.

As I got closer to Gardiner's Bay, a ribbon snake slid across my path. As the trail got closer to the water, I first heard the surf, then smelled it, and the finally saw it. It was a little disorienting to walk through an oak forest, and smell something as familiar as the beach without actually seeing it. Eventually the trail reaches a spot where you can see the beach slightly below you, and the water beyond. Looking over the bay, I spotted a kestrel perched on a tree branch. She paid no attention to me.

Tucked away in a swampy area I found a small pond covered in duckweed and populated by greyish colored green frogs, enjoying the last of the insects before digging deep into the mud to hibernate. As I walk closer to the pond, they jump away to the further end of the pond. Further along, the blue trail follows the edges of several ponds and wetland areas on the interior of the island. It is in this area that the blue trail meets up again with the green trail, which again joins the yellow trail back in the meadow. Geese, ducks and other waterfowl populate the open wetland areas.

As I walked past Sanctuary Pond, one of the preserve's larger ponds, I watched a harrier, also known as a marsh hawk dive unsuccessfully for a duck sitting on the water. The duck dodged the hawk in a lucky splash. After watching the mallard have a near death experience and the hawk go home hungry, I followed the trail along Smith Cove and through the meadow. Eventually the trail took me back through the pine swamp, and returned me to the visitor center.

Directions:

From either the north fork or south fork, take a ferry from Route 114. The preserve is on the east side of Route 114.

Hermit Thrush

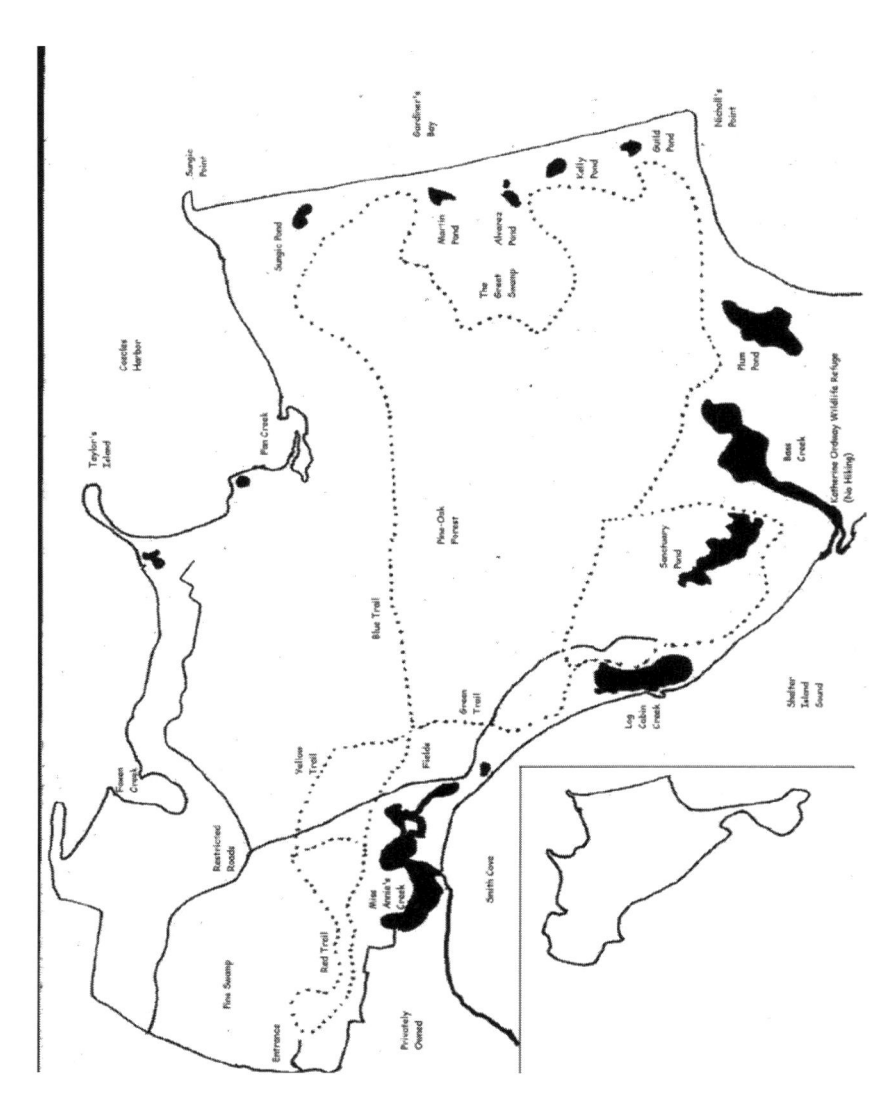

Figure 32 Mashomack Preserve

NOVEMBER

MILL POND

November 1st

  Ancient cultures considered November 1st to be the beginning of winter, when everything died, or rested until spring's first stirrings in February. Two days ago Hurricane Sandy struck Long Island, flooding Mill Pond in Bellmore along with most of the South Shore. Wind knocked down trees all over the Island. A thirteen foot storm surge reshaped the barrier beaches, breaking through to the bay in a number of locations. Nearly all of the South Shore experienced the type of flooding that happens once or twice a century. Mill pond sits less than a mile from the Great South Bay. Before developers built up the neighborhood, it stood immediately on the edge of the bay's tidal salt marsh, where the freshwaters from the creek mingled with the salt water from the bay. The same stream that feeds Mill Pond also feeds Wantagh's twin lakes, located north of Sunrise Highway and the railroad tracks.
  In addition to knocking out power, flooding homes and eroding shorelines, Hurricane Sandy knocked down trees...thousands of them. In all the preserves and along the sides of the parkways, downed trees lay everywhere you look. Driving here this morning, fallen trees blocked the right lane of Merrick Road.
  Two main trails circle the pond, a paved one, and another unpaved trail going deeper into the wooded area of the preserve. A white blazed trail incorporates parts of both and connects to the Twin Lakes Preserve north of Sunrise Highway. Fallen trees in the preserve won't be cleared for some time. The relatively short walk around the preserve, took much longer than normal, because I had to crawl under, climb over, or pick my way around fallen trees. Surprisingly, nearly all of them still hold onto their

leaves. On the east side of the preserve, the wind completely uprooted several enormous old maples, laying them on their sides. The flooding water softened the already moist ground, and the winds pushed them over. Greyish green rainwater fills in the holes left where roots once held the trees.

When the wind couldn't knock the trees down, it snapped their trunks. The winds even snapped a white oak with a trunk nearly two feet in diameter. In the trunks of some of the trees, you could see where they had been rotting from the inside out, waiting for a strong wind to break them into pieces. Walking through the preserve, I lost count of the fallen trees. Deeper in the wooded area of the preserve, trees knocked one another down like dominos. I counted a chain of fallen trees five trees deep. You had to look closely to see where the branches of one tree ended, and another began.

In addition to the damaged to damaging the trees, the storm flattened shrubs. The water receded, covering them with seaweed and marsh grass from the bay, branches from the trees above, and garbage from everywhere. Debris piled from several inches to over a foot thick. In addition to the natural debris, lawn furniture washed in, as did a portion of someone's floating dock, a child's playground set and a sign from a business on Merrick Road. The damage from the hurricane makes today's walk through a familiar park a surreal experience.

Under normal circumstances, the preserve provides a relaxing place to take a short walk. This time of year the leaves reach their peak colors. In the spring, flowers surround the edges of the pond. In the back woods area, a number of smaller streams feed into the pond. You can also find old piping in the ground and a graffittied brick building. The building and pipes remain from a time when the City of Brooklyn pumped groundwater from this area to satisfy its growing needs.

It appears that the ducks and other birds weathered the storm. God bless them. On the pond today scores of paired off mallards, several blue winged teals, a few herons, cormorants, and, of course, the ubiquitous Canadian geese all enjoyed the water. Most likely, the birds flew further into the island. Animals detect natural dangers, and respond to them quickly. The pond awaits the arrival of its winter ducks. Like Fort Lauderdale attracts Long Islanders during the winter, Mill Pond attract ducks and other birds from the artic during the winter months. Both Mill Pond and the three ponds that make up the Twin Ponds Preserve offer great duck watching opportunities during the winter months.

Directions:

From Wantagh State Parkway, exit at Merrick Road, heading west.
The preserve is a short distance away on the right side of Merrick Road

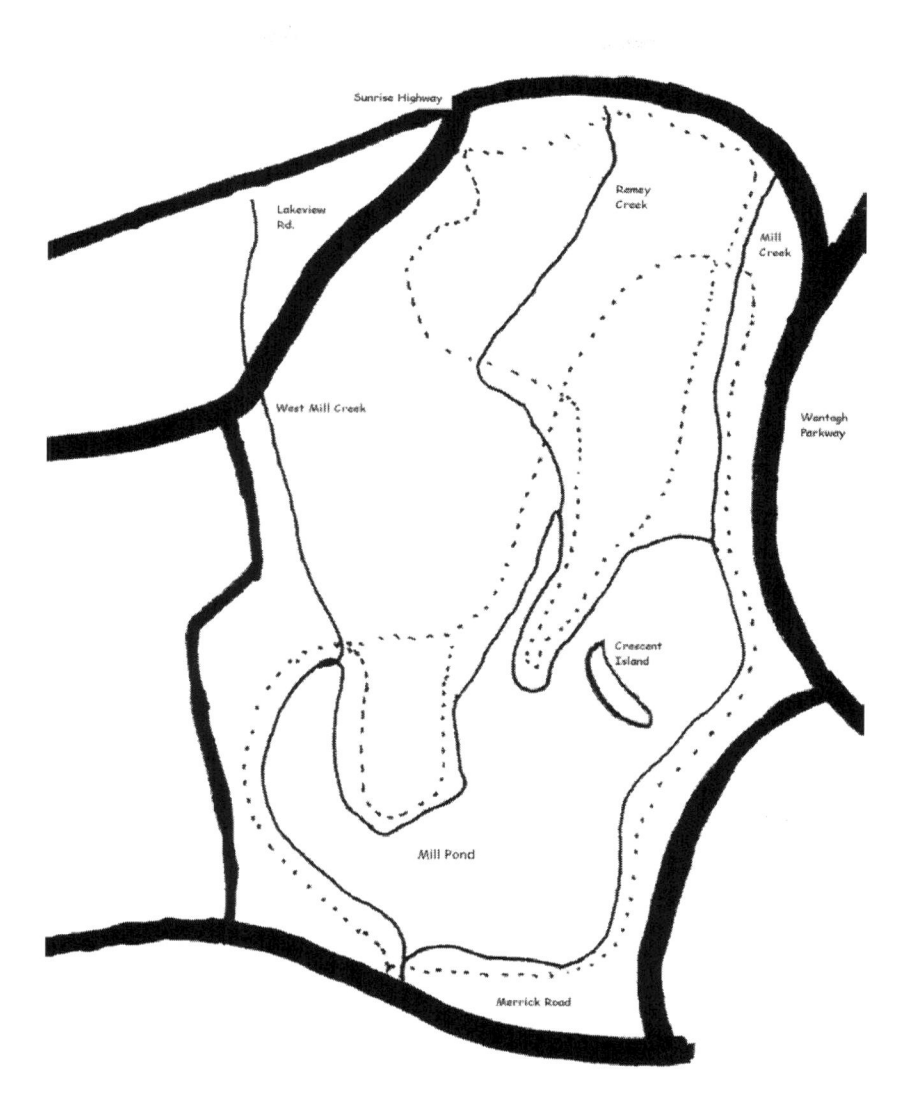

Figure 33 Mill Pond

EDGEWOOD OAK BRUSH PLAINS PRESERVE

November 14th

The preserve occupies the remainder of what was once a transition area between the plains of Nassau County, and the pine barrens extending eastward into Suffolk County. Covered with sandy soil, grasses, scrub oak, shrubs, and pitch pine, it once provided a habitat for the now extinct heath hen. A flightless bird closely related to the prairie chicken, heath hen owe their disappearance to a lethal combination of over hunting and habitat destruction. Prior to development, an estimated 60,000 acres of oak brush habitat covered western Suffolk, from about Farmingdale in the west, to Brentwood in the east. Today, about 2000 acres remain. The preserve was saved from heavy development, because Edgewood State Hospital and Pilgrim State Mental Hospital occupied the property. Much of the land was never touched. When the state no longer had use for the facilities, it tore town the buildings and returned the land to nature. Over the past several years I've been visiting this preserve, I've watched the areas where buildings formerly stood gradually turn from stretches of sand, to grass covered stretches of sand to semi-wooded areas consisting of young pitch pine and various shrubs.

In the preserve, you will also find the remains of Old Commack Road, lined with lights, no longer connected to the grid, and fire hydrants, disconnected from any source of water. You will also find abandoned railroad tracks leading nowhere. When the state used the grounds as a hospital, it had its own train station. You can walk along the old tracks, most of it raised up on a mound, and see pitch pine growing from between the railroad ties. A portion of the preserve is also recovering from an old forest fire. The bare trunks of dead pitch pine rise above much smaller scrub oak. On the same hike you can see how a wooded area recovers from both development and fire. The sandy areas and the train tracks offer a glimpse of nature's ability to heal and very easily take back what was hers to begin with.

    Officially, the preserve includes just over 700 acres, but its connection to other wooded areas makes the whole preserve bigger than it appears. The diversity, and the many trails, both marked and unmarked, make it ideal for repeated visits throughout the seasons. In the fall the leaves change, in the winter, everything sleeps, through spring and summer you can watch wildflowers bloom along the sides of the trails, and in the fields.

    The blue trail constitutes a three mile loop, and is the best way to see a little of everything in the preserve. Edgewood is one of the few preserves on Long Island without any streams, ponds, or shoreline. As I make my way around, I keep being followed by a mysterious west highland terrier. Curious but apprehensive, she disappears for a little while into the brush, and then returns, never getting any closer to me than ten or fifteen feet. Feral dogs do appear in preserves every now and again, but I don't believe this westie poses any threat. By now, the oak leaves shrivel dark brown on the branches. Arrowwood berries are a dark blue, almost black. Seed pods hang off black locust trees similar to dried string beans. The grasses are yellow, and the only green left comes from the pine and hollies. During spring and summer, the thickets make a great home for a variety of birds. Volunteers placed several bird blinds in strategic location, so visitors can discreetly set up a spotting scope or camera equipment.

    While visiting today, I was lucky enough to spot an orange crowned warbler sitting on a thin stump. This bird isn't an annual or, even a seasonal, resident. It's stopping over on its way from its summer home in Canada or Maine to its winter home in the tropics.

    Bats make use of the fields and open areas for hunting. About this time of year, the brown bats on the island congregate in caves in the Hudson valley and hibernate. Over the past several years, a fungus, has been killing bats by the millions. Bats suffered a ninety percent decline since 2006. During the summer months, bats eat thousands of insects in places like Edgewood Preserve, and store the energy for hibernation. During hibernation, their metabolism slows down drastically, allowing their fat reserves to last them through the winter. The fungus, carried over from Europe, disrupts their hibernation in such a way that they continually wake up throughout the winter. Because they repeatedly awaken during hibernation, their metabolism remains at its active level. The bats use up their fat reserves, ultimately starving to death while in their caves. Some of the bats venture out of their caves in midwinter in search of insects which are nowhere to be found. As their populations decline, the populations of mosquito, ticks and other insects during the summer months increase drastically.

    This preserve is almost big enough to get lost in. The northern end is forested by pine and oak. You will also find an extensive red cedar grove tucked away south east of the field area. It is big enough to spend a whole day in. The preserve has one of the more diverse ranges of habitat on the Island. Besides the thickets of various heath and other shrubs, you will find willow, magnolia, honeysuckle, juniper, red cedar, cherry, quaking aspen, and a variety of other types of trees.

Directions:

From the L.I.E., take Exit 52 south (Commack Road). Proceed south on Commack Road. The preserve is on the left side of Commack Road.

Figure 34 recovering from an old fire at Edgewood Preserve

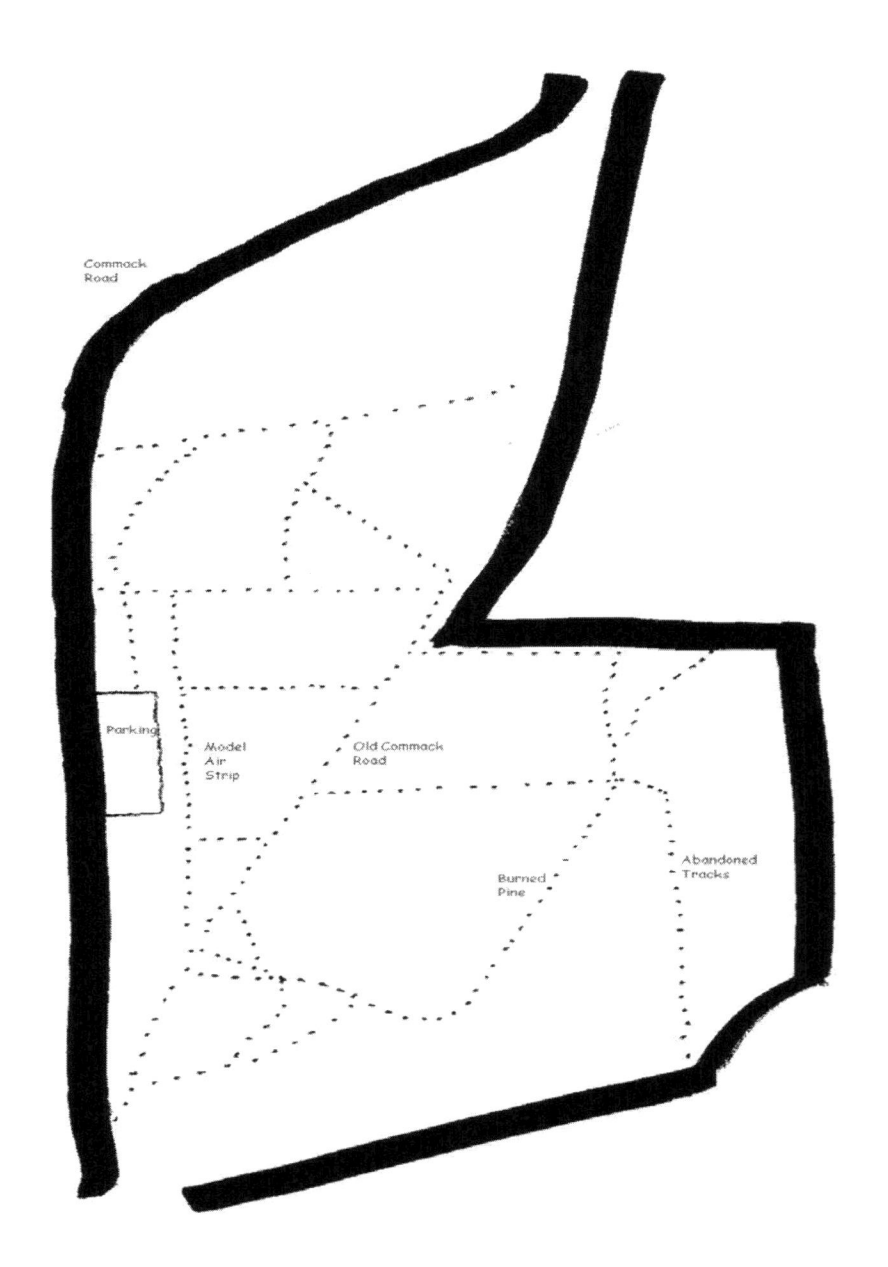

Figure 35 Edgewood Preserve

PROSSER PINES

November 23rd

On the east side of Yaphank-Middle Island Road, across from Cathedral Pines Preserve sits Prosser Pines, an extensive grove of white pine, planted approximately 200 years ago by a man known to history as Uncle Billy Dayton, a local farmer and war hero. The grove later came under the care and protection of the Prosser family.

Before entering the shady grove, take a moment and visit the witch hazel shrub in the grassy area north of the parking lot. In late November, its spindly pale yellow flowers bloom before winter fully sets in. Witch hazel is somewhat uncommon, but can be found throughout the island. Its bark and leaves produce a strong astringent, and have a variety of skin care uses.

The pine grove outgrew its original boundaries long ago. Several long ditches dug into the ground mark the original boundaries, as do "boundary trees", trees with trunks permanently bent into unnatural shapes marking the corners of old property divisions. On the east side of the preserve a straight line of beech trees also marks an edge important to the planter, but long since forgotten. As for the white pine, the tallest and oldest trees, possibly from the original planting, rise comfortably above 100 feet. A good number of the original trees fell long ago, and rest on the carpet of needles covering the forest floor. Breaking down to dirt, they slowly return to the earth, nourishing newer growth. Open spaces in the canopy let sunshine filter down, allowing younger trees to grow and compete with one another for their place in the sun. If you visit here on a hot summer day, shade from the upper canopy keeps the air underneath noticeably cooler.

Like a spell, the pines cast such a serene mood

beneath their branches, that the passing cars keep quiet out of respect. The aroma of the pine needles sooths the air. The meditative quality of the grove is lost on no one. A church owning a portion of the grove keeps pews and an altar set up under the trees for outdoor services.

    The lack of a pronounced understory through most of the grove shows a gradual upward slope of the ground. At the top edge, a farm extends for acres. Slightly down hill, and across Yaphank-Middle Island Road, dense undergrowth marks the beginnings of the Carman River. Sandy soil drains quickly, perfect for the growth of white pine. You can casually walk through the whole grove in less than an hour. The trails are wide and fairly simple to follow. As you stroll through the grove, contemplate the time it takes the pine to grow. White pines grow only a foot in their first five years. By the time they are ten years of age, the trees are barely five feet high. Between the ages of ten and twenty, they can grow as much as five feet per year. Reaching for the sun, the trees continue growing as they age. As you explore, you will notice groups of trees around the same height and width. These stands gradually thin out as the trees compete for sunlight, the smaller ones dying out. Previous visitors made teepee structures from the trunks of smaller trees around some of the larger trees. These structures have been standing for years.

    Hurricane Sandy's winds made a noticeable impact on the grove. Fallen branches, their needles still green, cover the floor. It's unusual to see so much green on the ground here; it seems out of place. Eventually, the needles will turn to orange, and blend with the rest of the forest floor. Besides the white pine, oak trees, particularly black oak, live here, as well as the remnants of American chestnut. Both were common when Uncle Billy Dayton planted the grove. From the storm, several black oaks had their crowns broken off from the wind. The wider leaves catching the force of the winds. The wind completely twisted the trunks of some of the trees before snapping them. When the oak fell, they took down smaller trees with them. From one fallen oak, I counted fifteen fallen pine, knocked down and uprooted. Looking at the roots of the pine trees, you could see the dry sand and soil that held them in place. Eventually, the impact of Hurricane Sandy won't be as obvious. Her marks will heal, and be forgotten like other large hurricanes which have come through the grove.

Directions:

From The Long Island Expressway:
Take Exit 66 (CR-101/Sills Road).
Head North on (CR-101/Sills Road).
Sills Road changes to Patchogue - Yaphank Road.
Patchogue - Yaphank Road changes to Mill Road.
Mill Road changes to Yaphank-Middle Island Road.
The preserve is on the right side of the road.

Witch Hazel

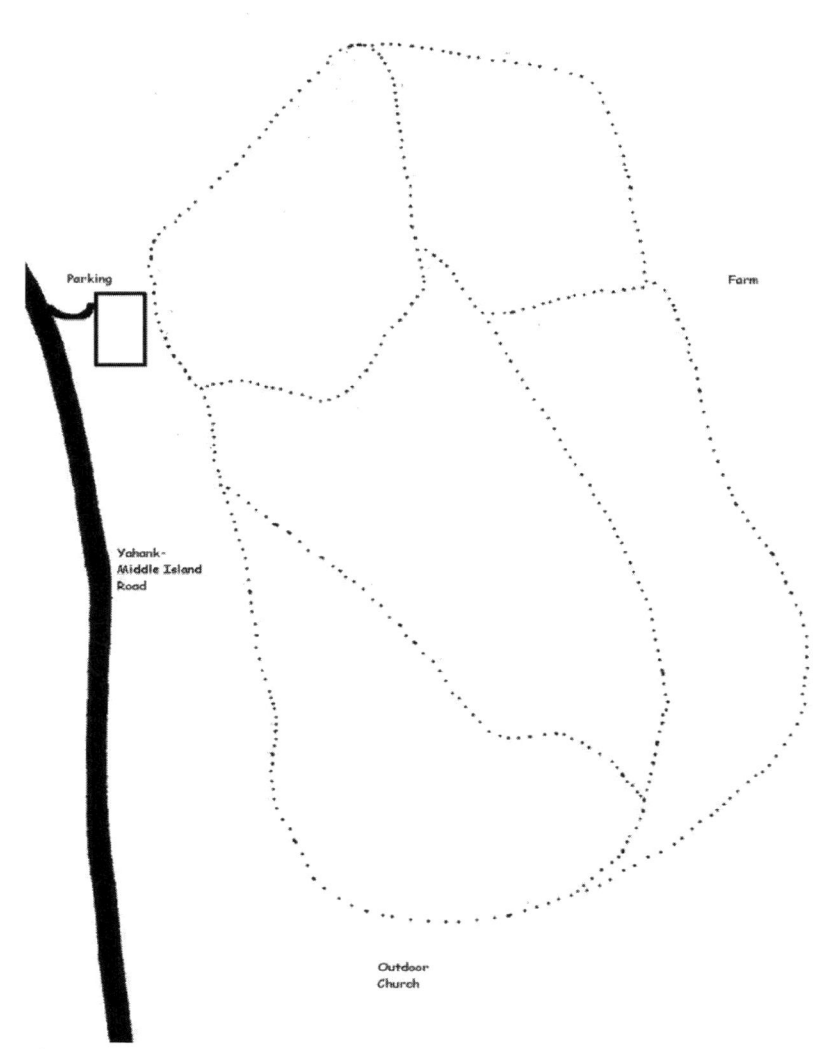

Figure 36 Prosser Pines

HECKSCHER STATE PARK

November 25th

  Winter trudges in with overcast skies and the temperature not quite hitting forty. Heckscher State Park occupies over 1400 acres on the Great South Bay. During the summer, you can camp, barbeque and enjoy the beach. The boat ramp and bike paths stay open all year round. Being a mixed use and developed park, it doesn't offer visitors a "lost in nature" experience, but the diversity of plant and wildlife in the varied habitats makes up for the developed and slightly crowded feel. Of course, if you are looking for place to jog or ride your bicycle, the paved trails provide plenty of room. During the summer months, ticks and poison ivy present a common problem, so take appropriate precautions. The signs at the entrance to the park declare that Heckscher is "The Home of the White Tailed Deer". Fairly tame, almost to the point of domestication, deer populate the preserve and surrounding neighborhoods. I notice several trees with bark rubbed off by male deer polishing its antlers. Deer mate in the fall. Bucks compete for dominance and does. The deer scent their rubs to communicate which males live in a particular territory. Deer have multiple scent glands and use scent to communicate with each other, the way some birds vary their calls to convey different messages.
  Starting near the marina, I follow a trail heading west. The trail traces a stream on the north edge of a salt marsh. Puffy white flowers on the groundsel bushes prepare to be taken by the wind. Other seaside plants include holly, juniper and a few cedars. Further from the salt marsh area, oak and pitch pine become more prominent. I spot a black throated blue warbler on a fallen tree. Over 250 bird species visit Heckscher throughout the

year, including osprey that nest in the less developed beach area and hunt in the bay. Most of the leaves have fallen, and the ones still clinging to the trees are a bland brown color.

Following the trails behind the picnic areas, into the interior of the preserve, you can reach one of the few areas where it is possible to forget how developed the park is. The area is mostly swampy, and the trails are not marked, so, if you feel adventurous, you can spend several hours exploring. During the summer, expect ticks, poison ivy and sticker bushes throughout this area. With those threats asleep, fall and winter make for safer hikes.

On the eastern side of the park, north of the campground, the Long Island Greenbelt trail enters the park through some wooded areas north of the camp sites. White blazes mark the Greenbelt Trail as it goes through some open grass areas. In late November, the grass is pale brown in color and flowering. As the Greenbelt Trail gets closer to the water, pine and oak become less prevalent, and cedar and holly become more pronounced. During the summer months, the undergrowth is thick with catbrier and raspberry. Taller phragmites indicate the presence of water on the ground.

Two miles of shoreline trace the edge of the bay. The more eastern areas of the shore, closer to the camp sites, tend to be less crowded, even during the summer. A model airplane club converted one of the older beach parking lots into an airfield for model planes. Surprisingly, the model planes don't scare off the osprey and other shorebirds that spend their summers at Heckscher. Walking along the shore, you can see Fire Island and its lighthouse. Smooth grained sands forms a mini-dune type of environment, similar to what you find on the barrier beaches, but scaled back. Included you'll find beach grass, heather, and smaller pitch pine taking root in the sand as best as they can. The effects of the flooding from

Hurricane Sandy can be seen all along the beach. The bay water pushed the grasses down, and the receding tide left debris piled everywhere. Seagulls along with other shorebirds pick through the debris left by Sandy. Enjoying the cool bay water, a small group of bufflehead ducks and hooded mergansers swim along the shore. These ducks like to spend their winters in Long Island's estuaries. Also paddling in the waters of The Great South Bay during the winter months is a type of duck called an oldsquaw, or long tailed duck. The long tailed duck dives for mollusks, and can dive up to 200 feet into the water if they need to, using the edges of their partially folded wing like flippers, propelling themselves through the water. Further down the beach, a sandpiper lingers, picking through the sand for a bite to eat. A sign near the beach marks the beginning of the Long Island Greenbelt Trail, which extends north across the island for 31.6 miles, passing alongside the Connetquot River, both moraines, the Nissequogue River, until it ultimately reaches Sunken Meadow State Park on the north shore. A smaller trail traces back to the marina, which sits at the end of a small deep cove between the sandy beach area and an extensive salt marsh covering the western portion of the preserve. The marina is quiet, and a few joggers pass by once I return to the paved portion of the trail.

Directions:

Follow the Southern State Parkway east, until it changes to the Heckshire State Parkway. Follow it until it ends at the park entrance.

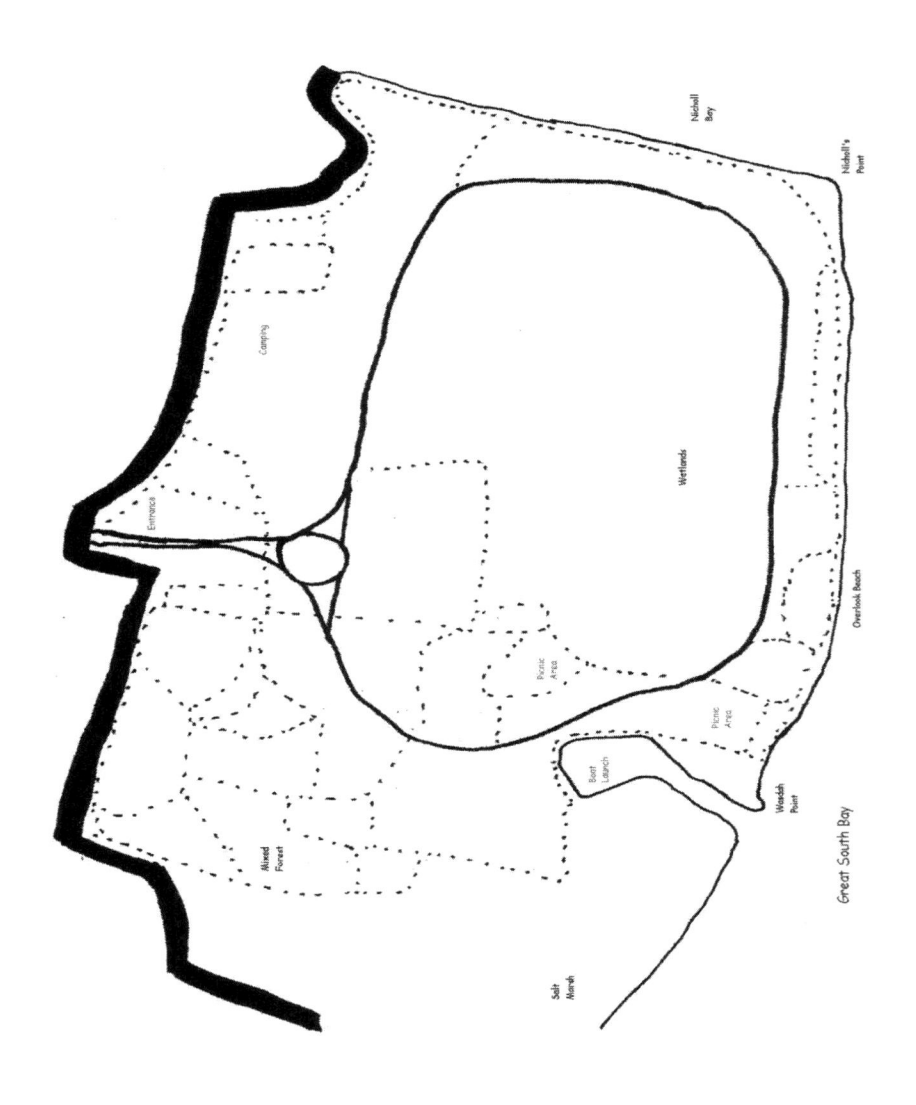

Figure 37 Heckscher State Park

DECEMBER

American Chestnuts

SANDS POINT PRESERVE

December 1st

  Winter clouds fill the skies and the temperature barely reaches forty degrees. Except for the evergreens, the trees have dropped most of their leaves. White oak and beech, fall's last holdouts, still hold their dead leaves, and will until spring returns. Nassau County owns the 216 acre preserve, formerly an old estate, reputed to be the inspiration for "East Egg" from F. Scott Fitzgerald's <u>The Great Gatsby</u>. People make fortunes, enabling them to create an estate like this. They live there a short time, and when they die, their heirs lack the resources or inclination to maintain them, so they end up in public hands, where the tax payers foot the bill for their upkeep. The lavish buildings are considered to be more of a treasure than the land they are built on. Like other preserves in Nassau County that endured previous incarnations as wealthy estates, the buildings remain. Groundskeepers continue maintenance on the areas closest to the buildings. The remaining areas have, over time, slowly been reclaimed by natural processes, but the old estate holders left their mark.
  Unlike the other preserves in Nassau, The County charges ten dollars to every car entering the grounds. They charge a two dollar fee to each person walking in without a car. The surrounding village of Sands Point prohibits parking, so don't expect to save some money by parking on the street and walking into the preserve. Sands Point is not the type of inviting place you can visit on a daily basis to jog or walk your dog. No unique features set it apart from other nature preserves on the island. One might suspect that the blue bloods living in the neighborhood requested the county to charge the unusual entrance fee for the purpose of discouraging riff-raff from less affluent

communities from visiting too frequently. Honestly, Welwyn Preserve and Garvies Point, both fairly close by, provide a similar view of the sound, a better natural experience, and don't charge an entrance fee. To their credit, the overseers marked five easy to follow trials, which can be combined and explored in under two hours. A fifth trail, called "The Dino Track Trail" and designed for children, lacks authentic dinosaur tracks.[2]

 A small pond serves as the centerpiece of the preserve. Vines surrounding it work hard to pull down the few trees on its edges. Clearly manmade, a stream leading past Castle Gould feeds it. A trail goes around it, and another leads past it to the Sound. Not even a goose swims in the pond, and no seagulls fly over the water. The effects of Hurricane Sandy can be seen on the beach. The clay and sand under a paved road leading to the beach washed away, causing sections of it to cave in. The waves also pulled down sections of the bluffs. Today, a strong wind can be felt when walking along the beach, making for strong waves in the sound.

 While one of the trails brings you along the beach, another brings you along the bluffs overlooking the sound. Like elsewhere on the north shore, a few sizable tulip trees managed to remain on the grounds as the property changed hands through a succession of owners. A number of glacial erratics scatter around the grounds. On the southern portion of the preserve, you'll find a ravine, with fairly steep sides. The rhododendron growing here are a native species. Their leaves stay green throughout the year. In summer they put out clusters of white flowers, and fill the

---

[2] Across the Long Island Sound in Connecticut, Dinosaur State Park offers authentic dinosaur footprints, and doesn't charge an entrance fee for the park grounds. They only charge for an exhibit center which provides a very enlightening view of how this region was millions of years before glaciers scraped sand and debris from New England forming Long Island.

air with their aroma. For people who prefer landscaping with indigenous plants and shrubs, the rhododendron is an excellent and popular choice. In addition to the black and white oak, sweetgum trees grow here as well. You can identify them this time of year by their fruit, a hard spiky "burr ball" which hang from the branches and eventually falls to the ground. Sweetgum gets its name from its resin which manufacturers still use to make gum. Through history, people believe the resins to have medicinal properties, particularly for the treatment of respiratory ailments.

   As the trails lead back to the entrance, you can see Castle Gould on the hill at the top of the ravine. Its designers fashioned it after Kilkenny Castle. It's reminiscent of the castle in <u>Monty Python's and the Holy Grail</u>. I expect a Frenchman to show his head above the ramparts and start shouting insults. Slowly, I walk past the castle to the parking lot, managing to avoid any taunting or projectiles thrown from the ramparts.

Directions:

From the L.I.E. take Exit 36. (Searingtown Rd./Shelter Rock Rd.)
Proceed north on Searingtown Road.
Searingtown Road will change into Port Washington Boulevard, and then Middle Neck Road. The Preserve will be on the right side of the road in Sand's Point.

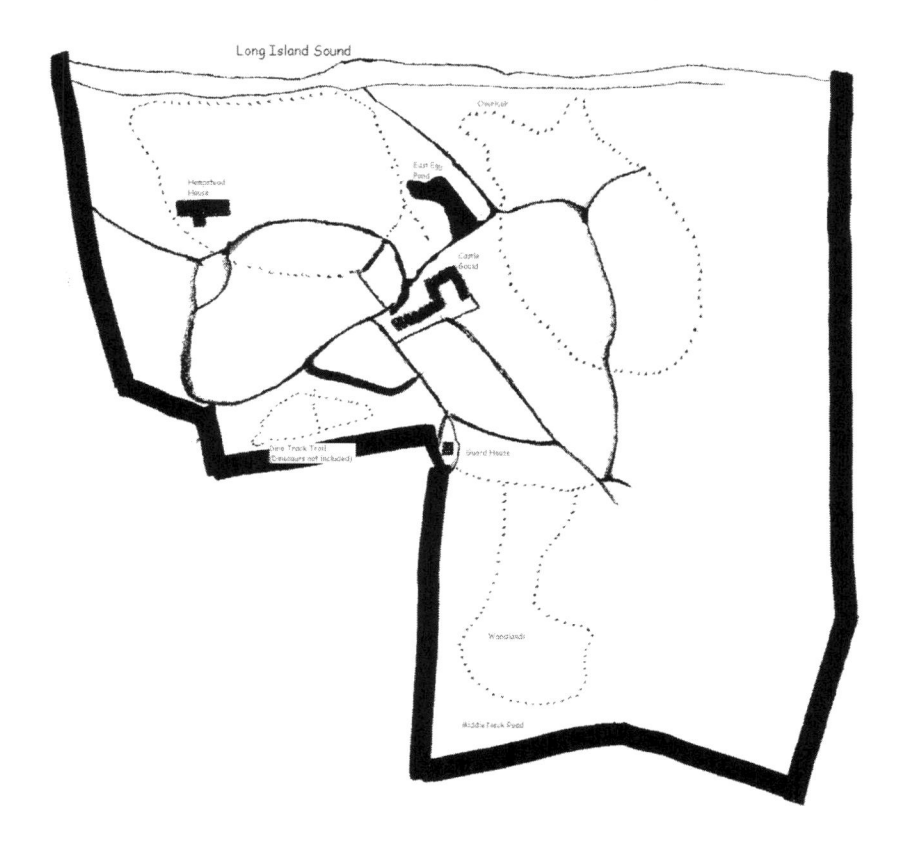

Figure 38 Sands Point Preserve

PINE MEADOW PRESERVE

December 9th

On the east side of route 51 sits the little known Pine Meadow Preserve. Set aside primarily as a hunting spot, the county permits hunting here from the beginning of October to the end of December. The hawks get to hunt here year round without permission from the county or state. Be careful and courteous to the hunters during hunting season. This preserve is their domain. Like the hawks, they fill an important ecological niche on this Island. As the preserve's name suggests, it is essentially a pine meadow. The trail is not a loop, but a dirt road less than a mile in length. It hooks up with other unmarked trails, allowing for a much longer hike, provided you have a map of the area. David Sarnoff Preserve and the Cranberry Bogs are both nearby. The north and east sides of the trail consist of mainly oak and pitch pine. The southwest corner consists of a wet meadow, with pine and other trees scattered about. The sandy ground stays saturated, without forming ponds. The wider, unobstructed, view allows for some great bird watching opportunities, and the open field allows room for birds to perform courtship displays. The wet meadow attracts ticks and other insects during the spring and summer, but also provides opportunities to enjoy the wildflowers when they bloom. I personally like the feel of this preserve in the fall and winter. A day like today with a hint of rain and cool, but not cold, temperatures is ideal. The place feels alive, but placid. A cinnamony scent hangs in the air, and mixes with the smell of the pine needles on the path.

My first visit here several years ago was late in the summer. On that visit, I spotted a groundhog on the edge of the field. He rests in a state of hibernation now. He saw me before I saw him, and ran into his burrow before I could turn my camera on. When people show grainy pictures of The Loch Ness Monster, or talk about how they almost got a picture of Sasquatch, I think about the groundhog, and all the other near misses I've had trying to photograph wildlife on different parts of the Island. Getting a good picture of any living, moving animal is not as easy as it seems. The key to wildlife photography is patience. If I really wanted to get a good picture of the groundhog, I'd come back in early February, set up my camera on a tri-pod and stake out the entrance to his den. With my luck, I'd be waiting around, and he'd come out the secondary entrance when I wasn't looking. A tiny little critter like a groundhog moves about two and a half tons of dirt while digging its extensive burrow. Groundhogs love to place the entrances to their burrows on the edges of fields. The meadow provides the grasses and wild berries they feed off of. Its proximity to the field also attracts hawks, which frequently hunt at Pine Meadow. Hawk sightings are pretty much guaranteed to visitors who come here. The open fields make ideal hunting grounds for avian predators. Groundhogs and other rodents breed prodigiously, quickly replenishing their numbers, and providing plenty of food for the hawks.

  Juniper and pitch pine grow scattered in the field, their seeds deposited with the help of songbirds. On the branches of an oak, I spot a blue jay. He dives into a puddle and washes himself off, taking a drink. The grasses in the meadow are light brown this time of year, as are the ferns that also grow in the wet soil. Walking through the fields I get an appreciation for the wet meadow. Lichens grow on trees, and on the sand. Parts of it are too saturated to walk through. The soil underneath, like most of the soil consists mostly of sand.

Directions:

From Sunrise Highway take Exit 61 (County Route 51). Head north on Route 51. The entrance to the preserve will be on the right side of the road.

Blue Jay

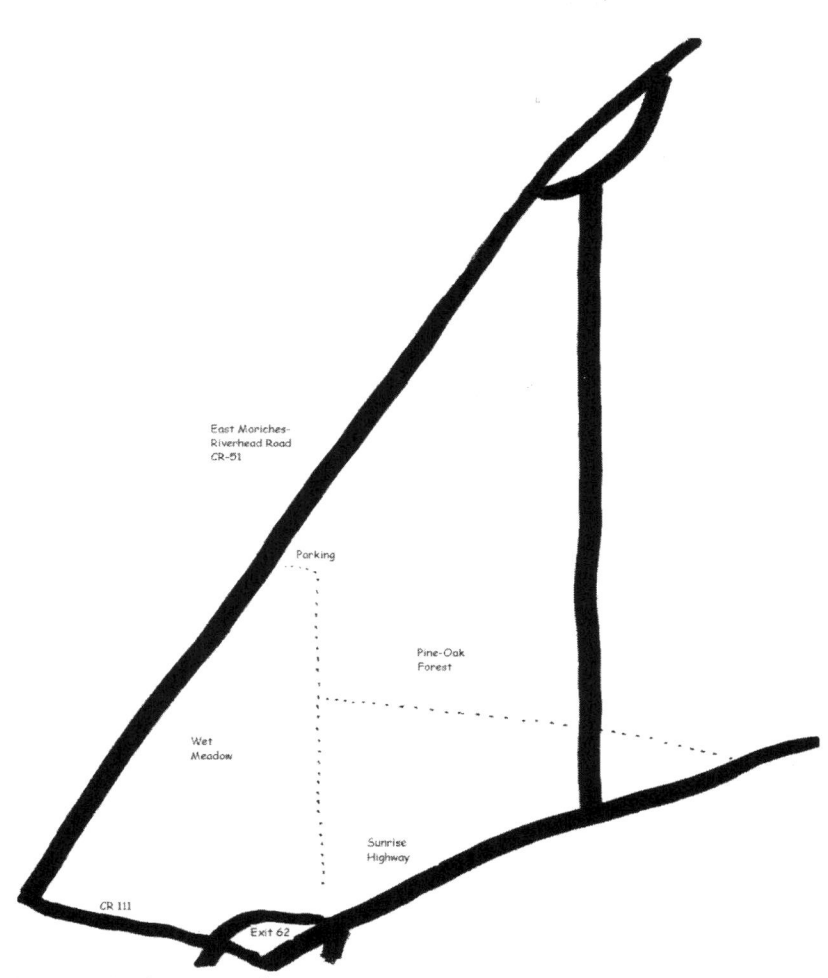

Figure 39 Pine Meadow Preserve

GARDINER COUNTY PARK

December 21st

  I decided to commemorate the Winter Solstice by visiting Gardiner County Park where I can watch the sun rise over the Great South Bay. Gardiner County Park occupies 230 acres between Montauk Highway and the Great South Bay, just east of the Robert Moses Causeway. A number of different trails allow access to different areas of the preserve. The parks department gave the trails names like Beach Road, Gull Lane, and Beaver Way. Different habitats in the preserve include an old field, a maple swamp, and of course an extensive salt marsh leading to the bay. Beach Road, the main trail, leads directly through the woods and salt marsh to the sandy beach. From the beach you can see the Fire Island lighthouse, Captree, and, on the right, the Robert Moses Causeway.

  For millennia, people celebrated the winter solstice, or mid-winter, as the return, or re-birth, of the sun. Although today has the least amount of sunlight for the year, each day between now and the summer solstice brings with it more and more sun. The night is as long as it will ever be. The solstice is the day in the year when things start to turn around and change. According to older European myths, the reborn Sun God brings light and hope into the world. In ancient times, people celebrated the solstice with candles, symbolic fires and wreaths of holly. The wreath symbolized the wheel of the year, understood as the perpetual change of seasons. The holly, an evergreen with bright red berries, emerges this time of year. The wheel of the year continues to spin. Spring and the fertility that accompanies it will eventually return as the daylight grows longer. Consider the original reason for the season the next time you light a candle in the darkness on Christmas Eve.

Today the clouds take in most of the sun, and drop rain by the gallon. Here and there, the sun manages to shine through, in spite of the rain coming down. The tides and winds pushed the bay water up past the salt marsh, and into the woods.

I recommend the park to anyone looking to take a short walk on the South Shore. A popular spot for dog walkers, coming here on a day with good weather can be an unofficial dog show. Proud dog owners come here eager to show off their pooches, and their dogs eagerly greet each other with the usual formalities.

Surprisingly, the dogs don't scare off the shorebirds. In season, the open salt marsh provides a home for egrets, cormorants, herons and a variety of ducks. The beach area at lower tides is a great place for shell collecting, if you are so inclined. Even at the busiest times, you can still find a quieter spot on the beach, particularly on the west side of the preserve to enjoy the sights and smells of the bay. During the summer, expect to see fiddler crabs scurrying across the sand.

Phragmites and dense brush hide a small freshwater pond near the parking area. In December, you'll need to look for the winter ducks, including buffleheads, mergansers and northern shovelers. You'll also find these ducks swimming on the bay when the water's not too rough. On the northern side of the preserve, along Montauk Highway, ground crews keep an area mowed, but allow a few islands of shrubs and small trees to grow free in the field. Like the salt marsh, this area is great for bird watching during the spring. Instead of shorebirds, you will find song birds in the brush. Twenty one species of warblers breed on the Island, add to that a myriad of other species, such as blue birds, indigo buntings, thrushes, orioles, and there are hundreds of bird species that breed around the island, and hundreds more that just pass through when migrating. Birdwatchers certainly have something to look forward to in the spring.

 A maple swamp covers the area north of the salt marsh. Off the paths the swamp gets quickly overgrown with various vines and shrubs, colored brown and grey this time of year. A number of smaller streams cut through the preserve, allowing for some drainage. Without the streams this area would flood constantly. Instead, it only floods frequently. A fair amount of cedar and pitch pine grow in raised areas throughout the swampy area. Oak and beech are also well represented.

 Here and there, holly trees show themselves. In the spring, the hollies silently blend into the green around them, but this time of year, their spiky green leaves and soft red berries contrast with the brown and grey colors of winter. Although toxic to humans, the berries provide winter food for birds. The spiny leaves also provide a hiding place and a refuge from predators all year round. In Medieval Heraldry, holly symbolized truth. In pre-christian Europe, holly became associated with the mid-winter solstice holiday, because it showed life in an otherwise dead time of year. It represented hope, and reminded people that even if the nights were at their longest, and the days the darkest and coldest, that new life, and warmth would eventually return with the inevitable coming of spring.

Directions:

From The Robert Moses Causeway, take the exit for Montauk Highway heading east.
The preserve will be on the right side of Montauk Highway.

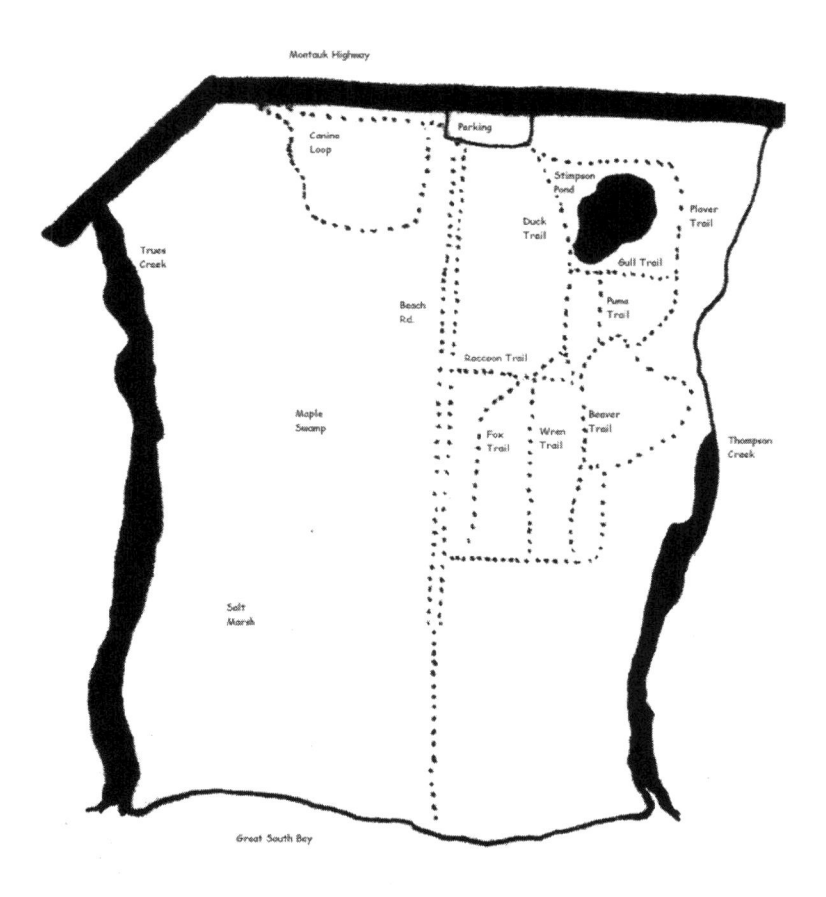

Figure 40 Gardiner County Park

DWARF PINE PLAINS

December 25th

Mother Nature blessed Long Island by placing one of the few existing dwarf pine forests in Westhampton. Only three dwarf pine forests exist. The other two can be found in along the Shawangunk Ridge in the Hudson Valley in the New Jersey pine barrens. The Dwarf Pine forest in Westhampton consists of dwarf pitch pines and similarly stunted scrub oak. Consisting of exactly the same species of pitch pine found throughout the pine barrens, natural breeding combined with dry, sandy and acidic soil conditions dwarfed these trees. Most of them stand smaller than eight feet. The forest itself is much larger than the preserve. Some if it grows on private land. Sunrise Highway passes through the forest in the vicinity of exit 63. Laws protect the forest and surrounding areas from further development. Protecting the forest also protects the aquifer collecting water in the sand below it. Individual stands of dwarf pine can be found elsewhere on the Island, particularly on the barrier beaches. The forest in Westhampton covers approximately 1300 acres.

As in the rest of the pine barrens, fire plays an essential role in perpetuating this habitat. As you walk through the preserve, keep in mind, nearly all of the forest around you was burned to the ground by the extensive wild fires that swept through the area in the summer of 1995. A number of the plants contain flammable resins that promote fires. A relatively low water table and a near absence of ponds, streams or other wetlands also facilitate the spread of fire in this part of the island. The fires actually allow seeds of fire dependent communities to take root, and rejuvenate the forest.   The real threat to a forest like this isn't forest fires, but human intervention through development and fire suppression. Controlled burns perform an essential role in protecting this habitat, just as it does in the rest of the pine barrens.

Winter hikes here are ideal, because the pine trees are always green. Also, the ticks sleep underground this time of year, so you can really explore the forest, without picking up any unwanted hangers-on. It snowed a few inches yesterday, and the snow drained through the soil as quickly as it melted. The soil here is probably some of the driest, sandiest soil on the Island, excluding beach areas and adjoining dunes. In many ways this forest is like the maritime forests elsewhere on the Island, but without the influence of sea spray and heavy winds. The plants reflect those conditions, and are more similar to what you find in the beach areas, than in a typical forest. Only the most tenacious plants flourish. Bearberry and heather cover the ground, pushing their way up through various grasses and lichens. The understory shrubs consist of low bush blueberry and huckleberry.

Although they usually shy away from people, deer can be found year round, their tracks easy to spot in the sand. Kestrels and hawks, including the endangered northern harrier, also nest in the preserve. The thin canopy allows them to easily hunt the rabbits and other small animals that live here.

Visiting the forest during the spring and early summer provides great opportunities for bird watching. In the thickets, a variety of warblers and other song birds can be found breeding. On the west side of Route 31, you will find extensive clearings where heather covers the entire ground, and only a few isolated trees break up the clearings. During the spring and summer the heather blooms, covering the fields with tiny yellow flowers.

The Autumn months bring out a variety of

butterflies and moths which breed and feed here. One of the more notable species is the buck moth. During the winter, you'll find their eggs on the scrub oaks branches. The eggs look like a string of white beads wound tightly around the smallest branches. The caterpillars look like painful living torture implements. Spines cover their squirming little bodies, and you may get a rash if you touch them. During the spring and summers the caterpillars spend most of their time underground, and emerge for a brief period in the fall so they can mate. The full grown moths can be identified by their brown and white wings, with markings that look almost like eyes.

     Any time of year this preserve can be explored fairly quickly, particularly the shorter path on the east side of Route 31, covering slightly more than half a mile. For people driving further east to Montauk the preserve sits close enough to Sunrise Highway that you can stop and stretch your legs here. The larger, unmarked trail loops for three miles on the west side of Route 31. The forest extends northward to David Sarnoff Preserve.

Directions:

Take Exit 63(Route 31).
Head south. Parking for the Preserve is immediately south of Sunrise Highway on the right side of the road. The smaller trail is next to the Suffolk County Water Authority building on the left side of the road.

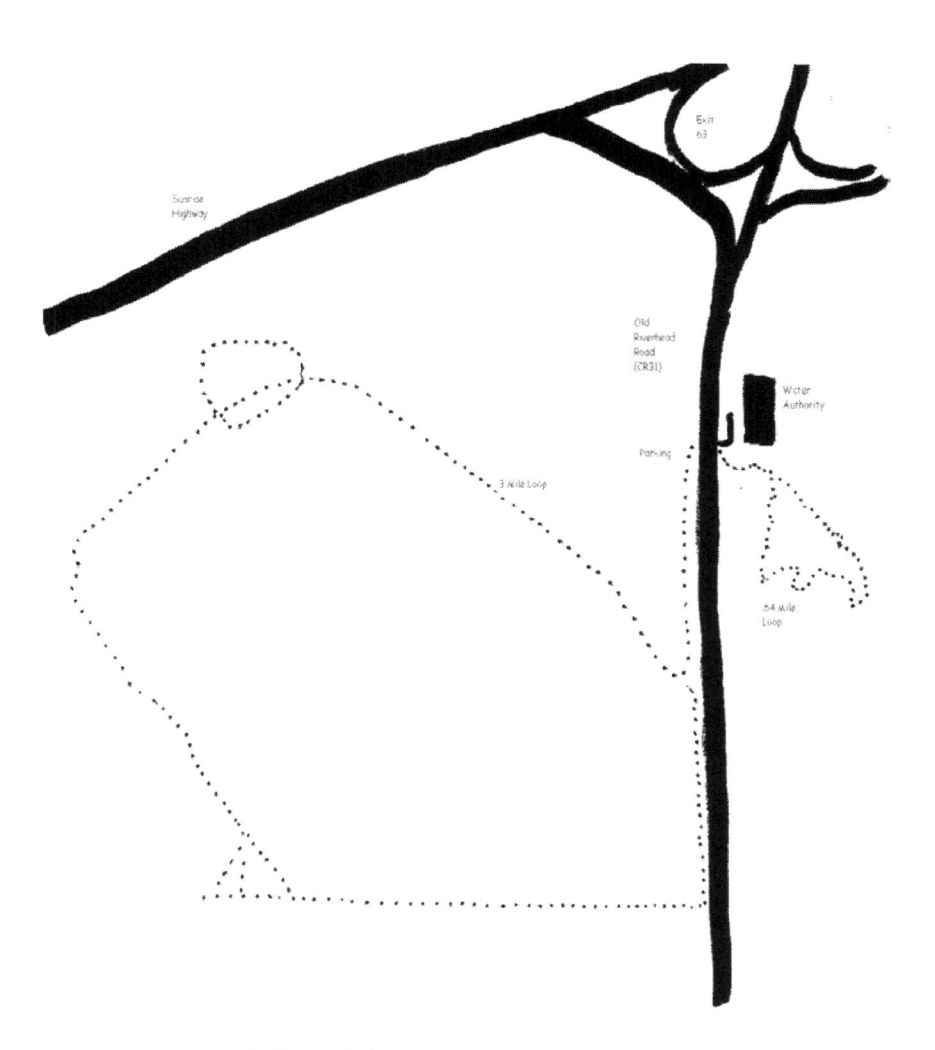

Figure 41 Dwarf Pine Plains

FOREST PARK PRESERVE

December 29th

The temperature hovers at thirty two degrees. Little flakes of snow drift in the air. Gradually the snow fall gets a little heavier, and the air warms slightly. By the time I finish my walk around Forest Park, the snow turns to a cold rain. The orange trail takes a little over an hour to walk. A shorter blue trail covers about half the distance of the orange trail. A number of side trails allow for additional exploration for people interested in avoiding the beaten path.

Unfortunately, Queens offers very few places where you can enjoy a taste of the natural world, and see the western end of the Island the way your great grandparents, or maybe their grandparents saw it. The City of Brooklyn saved the preserve from development when it purchased it from Queens County for use as a public park in the late 1800's. At the time, Brooklyn and Queens hadn't been incorporated into New York City, and white tailed deer ran through the forest underneath a canopy of chestnut and oak trees.

Today, New York City uses most of Forest Park for typical park uses, such as picnic and athletic fields. They also maintain greenhouses to raise seedlings of trees that they later plant throughout the city. The Million Trees NYC planting initiative sources most of its trees from the greenhouses here, and provides a great way for people in the community to get involved in making their city a little greener.

Developers left approximately one hundred and sixty acres of mature oak forest intact. Growing beneath the oak, you'll find hickory, pine and dogwood. At the time the City established it as a park, American chestnut grew as plentiful as the oak, but they died off years ago. In one corner of the preserve, the city planted a white pine grove which provides a much needed splash of green this time of year. Visiting in the winter, the vegetation is all down, and you can see very clearly why geologists consider this type of terrain "Knob and Kettle". The preserve, like most of Queens, sits on the western end of the Harbor Hill moraine. The knobs refer to the mounds and hills, and the kettles refer to the large depressions between them. The ups and downs give the walker a fair amount of exercise. With the trees bare, you can walk along the top of the moraine, and catch a view looking south west, as far as Rockaway Beach.

Even though you can hear the traffic from nearby streets, the acreage is large enough for a visitor to imagine themselves as being somewhere other than the middle of Queens. Strack Pond, a kettle pond, sits in a lower lying part of the preserve. It attracts great blue herons, egrets, various ducks, and Canadian geese. The pond, along with the rest of the preserve offers one of the few good bird watching spots in Queens.

Strack Pond benefited from a recent restoration project, which allowed for the removal of debris and various invasive plant species. Being in a densely populated area, not everyone who visits the preserve is particularly concerned with preserving its natural character. Just like in Marine Park and Udall's Cove, occasional restoration projects become vital to the preservation of the park. With a little imagination, and smart, realistic practices, nature can be brought into a generally urban area, benefiting all the city's residents, whether, animal, vegetable or mineral.

Directions:
From Jackie Robinson Parkway, take Exit 4 (Forest Park Drive).

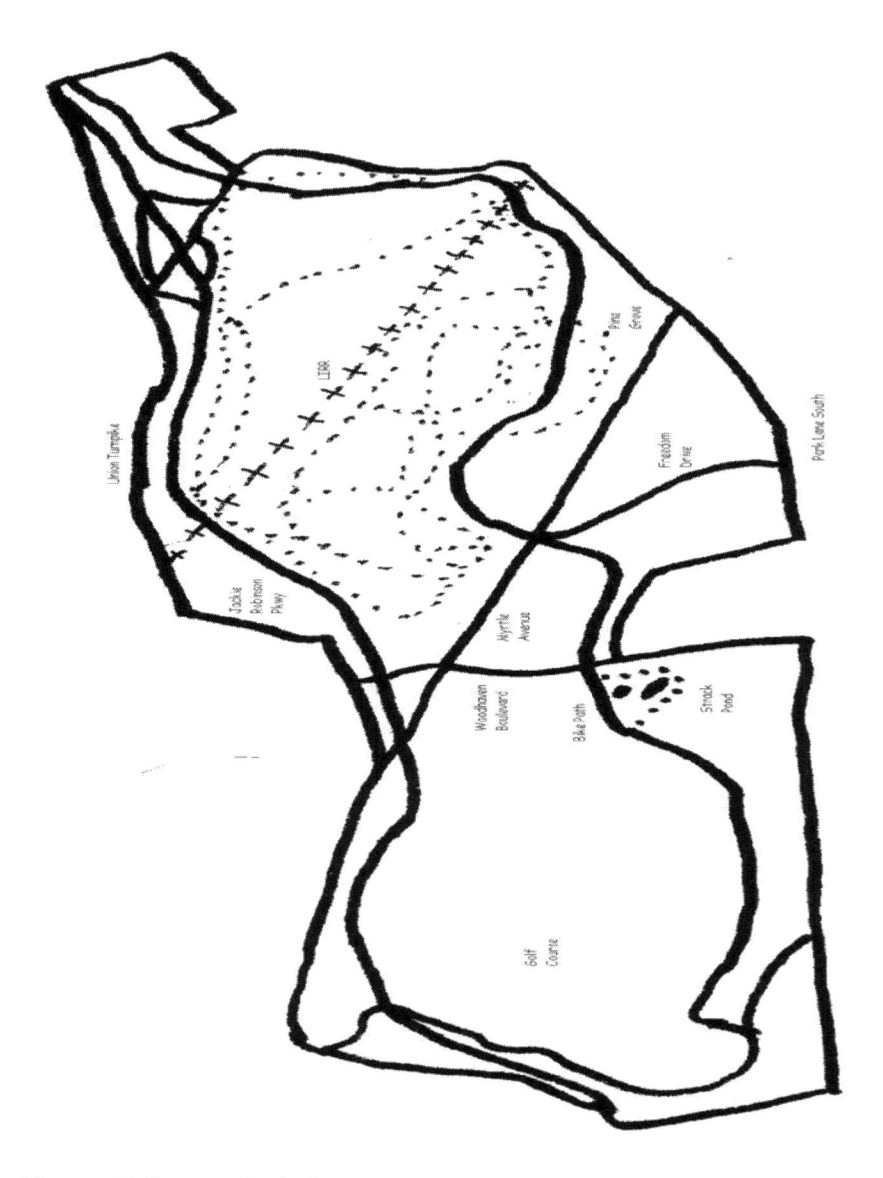

Figure 42 Forest Park Preserve

JANUARY

Figure 43 Nassau Suffolk Greenbelt Trail in Massapequa Preserve

GARVIES POINT

1/6/13

     Forty degrees and sunny -- warm for January. Patches of snow remain from earlier in the week. Garvies point occupies seventy acres on the west side of Hempstead Harbor, immediately north of Mosquito Cove. Covering forest, old fields and 2000 feet of shoreline, Garvies Point can be explored in under two hours, even if you take your time. Like most of the preserves in Nassau, it served as an estate before falling into Nassau County's hands. Since the county established it as a preserve, nature has been taking it back. The Garvie family cemetery remains tucked away on the grounds. A glacial erratic marks the location.

     Prior to being settled by the Cole and Garvie families, Native Americans inhabited the site. The water provided fish and mussels, and the beach provided valuable clay. Tulip trees, perfect for making dugout canoes, grew in the woods above the beach. The sandy glacial deposits are part of the Harbor Hill Moraine, which starts in Queens, and ends at Plum Island. Small bluffs mark the edge where the woods meet the sandy beach. The actual Harbor Hill glacial deposits from that period are fairly thin compared to the rest of the island, allowing the emergence of much older clay from sides of the bluffs. Nature created the clay long before the Wisconsin glaciers formed the moraines that make up the back bone of Long Island. While the Wisconsin deposits go back 20,000 years, the clay they rest upon go back 70 million years, to the cretaceous period.

     European settlers mined the clay, as did the Matinecock who lived here prior to European settlement. Iron oxide colors the clay its distinctive orange to red color.

Clay containing less iron is colored greyish white. Shale and sandstone from this period can be found along the beach also. Among the rocks on the beach, you will find concretions called "Indian paint pots" and "rattlestones". Through oxidation and erosion caused by being tossed around in the surf, lumps of pyrite become bowl shaped stones called "Indian paint pots". Nature creates "rattlestones" when iron oxide coalesces around a clay core. The clay core dries within a hardened mineral shell, and can be heard rattling in the stone. The iron oxide in both can be used as a pigment. Ambitious folks can look through the shale for fossils, but the preserve's rules protect the beach for future generations, and prohibit removing samples.

    The preserve's museum focuses on local geology and the natural history of Long Island. The displays make the visitor feel like they are stepping back in time. It seems as if they haven't been changed since the early 1970s. Of course, the geological history of Long Island hasn't changed either, so the displays are still informative. Near the museum is an outdoor classroom and small trail for the visually impaired. Marked by a rope, it contains signs in Braille and raised text identifying various trees common in the preserve. The signs offer a good starting point for anybody learning to identify local plant life.

    The forested parts of the preserve consist of a mix of cherry and locust. In the branches, I spot a downy woodpecker, a non-migratory bird. One of the more diverse wooded areas around, it also contains a good mix of oak, beech, and maple. In the nineteenth century oak and chestnut lived in the forest, but these were either cut down by settlers or destroyed by chestnut blight. The ground on the north side of the preserve is steep, whereas, the southern portion of the preserve is a little more even, having been cleared for either farming or grazing at some point in the past.

On the south side of the preserve, a sheet of ice covers a small kettlehole pond. A cardinal sits on a nearby tree. In a few months, when spring starts, the bullfrogs living in the pond will come out and sun themselves on the edges of the pond. Right now, they quietly hibernate in the mud. The bullfrogs living in this pond grow to about the size of a softball, and have dark brown, almost black, skin, making them different than the brighter green bullfrogs found elsewhere on Long Island. In the spring the pond and nearby thickets also attract a variety of song birds.

Loons enjoy the beach in their winter plumage, which is mostly black with a white throat and breast. A long tailed duck rides the small waves alongside a small group of black scoters. For these birds, Garvies Point might as well be South Beach. They migrate here from much further north, enjoying Long Island's sunny beaches. Walking along the beach, a small group of snow geese, in both their white and blue phases, try to get my attention. Genetic variation with these geese allows for some to be nearly completely white, and some to have a bluish grey coloration with a white head.

Besides the winter visitors, the beach at low tide holds other treasures. In the sand one slow narrow trickle brings water from the moraine down into the bay. It's the best Mother Nature can do for a stream today. Mussels hold together patches of beach grass. Mostly rocky, with some larger glacial boulders, algae covers the beach. With the tide low, seaweed and shells wash up throughout the beach. At the southern end, near to the place where Glen Cove Creek empties into Mosquito Cove, the beach area gives way to phragmites at the water's edge. Beyond the creek, a busy marina and some industrial sites offer a reminder of how developed Western Nassau's become.

Directions:

From The Northern State Parkway, Go north on Route 107, until it ends.
Follow signs through a residential neighborhood until you reach the preserve.
The preserve is on Red Spring Lane in Glen Cove.

Snow Geese

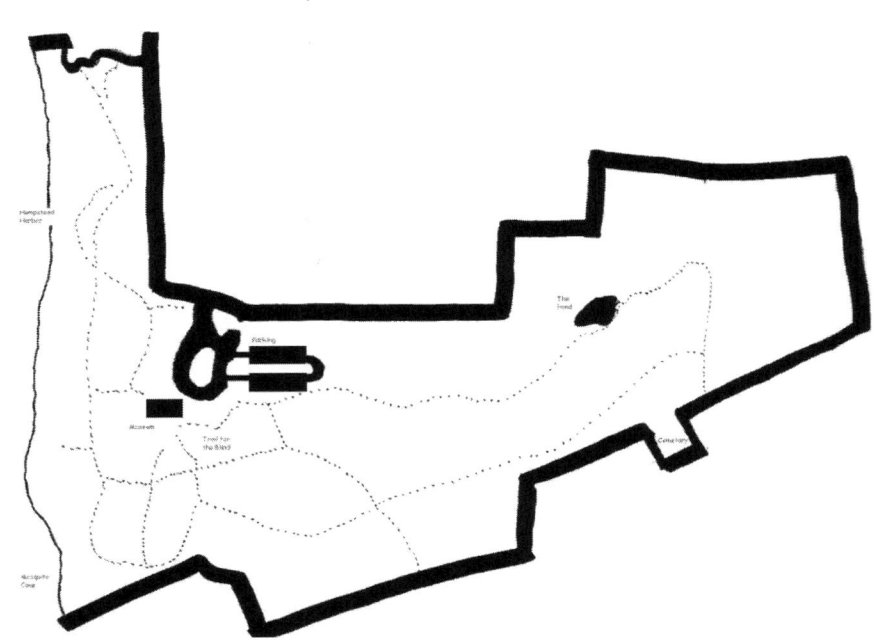

Figure 44 Garvies Point

ARTHUR KUNZ PRESERVE

January 13th

You can access the ninety-three acre preserve through a small dirt road at the end of Landing Avenue in Smithtown. The road leads directly to the Nissequogue River. The preserve follows The Nissequogue's western bank. Homes spread out on the eastern bank of the Nissequogue. Today a dense fog covers the river. At this end, close to where it flows into the sound, the river is wide. Mud flats covered in cord grass extend from the side of the river. This time of year the grass is all brown, most of it pushed down by the water. In the spring it will be back and green all over again. The Nissequogue, extending eight miles inland, is one of Long Island's four main rivers, and the fastest flowing. The Nissequogue starts as several shallow and unassuming streams, and ends as a wide estuary immediately east of Sunken Meadow State Park. The first Europeans to map the North Shore of Long Island mistakenly charted the Nissequogue as a lagoon and not a river.

Groundwater feeds the river, but the tides exert the strongest influence. Tides push the water inland. Because of the river's relatively short distance, and the quick rise in elevation between the edge of the shoreline and the top of the harbor hill moraine, its depth can fluctuate about seven feet with the tide. Water flows quickly, which, in addition to the fairly unspoiled scenery, makes it a popular spot for kayaking. The best way to enjoy the river is by paddling it, even on a January day in the low forties, such as today, several kayakers paddle along, enjoying the currents. At its northern end, the river serves as a nursery for fish and shell fish. Beds of oyster, clams and mussels live and breed in the mud flats.

Today, a "King Tide" influences the river, which means the water level will be at the highest it is during the year. Ten days ago, the Earth came to its closet point to the sun in its orbit, referred to as Perihelion. Additionally, this week, the moon came to its closest point to the earth for the month of January, referred to as its perigee. These two factors combined contribute to the king tide. The tides submerge sections of the trail closest to the river, making them impassible. Seaweed hangs several feet off the ground from some of the lower branches of trees along the river. This gives an indication of how high the tide rose. In warmer seasons, and at lower tides, the river bank attracts nesting diamondback terrapins, horseshoe crabs, fiddler crabs, and a variety of shellfish and shorebirds. Heron can be found year round, along with different types of ducks. This time of year, the river serves as a winter home for American black duck, lesser scaup, red-breasted merganser and other winter shorebirds. In warmer weather, Ospreys hunt along the river. You'll also find wild grapes along the banks during the spring and summer.

Being fed by groundwater, the river and its inhabitants are particularly susceptible to harm from oils, detergents, fertilizers, medications and other chemicals disposed of in the surrounding neighborhoods. At lower tides various kinds of debris can be seen along the river banks. At one spot, during low tide, you'll find the remains of a boat, including its motor, in the mud flats.

Marked by white blazes, the Long Island Greenbelt Trail extends through here. For the most part, the trail takes you through the hilly areas of the preserve, but at lower tides you can walk along the river bank. The hilly areas are part of the same Harbor Hill moraine that made Forest Park Preserve in Queens, and Garvie's Point in Nassau. Here, the woods are less populated and hillier than they are further west. Closer to the river, the forest consists of mainly beech and maple. Further away from the river, various oaks predominate. With the leaves down, you can make your way to the top of the hills and get fairly unobstructed views of the river and surrounding terrain. The lower kettle holes allow for a few shallow ponds and mud patches populated by fern and hibernating salamanders. In a few places, deer scat can be seen on the trial, but the deer tend to stay hidden from people. I don't see any out today, but they are certainly here. Along the trail you will find a stone foundation from a house abandoned long ago. Near it, several cars slowly rust into the ground.

On the trail you'll pass an enormous glacial erratic split in two. Two grey birch trees grow out of the split. It tells a story. Nature placed it in that spot between ten and twenty thousand years ago, before the Atlantic Ocean inundated the Long Island Sound, and before the groundwater feeding the Nissequogue fell as rain. Its size makes it a natural landmark, which was likely used by the first people to settle here. The children of all the generations who've lived along the river found the boulder an attractive place to play. The trees slowly tear the boulder apart. The process started thousands of years ago when lichen seeped into small cracks on the boulder's surface. These trees are not the first to take root in the boulder. In time the trees will die and decompose, only to be replaced by other trees, which will continue the process of erosion started by the glaciers that left it here. The trail at Arthur Kunz continues down until it reaches the parking lot of the aquatic center, and the white blazes of the Long Island Greenbelt continue to Heckscher State Park on the Great South Bay.

Directions:

From Sunken Meadow Parkway, take exit SM4E (East Northport Road).
Proceed east. Make a right on Main Street.
Make a left onto St. Johnland Road.
Make a right on Landing Road.
The entrance will be on the right.

Figure 45 Patience

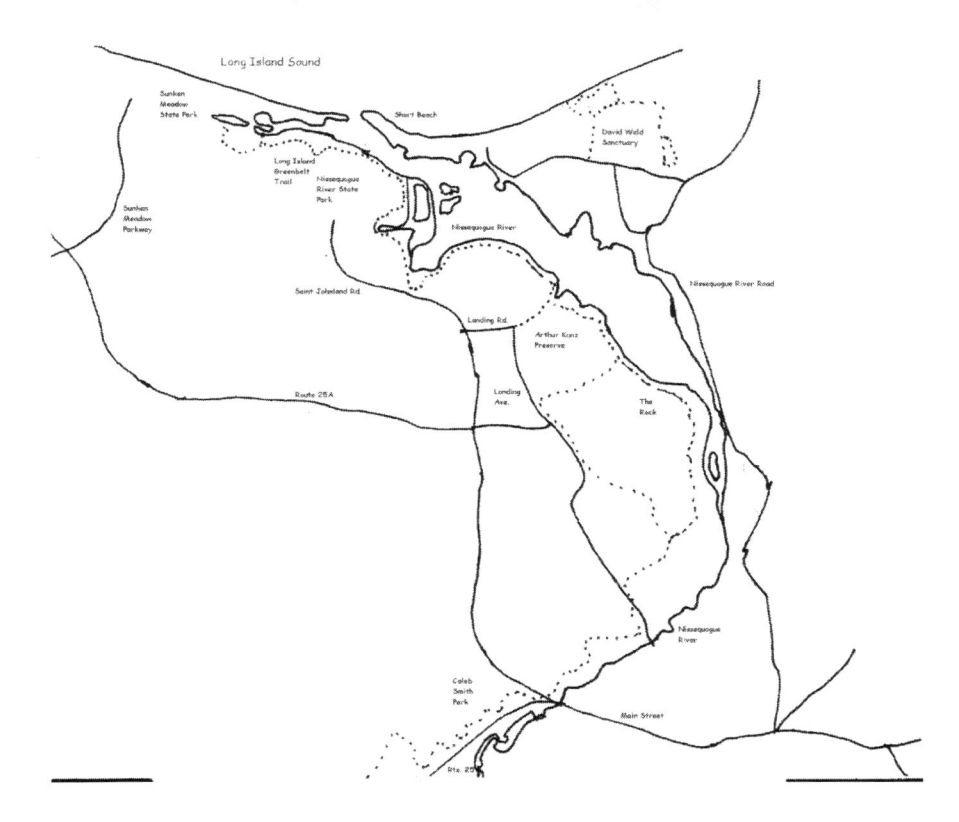

Figure 46 Nissequogue River

CUPSOGUE BEACH

January 20th

There is nothing cooler than walking along a beach in the winter. In the winter, the waves hit harder and with more determination. The wind means business, blowing hard enough to push the tiniest grains of sand along the beach. Cupsogue Beach occupies the western end of Dune Road and the east side of Moriches Inlet. Across Moriches Inlet the eastern tip of Fire Island beckons. You can quickly and easily walk around the tip of the beach from the ocean side to the bay side, and watch the waves go from forceful to gentle as they enter the bay. The shape and features of the barrier beaches change with every wave, every gust of wind and every storm. In a process called littoral, or long shore, drift, Atlantic waves gradually push the island's sand west, rolling the barrier beaches closer to Long Island.

When hurricanes and nor'easters hit they breach the dunes, forming inlets, which eventually close up. A nor'easter blew through here in 1931 creating Moriches Inlet. Prior to that storm, the strip of sand extending eastward along Dune Road was part of Fire Island. Today, it's a nameless barrier beach. Local fishermen find the inlet useful, so it's artificially kept open through the use barriers called groines which prevent sand from filling in the inlet. Without the groines, the inlet would have closed up within weeks or months of its formation. Sand piles up on the groines. Keeping the inlet open disrupts the natural process of long shore drift, causing beach erosion further west along Fire Island. On the positive side, keeping the inlet open also improves the health of the bay by allowing more water to flow in and out.

Interestingly, the name "Cupsogue" comes from a

native word meaning "closed inlet", suggesting that the original residents knew the ocean repeatedly punched through here, only to be closed by slow and constant efforts of long shore drift. As recently as Hurricane Sandy, another inlet formed, widened a few days later by a nor'easter, and subsequently closed with the help of the Army Corps of Engineers. That breach posed a threat to homes on Dune Road.

      Keeping Moriches Inlet open allows sandbars to form, making it easier for scallops and other mollusks to breed and attract a wider variety of shorebirds. The mix of salt and freshwater in the bay changes constantly. The open inlets allow for more saltwater. The calmer waters of the bay and the raised sandbars also attract seals during the winter months. More affectionately called sea dogs, harbor and grey seals migrate from the arctic, and visit our beaches in the winter. Today, on one of the larger sandbars, at least thirty seals sun themselves, warming themselves up on this January day. Mostly harbor seals, although a few grey seals can be seen. Harbor seals are whitish to yellow with dark patches. Grey seals, as their name implies, tend to be grey. Less frequently, harp seals and hooded seals can be found on the beaches. They grow larger than the grey and harbor seals. The largest hooded seals weigh up to 900 pounds. The seals look awkward on the land, but also relaxed. The seal community consists of extended families, pups and all. As if on cue, the whole pod of seals slides back into the bay at once. The water between the sandbar and the beach reaches a depth of ten feet. For a while, myself and my friend watch the seals pop their heads out of the water as they swim in the bay. The sea dogs stay under water for nearly a half an hour at a time. They eat fish, squid and other marine animals, and shy away from people. It's best not to disturb the seals. Like other wildlife, never feed them. Nature provides them exactly what they need to survive.

Suffolk County manages the beach, and during the summer allows camping on the dunes. Like Smith's Point further west, minimal light pollution and clear skies allow for awesome stargazing. The inlet is also a popular and productive fishing spot. On land, heavy grass and shrubs fill the bayside, holding the dunes together. A stretch of dwarf pitch pine, which thrives in sandy soil, lines the middle of the island, separating the bay side from the ocean side. On the ocean side, shells and seaweed wash up. During the summer piping plover and sand pipers make their homes on this beach, as do sunbathers and beach bums. During the winter, seagulls patrol the beach immune to the colder weather.

Directions:

Proceed west on Dune Road, until it ends in a parking lot.

Harbor Seal Pup

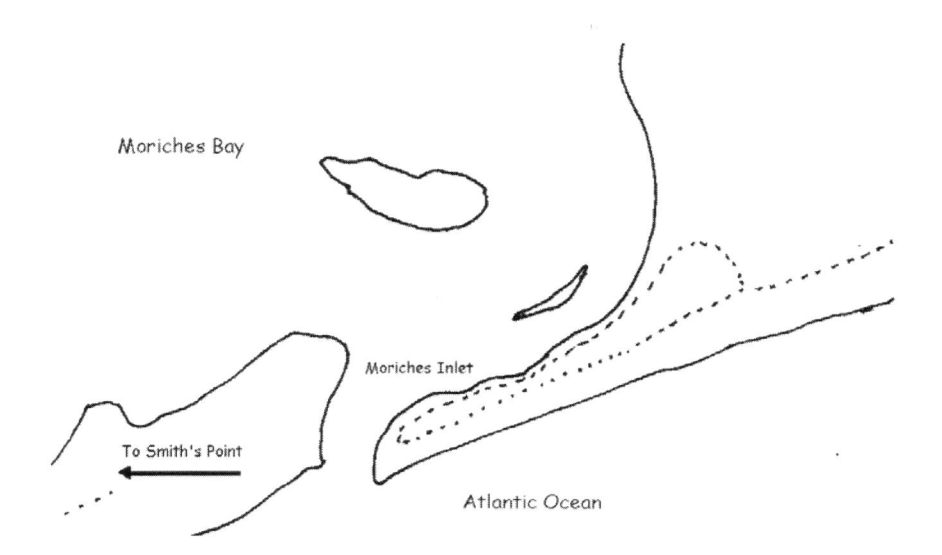

Figure 47 Cupsogue Beach

BROOKHAVEN STATE PARK

January 27th

  Winter in the pine barrens. The sun reflects off a thin covering of snow left on the ground from earlier this week. The temperature rests in the mid-twenties, preventing the snow from melting. Exhausted by cold weather, the whole forest sullenly waits for spring's arrival. Snow covers the sides of the trails and the bed of oak leaves and pine needles accumulated on the forest floor. People visit this preserve year round. Their footsteps wear most of the snow off the path. Brookhaven State Park connects to other state owned land, as well as town and county owned preserves, allowing for much larger, and less structured hikes for people wanting to leave the confines of this preserve. The preserve offers four marked trails. The blue trail is the shortest at 1.7 miles, and the green trail is the longest at 5.3 miles. The red trail loops for about three miles. The Brookhaven Trail, marked in yellow, passes through, beginning at Shorham-Wading River High School, near Route 25a, and ending 5.25 miles later south of Route 25 in Robert Cushman Murphy Preserve where it connects with the Paumonock Path.

  Besides the marked trails, several fire breaks cut through the preserve, and some smaller trails can be explored. The trails are wide, and fairly well marked. The state provides maps at a kiosk near the parking lot. The gates close at 4:00pm on the weekends, so it's best to get here early, so you can take your time and not be rushed. What the preserve offers is pitch pine, pitch pine, oak, and more pitch pine. On the western side of the preserve, flowering dogwood trees create an understory beneath the oak. In early spring when they blossom, the flowers are a welcome sight. Deer and wild turkey can be found throughout the preserve. In recent years, hikers spotted albino deer here, and in Robert Cushman Murphy Preserve to the south.

While the albino deer are a rare occurrence, wild turkey are not. The Department of Environmental Conservation re-introduced wild turkey to Long Island twenty years ago. In the nineteenth century, turkeys were common, but through habitat destruction, they, like otters, beavers and heath hens, disappeared from Long Island. In 1992 and 1993 The DEC brought seventy nine wild turkeys from Albany and Saratoga releasing them in Southhaven County Park and Heather Hills, both south of here. The population spread, and Long Island now has about three thousand wild turkeys and counting. The population's grown enough to allow limited turkey hunts around Thanksgiving. The wild turkeys released by the DEC in the early nineties shouldn't be confused with the turkeys found in Connetquot, Bethpage and elsewhere. Those populations escaped from farms and went feral. They are not the same as the wild turkeys in this preserve and elsewhere in eastern Suffolk County. If you seem them, they will be in small groups. Bear in mind, the wild turkey released in Suffolk can be quite elusive. They blend quietly into the brush when they hear people walking in their vicinity. You must be very, very quiet, regardless of the season.

On the eastern side of the preserve, near the power lines, you'll find a series of ponds. Shallow and sandy bottomed, they are a prelude to the numerous coastal plain ponds found further south in Cushman Preserve. Slightly grown in with grass and shrubs, their water levels fluctuate with the amount of rainfall. The ponds offer some of the few open areas in the preserve. In the spring and summer the ponds can be a great place for viewing wildflowers, and a great breeding ground for insects. You'll even find turtles and tiger salamanders.

Occupying the space between the two moraines, the terrain in the preserve stays relatively flat. Periods of glacial advances and retreats have been leaving deposits at this latitude since the early cretaceous period, approximately 3 million years ago. Clay deposits reveal that trees similar to the types of trees common in the pine barrens, have been growing here for tens of thousands of years. Pitch pine has been in this area for at least 10,000 years, and other types of pine were common prior to that. The two moraines currently making up the island are between 12,000 and 20,000 years old, but are made of sand much older than that. Like Gaia's Zen Garden, glaciers have been reshaping the land, pushing up and leveling different moraines in this area for millennia. In that manner the pine barrens, like the rest of the island, have been here, in one form or another for millions of years, and ponds like the ones here have been forming and eroding away for just as long.

Directions:

From the L.I.E., take exit 68 (William Floyd Parkway).
Head north on William Floyd Parkway.
The entrance to the preserve is on the right side.

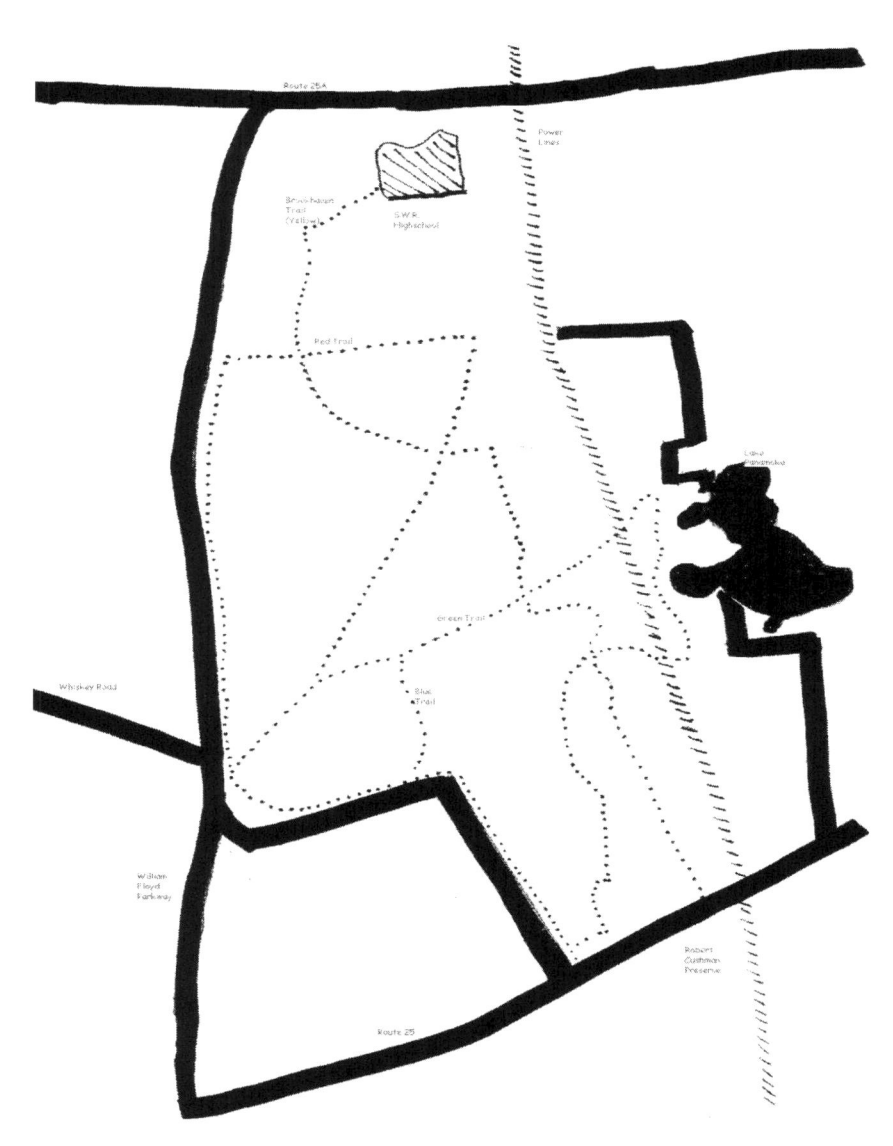

Figure 48 Brookhaven State Park

FEBRUARY

Westbrook Pond

CONNETQUOT STATE PARK

February 2nd

Located in Islip, Connetquot State Park can be easily reached by most Long Islanders. Big enough to get lost in, the preserve is home to tremendous diversity. You can easily take a different hike and see something new with each visit. A sign near Bunce's Bridge is dedicated to a man who enjoyed every square inch of this preserve, hiking it daily until he passed away at the age of 94. The advantage to visiting a place like this throughout the year is that you can feel the seasons gradually fade in and out of each other.

For most of the 19th and the early part of the 20th centuries, it served as an exclusive rod and gun club. For that reason, the Connetquot River, and nearly 3500 acres surrounding it were spared from development, and left in an unpolluted, unspoiled state. I visit on Febuary 2, 2013, the halfway point between the winter solstice and the spring equinox. Currently known as Groundhog's Day, and traditionally known as Imbolc, or Saint Brighid's Day, some older Celtic traditions regard early February as the beginning of spring. It makes sense, if you think about it. In the next six weeks the trees will push out the first leaf buds, the forest floors will start to turn green, birds will return, and the first flowers of spring will blossom.

The modern view places the beginning of spring on the same day as the vernal equinox, when the daylight hours start to grow longer than the night hours. Some European traditions reconcile this conflict by leaving the determination of whether spring starts now, or six weeks from now up to the badgers. In North America, we trust the groundhogs to resolve this dispute. They never agree, and for some reason, even with the leaf buds and the returning green, February always seems to be the coldest and snowiest month, no matter what the groundhogs have to say about it. Even with snow and cold temperatures, life re-emerges. Today the air is in the twenties, and the skies are clear and dry. Most groundhogs see their shadows, and assure us of another six weeks of winter.

    Near the entrance to the preserve, an extensive grove of white pine grows along the river, most likely planted by the gun club. Five marked trails, including the Long Island Greenbelt, make their way through the preserve. Horseback riders share the trails, adding to the experience of hiking here. The longest, the blue trail, loops for 8.4 miles, and the shortest, the yellow trail, connects the entrance to the hatchery complex, about a mile away. At the hatchery complex it connects with the other trails. Combining it with the western half of the red trail gives you about another mile, and a nice view of the main pond and some of the swamps. The Green trail crosses the Connetquot River at Bunce's Bridge, allowing for a scenic view of the river at that crossing. Combining the green trail with either side of the blue trail allows a full view of what this preserve has to offer. Firebreaks with quaint names like Shanty Lane and Poachers Path intersect the trails. These can be traversed to make a particular hike shorter or longer. Another worthwhile excursion is to follow the Long Island Greenbelt Trail south, past the park entrance.

    Marked by white blazes, the Long Island Greenbelt Trail leads to Westbrook Pond, just west of the main entrance of the park, and goes underneath Sunrise Highway, along with the pond. Engineers squeezed Westbrook Pond under Sunrise Highway through a culvert. A metal catwalk allows hikers to walk through the culvert with the pond beneath them. A popular fishing spot, the pond remains fairly shallow, and in the spring and summer grows thick with duckweed and water lilies. In early February, the pond's turtles hibernate in the mud, but once the weather warms, you'll see painted turtles sunning themselves on the sides of the pond, and snapping turtles lurking at the bottom of the water. The trail, unfortunately, doesn't go completely around the pond. Westbrook Pond eventually flows into a stream which joins with the Connetquot River south of Montauk Highway. On the south side of Sunrise Highway, the Connetquot River widens, passing the Bayard-Cutting Arboretum, and flows out to the Great South Bay. Forcing the Connetquot and adjoining streams under Sunrise Highway at this point creates a low lying stretch of Sunrise Highway prone to flooding during heavy rainstorms. Patches of fog frequently appear when the air temperature is just right.

  North of Sunrise Highway, the preserve waits. The pond near the entrance to the park was man made, and used to power a grist mill. It's become a great spot for bird watching and fishing. On the west side of the pond, a bird blind allows for an easy view of the flocks of ducks and geese living on the pond year round. Today, I see small groups of Canadian geese and buffleheads on the pond. Buffleheads visit Long Island from further north. At the south end of the pond, I startle a great blue heron, which flies south towards the Great South Bay. The trail leads to the hatchery complex, about a mile north of the pond. New York State farms brook trout here, and uses them to stock ponds and streams throughout Long Island and New York. The Connetquot River runs clear and fast. Traveling the boardwalks around the hatchery, you can look in the quick moving water and watch the fish. Going north, the river gradually narrows until it reaches its source, Honeysuckle Pond in Lakeland Park, north of Veteran's Memorial Highway. A number of smaller streams cut through the preserve, feeding into the Connetquot River. The swampy areas can be thick with undergrowth. The red maples enjoy the constant supply of water. This contrasts with the pine and oak in the north and eastern sections of the preserve. Today, the slower moving water in the swampy areas stands frozen. A thin sheet of ice extends from the edges of the ponds. The normally soft sand on the paths is frozen hard.

Before reaching Bunce's Bridge, which crosses the river, the trails pass through a few open grass areas, where the resident herd of white tailed deer often congregates. No visit to Connetquot would be complete without spotting deer. It's not unusual to see thirty or more deer foraging together. Even on the east side of the river, deer can be seen in smaller groups. Besides the deer, a flock of feral turkey make their home here, as do fox and, of course groundhogs.

Directions:

The entrance is on the westbound side of Sunrise Highway between exits 46 and 47.

White Tailed Deer

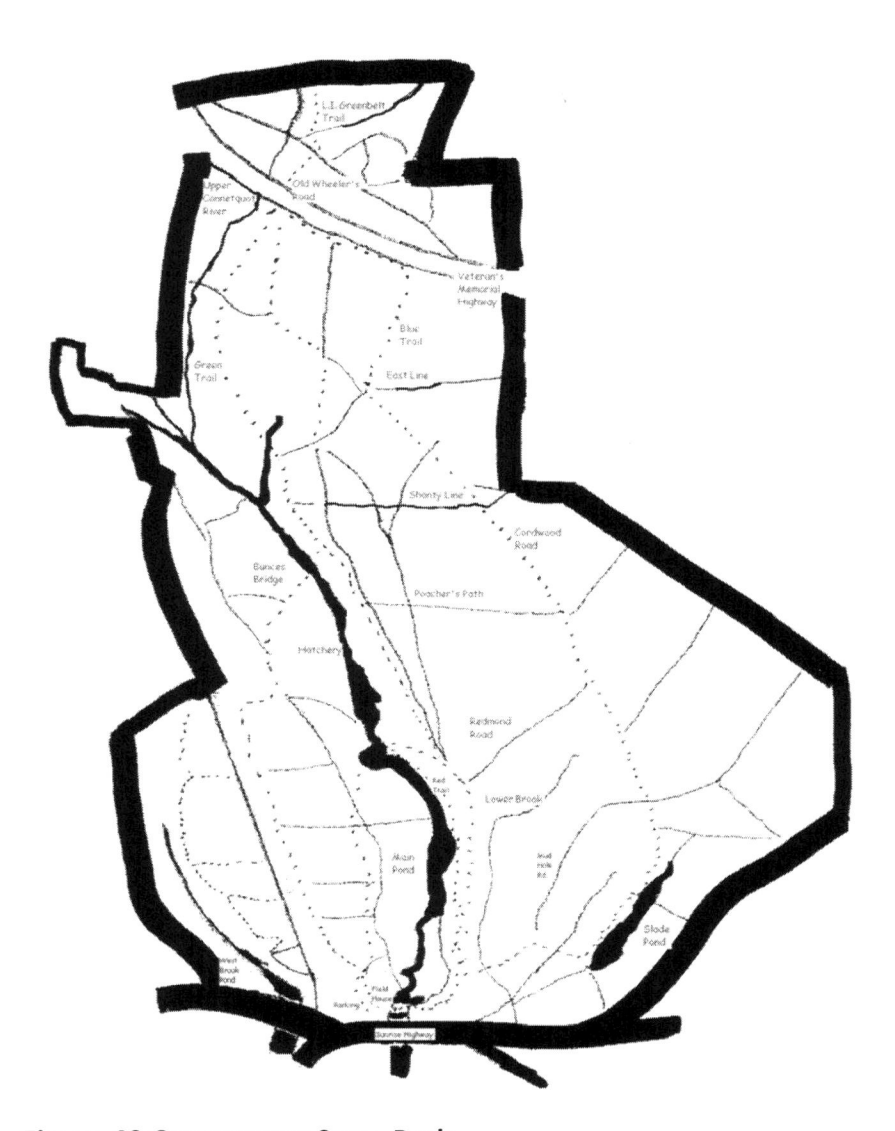

Figure 49 Connetquot State Park

TWIN LAKES PRESERVE

February 10th

      Yesterday Mother Nature left over a foot of snow on the ground. The temperature hangs in the twenties, and ice covers much of the surface of the lakes. Twin Lakes Preserve contains three lakes, but who's counting. Water flows a bit more freely toward the center of Seaman Pond, and the ducks make the most of it. The lakes fit neatly between Wantagh Parkway and Old Mill Road. Park Avenue separates the two main ponds, Seaman Pond and Wantagh Pond. The smallest pond, Forest Lake sits northwest of Seaman Pond, connecting to it with a small creek. Walking around the ponds in normal conditions takes less than an hour. With the snow it takes a bit longer. The white blazes of the Wantagh Nature Trail continue past the train tracks, south of Sunrise Highway to Mill Pond, another popular spot for duck watching. A robin hops in the underbrush, which will start pushing out leaves in a week or two. Around the edges of the pond the red maple, cherry and black tupelo all quietly wait for the air to warm up enough for them to start pushing out leaf buds, followed by flowers and fruit.

      A few smaller beech trees get a head start, pushing out the beginnings of leaf buds. The white oaks still hold onto their dead leaves from autumn. There leaves will fall once newer spring leaves push them out. A downy woodpecker clings to the side of a tree. In the grassier areas, the greens of the juniper stand out against the snow and dried grass. Being squeezed between the parkway and a residential area, the preserve isn't vast enough to get lost in or provide a serene escape, unless, of course, you happen to be a duck. In that case, you don't care about the messy neighbors or the noisy parkway, and find the lakes an excellent place to call home.

During the summer months duckweed and lilies cover the shallow, sandy ponds. Painted turtles also make a home for themselves, but for now, they sleep in the mud. Trout and sunfish can be caught here. Any time of year, ducks congregate here in the hundreds. Large flocks of ducks and geese can always be seen here, as can smaller numbers of both great white heron and great blue heron. The mallards and Canadian geese live here year round. The different flocks intermingle, as birds often do. Visiting us for the winter, northern shovelers swim alongside the mallards in pairs. They look similar, but the shovelers have a wide, flat bill.

Green winged, or common, teal, a year round resident also join the megaflock. The teal can be identified by a reddish brown head with a green patch around the eyes. Their females look similar to mallard females, with dull brown and white feathers. Dozens of American coots, also known as mud hens, swim with the ducks. Technically not ducks, coots lack webbing on their feet. The coots are colored black with stubby yellow bills and red eyes. It's difficult to tell whether the coots are returning early from down south, or have spent the whole winter here. Their winter range has gradually been extending further north over the past several years.

A small flock of hooded merganser, an attractive winter visitor, swims together on the stream connecting Forest Lake and Seaman's Pond. The merganser's large heads are black with a large white disk on either side. American black ducks walk slowly on the ice. Black ducks look similar to female mallards. Black ducks and mallards frequently interbreed. Ruddy ducks visit also. They appear mottled with bluish black bills and tails that stick straight out of the water.

Even with the thick snow on the ground, and ice covering most of the water, I can feel spring waking up.

Robins stand out against the snow. Migrations are underway. The shrubs have a slight green color to them, making them look more alive than a few weeks ago. Spring comes back from the ground up. In the marshy areas around the ponds, skunk cabbage, the first plants to flower, melt the snow around them with their warmth.

Directions:

From Sunrise Highway, head north on Old Mill Road. Make a right on Park Avenue, where you'll find a few marked spots along the side of the road near the preserve entrance.

Northern Shoveler

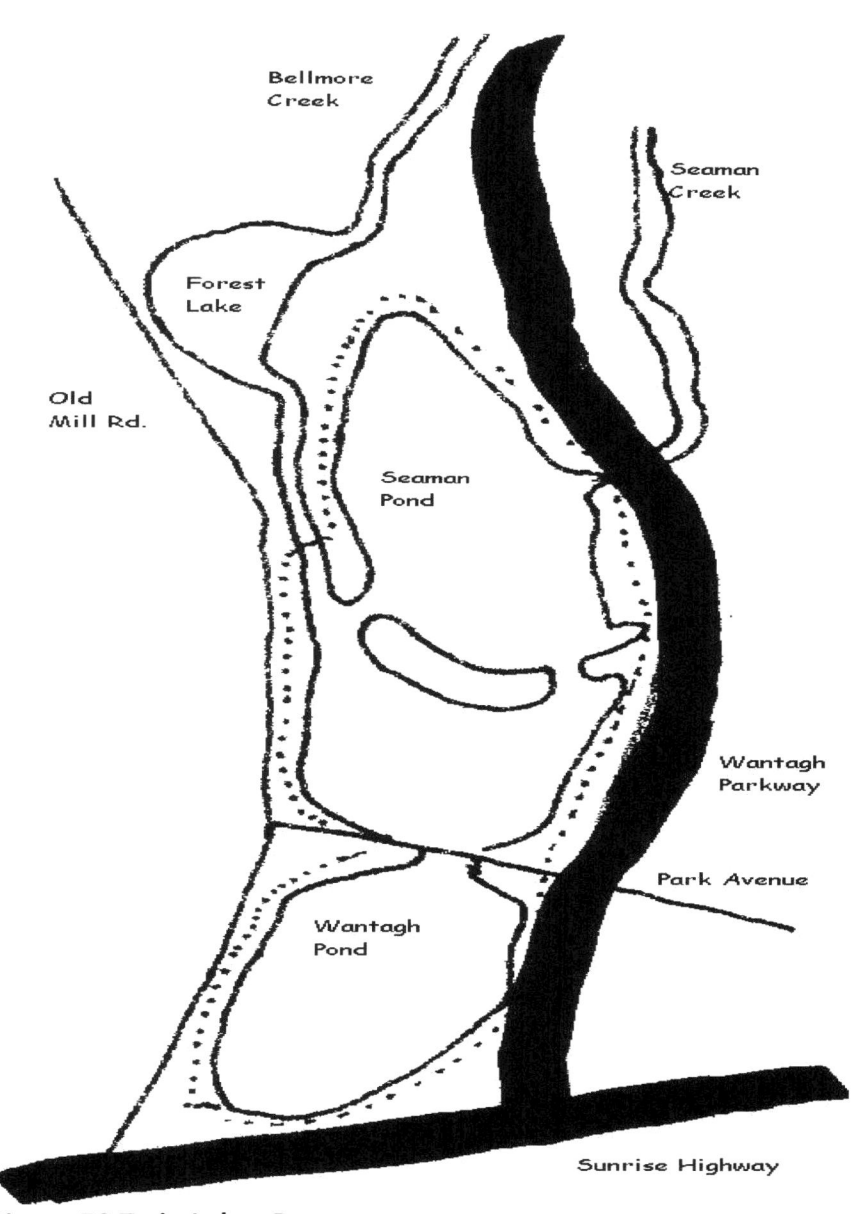

Figure 50 Twin Lakes Preserve

DAVID SARNOFF PRESERVE

February 18th

It's in the twenties, windy and sunny. Snow still covers the ground from the recent snow storm. The air warmed up a little during the week, but the temperature dropped again, leaving the snow with a heavy crust of ice on top. In areas, the crust is strong enough to support my weight, giving in only a little. In some areas, my boots crunch through the ice into snow five or six inches deep. The snow preserves tracks of deer, rabbits, raccoon and turkeys. In some areas, snow makes the heavily traveled deer trails visible. Deer follow their own trails, which can be harder to spot without snow on the ground. Nobody else walks on the paths, and there are no human tracks in the snow once I get a few hundred yards from the entrance. The advantage of hiking in winter, as compared to hiking in summer, is the lack of ticks. You don't have to deal with the heat slowing you down. The colder weather, however, can be much harder to dress for. I always wear layers, because as I move, my blood gets moving, and I warm up. The other very important thing to remember is to keep your feet dry. I carry an extra pair of boots and socks, because in the snow it will save me from having a miserable hike. The problem in winter is that you sweat, and don't realize it, until you stop for a rest. At which point, you will be cold and damp. This is the problem I'm having today. I'm dressed for very cold weather, but covering a lot of ground. The Red Loop on the west side of Route 104 covers six and a half miles, and the Blue Loop on the east side of Route 104 is nearly four miles in length. The preserve covers 2749 acres. Its trails connect with the Dwarf Pines Preserve and the Cranberry Bogs Preserve. At one point its previous owners used the preserve as an antenna field. With the technology obsolete, the property returned to the state's possession. You can still see the cement bases of the antennas along the trails in the preserve.

    Like the rest of the pine barrens, the forest is a pine-oak forest, with sandy soil and a very diverse population of oak. Keeping it open and undeveloped, helps replenish our aquifer. A few open savannah areas can also be found within the preserve. You will also find some kettle ponds and lower lying wetlands in the preserve. Wildwood Lake touches the western edge of the preserve, and the Cranberry Bogs Preserve is located across Route 63 on the northwest corner of the preserve. The Paumonock Path also cuts through the preserve. With that in mind, ambitious and energetic hikers can plan longer hikes incorporating adjacent sections of open public land. The State, County and Town properties are owned by all of us.

    The Blue Loop circles the eastern side of Route 104, and offers a little more diversity in a shorter hike. You have to follow the Yellow Trail from the parking lot on Route 104. The trail goes across Route 104, following along a firebreak, until it reaches the Blue Loop. Signs of an old fire can easily be seen on the tree trunks. East of Route 104, the trail gives a more open feel, allowing the contours of the land to be more visible than on the west side of the preserve. In the area where the yellow and blue trails meet, dead trees still stand, and their dead branches cover the forest floor. This is all fuel for the next forest fire to burn through here. Underneath the dead trees, smaller pine, standing between two and three feet high, start to grow.

    A few small shallow ponds are tucked away in the brush along the Blue Trail. These can be spotted by the suddenly thick undergrowth, and the lack of a tree canopy. Some of the ponds are nothing more than patches of mud and sphagnum moss, kept moist by the water pushing up from the ground. During warmer months, the thickets surrounding the pond come alive with the sounds various song birds, including pine warblers, blue warblers and various sparrows. Above the still ponds, a hawk circles in the sky, looking for a meal.

Directions:

From Sunrise Highway, take Exit 63 (CR-31).
Bear left on Route 104.
Parking is on the west side of the road.

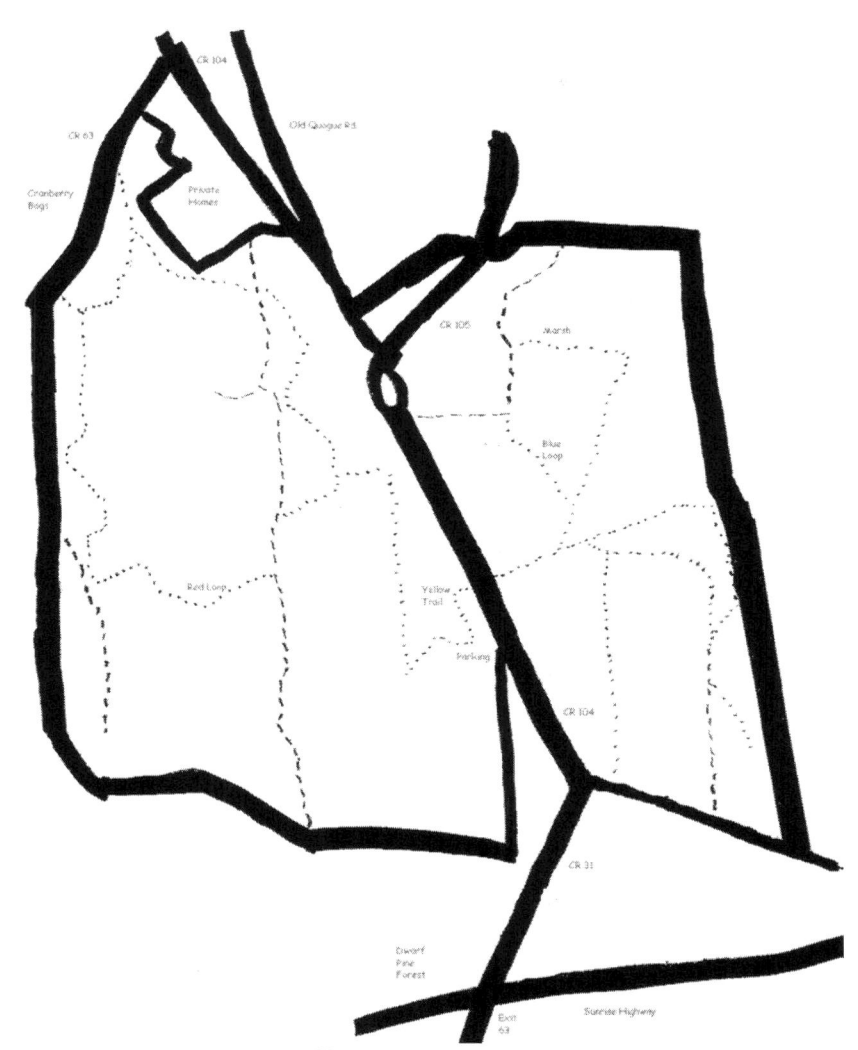

Figure 51 David Sarnoff Preserve

SEARS-BELLOWS PRESERVE

February 23rd

Covering 693 acres, Sears-Bellows lies immediately south of Hubbard Creek Preserve, and alongside other public park land. Visitors can combine different trails in adjacent preserves, and explore this nook of the South Fork. The Paumonock Path goes through it. More importantly the preserve welcomes campers and horseback riders. The Blue Trail connects with the Black Owl Trail, crossing over Red Creek Road and eventually leading to Flanders Bay. During the summer, ticks can be a problem, as they are anyplace else in Suffolk, but the quality and number of trails in the area make it worth a visit any time of year.

With spring starting to stir, the air warms to almost forty degrees. Rain fell this morning, melting much of the snow that accumulated several weeks ago. Clouds color the sky grey, dropping rain in short bursts. Adjacent to the parking lot sits Bellows Pond, the second largest of at least nine ponds in the preserve. A pair of deer tracks lead from the snow, onto the sandy beach, and right up to the edge of Bellows Pond. Ice still covers most of the pond, and slush covers the sides of the hills surrounding the pond. A sign at the water's edge prohibits swimming, because no lifeguard is on duty. I guess she called in sick today. I'm not planning on going in anyway. It's too cold.

Worn blue blazes mark the main loop going through the preserve. The main loop also intersects with the Yellow and Brown Owl Trails. Local hikers established these trails and continue maintaining them. Between Bellows Pond on the east side of the preserve and Sears Pond on the west side of the preserve hikers will find a number of small ponds connected by a series of streams.

The water allows denser growth, with thick areas of green in spring and summer. In season, these ponds attract a variety of dragonflies, and mosquitoes which, in turn, attract birds. A patient person can sit by the side of the pond and watch herons and hawks, as well as a variety of smaller song birds. The islands in the middle of some of ponds provide a protective area where birds can nest without being disturbed. Snow bunches around some of the trees on the water's edge. Small stands of Atlantic white cedar watch over the ponds, enjoying the stagnant water and acidic soil. Sphagnum moss covers the shallower edges of the ponds, gradually filling them in over the course of thousands of years. The ground is a little knobby, being on the eastern portion of the Ronkonkoma Moraine. The rises provide a fair amount of exercise, rewarding hikers with enjoyable views, especially in the winter. Oak and pitch pine make up most of the forest. A few patches of mountain laurel can also be found, their leaves green, but wilted. The heath push out the beginnings of leaf buds, adding a noticeable reddish hue, on what a few weeks ago was grey and brown. When green returns in the spring, it starts from the ground up, starting with the shrubs in the understory, and ending with the taller deciduous trees in the forest. The return of spring starts in February with smaller plants poking through the snow, and ends in May with rich shade trees like oak and maple fully leafed out.

    A sign on a wider portion of the trail points up a hill to Sears Pond, the largest pond in the preserve. A few duck blinds can be found on the edge of the pond, making perfect spots to stake out the pond with a camera. You can also enjoy the cedar towering on the edges of the pond. Ice covers two thirds of the pond. The northern corner of the pond, feeding Mill Creek still moves. Mill Creek ultimately flows through some marsh areas and into Flanders Bay. Puddles form on the ice from a combination of rain and melted water. A few ducks waddle across the ice, and a few more swim in the open areas of the pond. Slowly, I made my way back to the parking lot. At a relaxed pace, the walk lasted about an hour and a half. When I returned to the lot, the rain picked up again, bringing plenty of water in preparation for spring.

Directions:

From Sunrise Highway, take Exit 65North (Route 24).
Follow Route 24 (Flanders Road), until you reach Bellows-Pond Road.
Make a left on Bellows Pond Road.
The park entrance will be on the right side of the road.

An Ice Cold Drink?

Figure 52 Sears-Bellows Preserve and surrounding area

MARCH

A Mute Swan

HALLOCK STATE PARK

March 3rd

Hidden on the north shore of the north fork of Long Island, Hallock State Park consists of 230 undeveloped acres with nearly a mile of shoreline, two sizable ponds and hoodoos facing Long Island Sound. Hallock State Park, once called Camp Carey, served as a camp for teenagers, until a private corporation purchased it. Not being able to put it to use, it recently returned to the state. With no supervision or law enforcement, the bluffs continue to be torn apart by ATV riders entering the preserve illegally. Hiking trails remain unmarked, and there is no designated parking.

Last night we received a dusting of snow. Patches remain in the shady areas, and the cold air feels colder with wind coming off the sound. I reached the preserve by parking at Iron Pier Beach in Jamesport, and walking east along the beach. The Town of Riverhead manages Iron Pier Beach and charges a steep parking fee to non-residents during the summer. The low tide leaves rockweed and other sea plants washed up on the sand. A long, narrow tidal pool forms parallel to the beach, gradually being filled by each of the stronger waves washing in from the Sound. Strong winds make the surface of the sound unusually rough today. A red tailed hawk flies overhead, hunting alone on the beach.

After a short walk some trails lead off the beach, allowing you to explore the areas behind the bluffs and dunes. Prior to the erosion problems caused by ATV riders, the previous corporate owners mined sand here, removing all the vegetation and reducing sections of the bluffs to enormous sand hills. Some of the trails reach to the tops of the bluffs, providing views of the sound unlike any place else on the North Shore. On trails leading along the top of the bluffs you'll find deer tracks leading right to the edge, as if the deer wanted to relax for a moment and take in a sunset.

Behind the bluffs you'll find grasslands, and a successional forest composed of a mix of cherries, sumac, and sassafras. You'll also find several groves of white birch. The biggest trees you'll find are walnut and beech. Of course, oak and pine can be found throughout the preserve.

You'll also find a small forest of red cedar extending right up to the farms on the edge of the preserve. The cedars provide a refreshing amount of green this time of year. By early March, the colder dead winter weather has really worn out its welcome. Even with the shrubs starting to push out buds, the cold and the grey still seem to hang on. Much of the preserve was once farmed. The ponds, although fairly pristine and unpolluted, were once used for irrigation.

The larger of the two ponds, Hallock Pond covers four and a half acres on the west side of the preserve. Two rare plant species can be found in this pond; saltmarsh loosestrife, a small plant that sends out white flowers towards the end of the summer, and Farwell's water-milfoil, a submerged plant. New York State classifies both plants as endangered. During heavy rains, Hallock Pond frequently overruns its southern bank. Lily Pond is the smaller of the two ponds. Covering an acre, and grown in with shrubs and grass, it's more of a swamp than a pond. On the eastern edge of the preserve Howell's Spring flows for a short distance, not quite reaching the sound.

In areas where ATVs haven't destroyed the bluffs, you can see layers of different types of clay, and the slower action of natural erosion. The combination of clay, sand and natural erosion allowed hoodoos to develop in the preserve. Hoodoos are pillars of clay and sand. They form when the clay and sand combination are shaped by wind and water, forming layered formations, similar to what you would see looking at pictures of the badlands out west. These types of formations are extremely rare on the east coast. You'll also find hoodoos in Shadmoor Preserve on the South Fork. In addition to being rare, they are also extremely delicate. Most of the hoodoo formations that once stood along this beach eroded away. A few hundred yards from the water, you'll find a formation, about twelve feet high and twenty feet long, between a grassy area and a sand dune. The tracks from the ATVs go right up to the edge of it. Unfortunately, nobody stops them, and the riders don't care. Bureaucratic delays have, thus far, prevented the New York State from developing this as a preserve. All the state needs to do is maintain a small staff to monitor the area, and put in a few boardwalks to prevent further erosion of the bluffs. This preserve, and its hoodoos, can be enjoyed by everyone for years to come.

Hoodoos

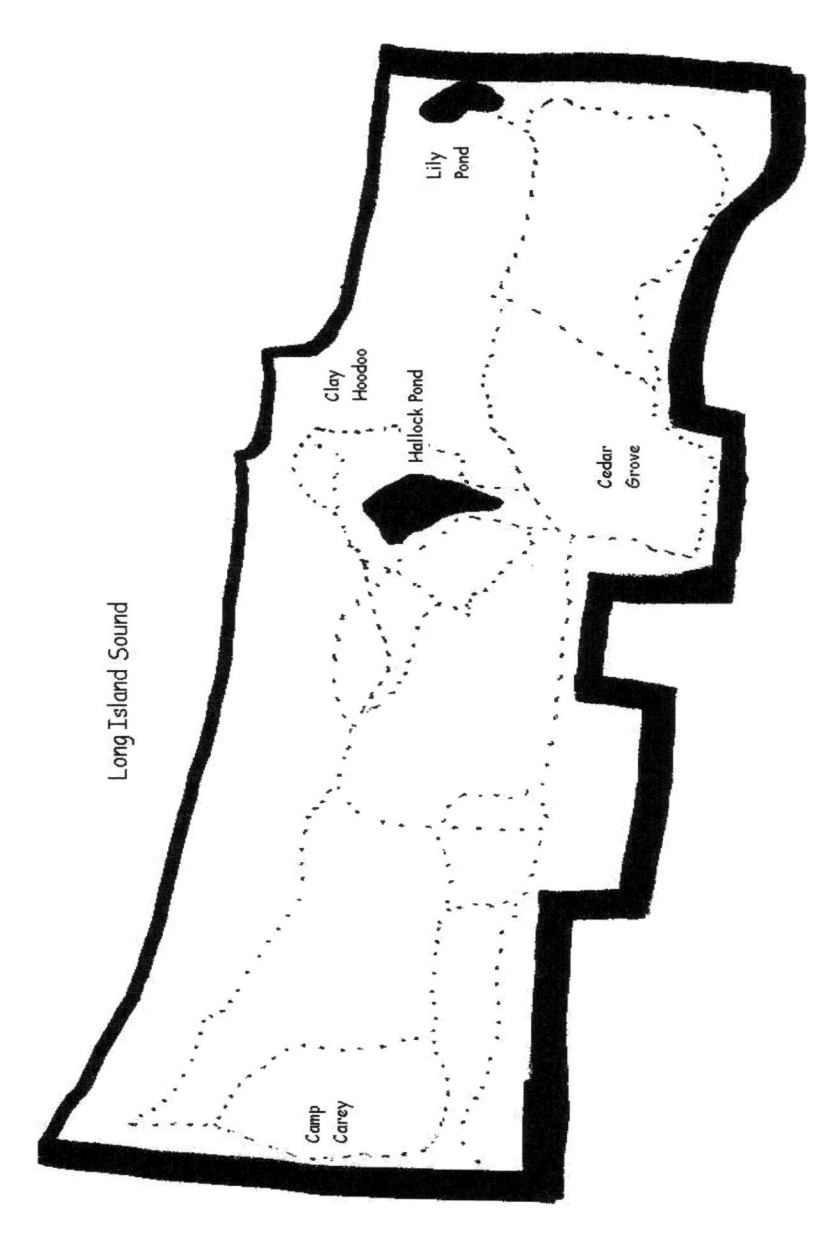

Figure 53 Hallock State Park

MONTAUK POINT STATE PARK AND CAMP HERO STATE PARK

March 10th

The End? ...or The Beginning? Journeying this far east makes Montauk a transformative experience. The park provides a wonderful destination to fish, meditate, or both. Words don't give it justice, and even the historic lighthouse seems small and insignificant when compared to the Atlantic bringing waves from far beyond, continually breaking them on its beaches. The air starts to warm, and it feels like a spring day. Starting with frost in the morning, it reaches the lower fifties by the afternoon. The sun stays out, and the waves stay gentle. The Paumonock path, like everything else, ends here. Theodore Roosevelt County Park lies immediately to the west, allowing longer hikes, if you are so inclined. Further west -- and unless you have a sturdy boat, you can only go west -- lies Hither Hills and Shadmoor State Park, both offering excellent hiking. Hither Hills is known for its walking dunes, and Shadmoor for its steeply carved bluffs. The South Fork arguably offers the best hiking trails on the Island.

    Going around Montauk Point is the best place to start. Starting from the parking lot near the lighthouse, you can walk around the point, through Camp Hero, cross back over Sunrise Highway, trace the edge of Oyster Pond and follow along the beach back to where the Peconic Bay ends and the Atlantic Ocean begins.

    Next to the gift shop near the parking lot, you'll find a stairway leading past a small pond to the rocky beach. You can follow this path around, until it reaches a large stone wall built to protect the lighthouse from eroding into the ocean. The path leads along the top of the wall. Walking along the wall, you can enjoy the spray from the waves reflecting back out to sea. Europe rises out of the Atlantic Ocean three and a half thousand miles away. On the other side of the seawall, you'll reach Camp Hero and its bluffs.

The bluffs are in amazing shape. Walking along the beach and looking up you can see layers in the clay. Looking down, the beach displays a mix of rocks. The sand has patches of red garnet blended in with the more common quartz sand. Winds continually blow ripples into the sand. As wind and sea erosion slowly pull down the bluffs, you can look for indentations where larger rocks once rested in the clay and, like a three dimensional puzzle, try to match the indentations with the rocks lying on the ground beneath them. Some larger boulders embedded in the bluffs hang precariously, waiting for their moment to fall. As I walk around, I spot a rock, about the size of a basketball and its matching home in the clay. Still moist from the clay, the elements haven't even cleaned the dirt off of it. It waited, embedded in the bluffs for millennia, until it fell to the beach that morning.

This time of year, the beach remains fairly empty. At Turtle Cove, the bluffs drop down and a fresh water stream lined with grass trickles onto the beach, cutting a delicate path in the sand leading to the ocean waves. Near the fishing access spots in Camp Hero, I'm able to leave the beach and explore the upland areas. On top of the bluffs you'll find a mixture of grass and shrubs. Holly and highbush blueberry, both well adapted to maritime environments, cover the highlands. Because the vegetation grows so low, you can easily see long distances, particularly as the elevation slowly creeps up. Further away from the ocean, the forest grows taller and thicker. Beech and maple become more common in the wetter areas. With spring arriving, the lower lying, moister areas away from the beach push out ferns. A few deer forage for whatever they can find after a long winter. Skunk cabbage, my favorite reminder of spring's arrival, starts to blossom in the mud. Beneath some of the rocks you'll find blue spotted salamanders.

As you walk through Camp Hero, cemented over gun emplacements and a large obsolete radio antenna remind you that it once functioned as a military base. The antenna can be seen throughout the park, and serves as a landmark for boats sailing around the point. The military installed the gun batteries during the Second World War, to protect the shipping lanes from u-boat attacks. When building them, the bunkers were buried under mounds of dirt, forming small hills, which, years later, look like they are part of the natural environment. Some areas of the preserve remain under military control and off limits. You'll also find other structures left by the military, and signs warning hikers to watch out for unexploded munitions. If you find any suspicious items, don't touch them, contact the State Park Police, and let them handle it.

This far east, Sunrise Highway consists of one quiet lane in each direction. Crossing over Sunrise, you'll find four color coded paths. Ogden Brook Trail, marked in blue, and Oyster Pond Trail, marked in red, both go west. Seal Haul Out Trail, marked in yellow, and Money Pond Trail, appropriately marked in green, head east. The east bound trails provide shorter hikes, eventually joining each other. The blue and red trails take you along Oyster Pond, and through some very wet area, until you ultimately arrive at the north side of the South Fork.

On the far side of Oyster Pond, a flock of at least one hundred seagulls dot the sand. On the interior part of the peninsula, woodcocks nest. Deer are everywhere. The ticks, fortunately, still hibernate, but will become more and more of a problem through the summer. Cherry and sumac trees become more common north of Sunrise Highway. Even when you can't see the Atlantic Ocean, you can hear it and smell it. The trails ultimately lead to the seal haul out area, a rocky section along Peconic Bay where the park provides guided seal watching tours during the winter months. Although it's still seal season, it appears that the large group of park visitors scared them off. Instead of seals, a few eiders swim on top of the water. Like the seals, these ducks also visit the bay during the winter. Their down is particularly soft, historically being used for pillows and comforters.

      Walking further east along Peconic Bay, I can look out and see Gardiner's Island, Shelter Island, The North Fork, Plum Island, and beyond that, Connecticut. Returning to the lighthouse, I pass a few small ponds along the beach. As I get closer, the beach becomes more crowded, and I watch the waves gradually strengthen as the Peconic Bay joins the Atlantic Ocean.

Directions:

Proceed east on Sunrise Highway until it ends at the park entrance.

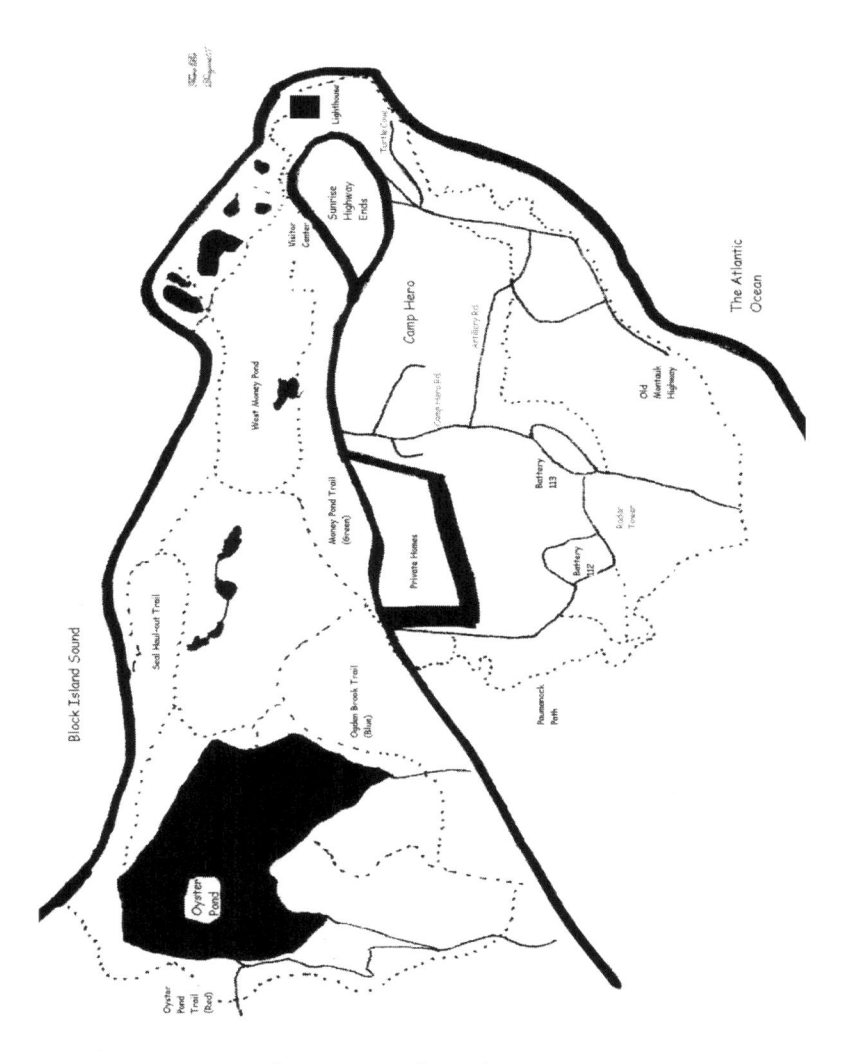

Figure 54 Montauk State Park and Camp Hero

WELLWYN PRESERVE

March 17th

March 17th, and I can't decide whether I want to find a pot of gold or a rainbow. Of the three preserves on Nassau's north shore, Wellwyn Preserve offers the most habitat diversity. Like nearby Garvies Point, it doesn't charge an entrance fee. A dusting of snow from the night before covers the trees. The snow on the ground melted, leaving the trails wet and muddy. I expect this dusting to be the last snow until fall and winter come around again. The oil magnates who previously owned the property landscaped portions of it. Nassau County's Holocaust center shares the property, occupying the mansion adjacent to the walled garden.

The preserve area can be found north and east of the mansion. It surrounds a small stream that gradually makes its way into the sound. Four marked trails can be combined to explore the whole two hundred acre preserve in about an hour and a half. Although Nassau County maintains the grounds closest to the Holocaust Center, it leaves the rest under the care and direction of Mother Nature. Trees and vines slowly pull down the few old buildings remaining on the grounds. Thankfully, the previous owners allowed sections of the estate to remain wild. Old growth tulip trees, mixed in with white pine, and oak remain untouched. Like nearly all of the other preserves on the Island, Sandy left behind a mess of fallen trees and broken branches. In time these will all return to the earth, nourishing new growth in the process.

The stream and its tributaries, fast moving in some places, sit at the bottom of a fairly big ravine, with trails leading around the edge. Mountain laurel grows on the edges of the ravine, staying green all year round. Closer to the streams, plants grow thicker. The years of water erosion left a number of glacial erratics on the property. In a few areas, the boulders rest in the sand, forcing the streams to flow around them. The trails lead to a small manmade pond, called Turtle Pond. Today water on Turtle Pond sits completely still. A thin film of algae covers the surface. Water flows under the path through a culvert flowing into a widening salt marsh. The path traces the edge of the salt marsh, until you reach the beach. The tide is out. The mud flats, and a few small and persistent streams, remain iced over around the edges. A few horseshoe crab shells can be found in the patches of flattened and dead cord grass. In a few weeks, the grass will start to re-grow, turning green. The osprey will return, and use the saltmarsh and sound as a hunting ground. Right now, the marsh is dormant, except for a flock of Canadian geese that live here year round.

  You can follow a stream connecting the saltmarsh to the sound. On the more natural parts of the beach, closer to the marsh, you'll find rocks covered with bright green algae below the high tide mark, east of a jetty. To the west of the jetty the previous owner removed the rocks and trucked sand in to make the beach more comfortable. On a good day, looking through the rocky area, you can find fiddler crabs, mussels, and a variety of other types of sea life. As I followed the trail back from the beach, through the wooded area, I saw snow drops blooming along the path. Imported from Europe, snowdrops have drooping white flowers, which are among the first to bloom in the spring. In a few weeks, their flowers will have withered, but the rest of spring's procession of flowers will continue to bloom.

Directions:

From the Northern State Parkway, take Exit 35N (Route 107).
Head North on Route 107 until it ends.
Signs will lead you through the residential neighborhood.
Make a right on Bridge Street, which changes to School Street.
Make a left on Cottage Row, which changes to Roosevelt Street.
Follow Roosevelt Street until you reach Crescent Beach Road, where you will make a right.
The preserve is on the right side of Crescent Beach Road.

Snow Drops

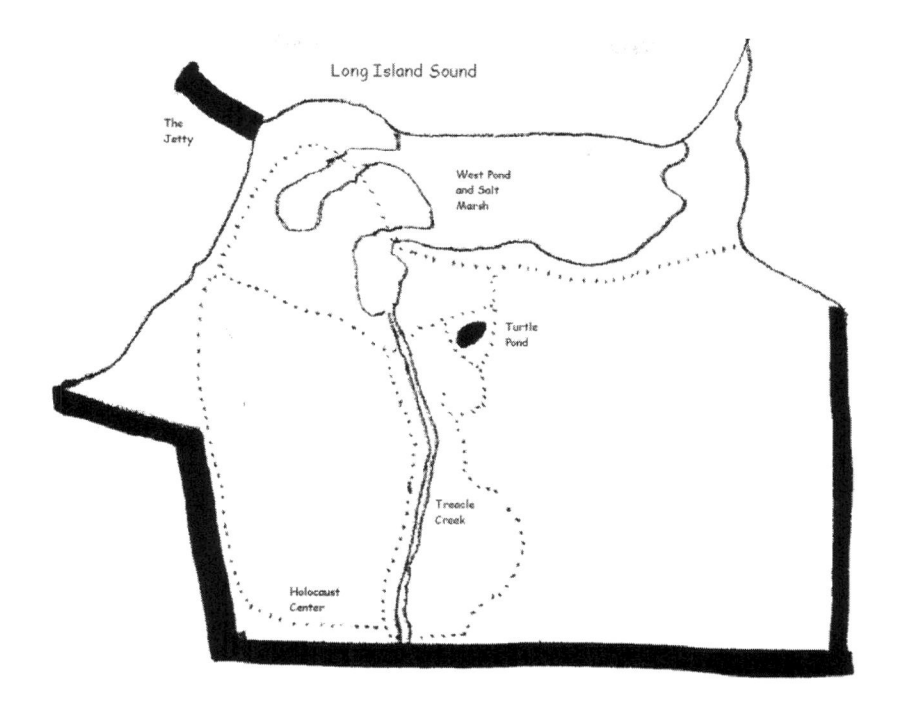

Figure 55 Wellwyn Preserve

WEST MEADOW BEACH

March 20th

    Snow fell two days ago, rain fell yesterday, and the temperature stays in the twenties. Ice holds the sand at West Meadow Beach together. It feels more like the last day of winter than the first day of spring. Strong winds push waves into whitecaps, crashing them onto the beach. A dynamic habitat throughout the year, wind and waves reshape West Meadow Beach moment by moment. Like the much bigger barrier beaches on the south shore, the shapes, size and location of the beach and accompanying sand bars change constantly. The beach consists of a 7000 foot spit of sand slowly being pushed southward from Crane Neck Point. On the east side of the beach flows West Meadow Creek, a tidal creek fed partially by a spring, and partially by the tides, similar to the Hudson River, but on a much smaller scale. The Harbor Hill moraine rises above the east side of the creek. On the west side of the beach, Smithtown Bay flows into Stony Brook Harbor via Porpoise Channel. The path to the end of the beach is easy enough to follow. You follow Trustees Road all the way to the green cottage at the end, and then follow the shoreline back up to the parking lot.

    Nature slowly reclaims the beach, creek and meadow from human influence. Developers dredged the southern edge of the beach at one point. Until a few short years ago, cottages lined the beach on the west side of Trustees Road. The state tore town all but two of the cottages. The Town of Brookhaven manages the beach now, using one of the old cottages as a ranger station. The other cottage, Listed on the National Register of Historic Places, occupies Shipman's Point at the very southern tip of the beach. A visit to West Meadow Beach makes it obvious why its former residents fought such a protracted legal battle to remain on the beach. The beach and meadow offer a serenely beautiful place, which can now be enjoyed by everyone.

Much of the creek falls under the protection of the Ward-Melville Heritage Organization, which maintains the Ernst Marine Conservation Center at the north end of West Meadow Creek. The privately operated conservation center runs a number of different educational programs and monitors wildlife in the preserve.

Year round, the creek provides a great spot for bird watching, offering every type of bird common on Long Island within a short walk. Herons, egrets, various ducks and geese all live here. Today, I spot a small flock of brants preparing for their spring migration to back to the artic. Ducks similar in coloration to Canadian Geese, brants feed primarily on eel grass and sea lettuce, both common along the beaches and in the saltier areas of West Meadow Creek. Black ducks, another winter visitor also swim in the calmer water in the creek. A flock of brewer's blackbirds congregate in the branches of a leafless tree along Trustees Road. Brewer's blackbirds look like small crows with yellow eyes. They use West Meadow Beach as a rest stop on their northward migration. Soon plover and osprey will return to the beach and nest. Seagulls and mallards stay throughout the whole year.

Cord grass surrounds the creek. The roots hold the sand and sediments together, making a home for a variety of clams and mussels, and providing battle ground for fiddler crabs. The creek also serves as a breeding ground for horseshoe crabs and diamond back terrapins, which lay their eggs in June and July. A few raised sandy areas in the meadow allow cedar and other shrubs to grow. The lower lying areas flood. In the sand along the sides of Trustees Road, salt resistant trees and shrubs, such as groundsel and beach plum, grow. This early in the season, beach plums push out buds. By the end of May, they will put out flowers, and by the end of August, edible fruit. Yucca and prickly pear cactus also grow out of the sand. With winter ending, the cactus look exhausted, shriveled up and slightly reddish. Like the beach plum, the cactus will also bloom providing edible fruit.

    On edge of the beach, the current and winds push harder than normal today. Long Beach Point and Young's Island rise out of Smithtown Bay on the south end of the beach. Less than a hundred yards from the beach, I spot a fox hole in the dune. The elusive red fox are common, but rarely seen. They hunt and forage at dusk and at dawn, avoiding daylight. They eat just about anything from mice, to gulls, to berries. Interestingly, cultures around the world incorporate the fox in their mythologies, and portray them as being tricksters and shape changers. Real life foxes are quite adaptable to different environments. They survive as well on the beaches, as they do in the woods.

    Walking further up the beach, grass grows where the cottages once stood, providing a nesting area for the plover and sandpipers. It's strange that the state went through the expense of removing the cottages, but didn't remove the non-native landscaping that surrounded them. The shrubs look over grown and out of place, providing the only obvious indication that a few short years ago a small community built their homes on the beach. Like the shifting sand patterns, the speed in which nature reclaims abandoned property works as a reminder of nature's strength. Its resiliency reminds us of our limited role in nature. Even when we leave, nature persists as she always has; pushing forward one wave, one gust of wind, and one sand grain at a time.

Directions:

From the Long Island Expressway, take Exit 62 (Nicholls Road).
Proceed North on Nicholls Road, until it ends at Route 25A.
Make a left at Route 25A.
Make a right at Quaker Path.
Bear left at Mt. Grey Road.
Turn left on West Meadow Road.
Turn Left on Trustees Road.
A parking lot is on the right side of Trustees Road.

West Meadow Creek

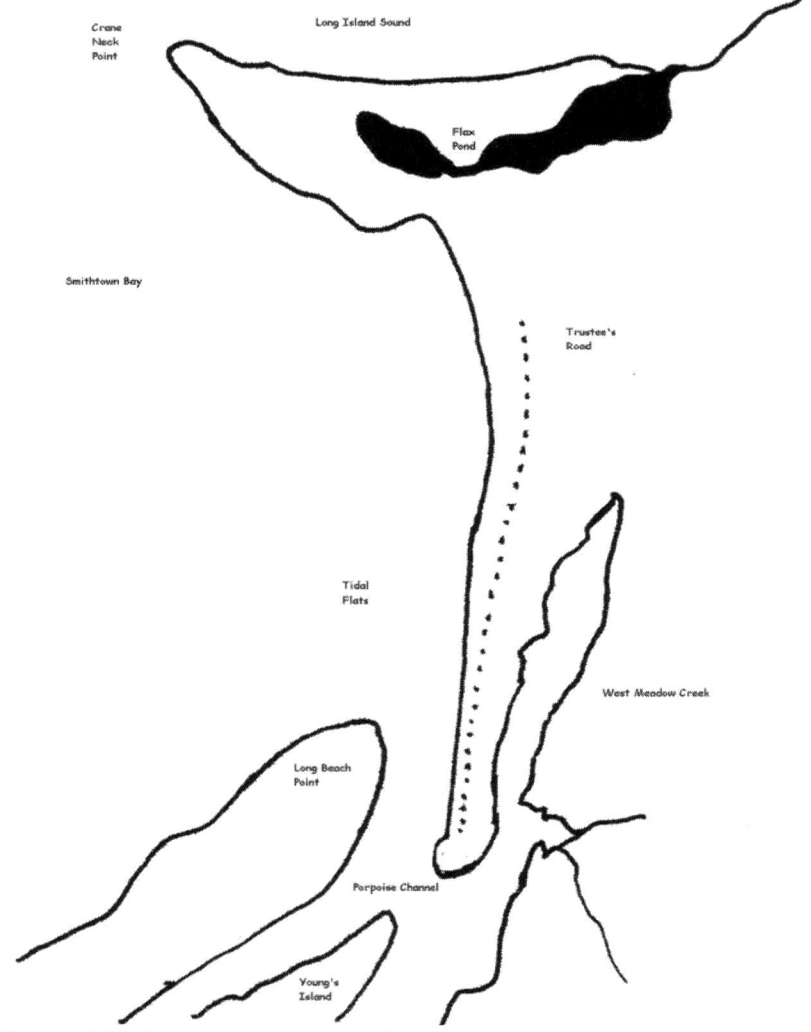

Figure 56 West Meadow Beach

LEAF GALLERY

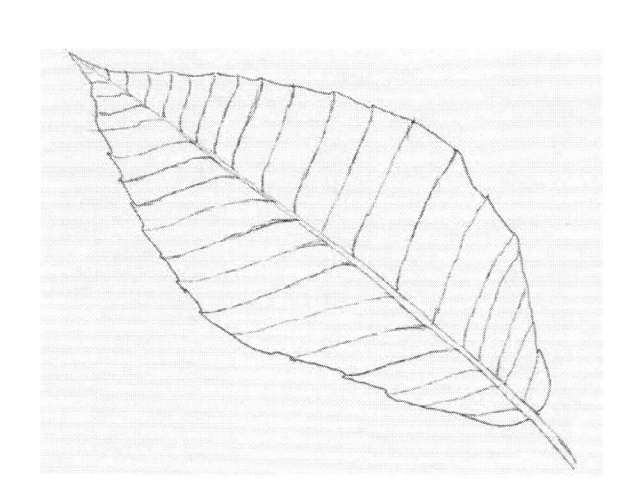

BEECH

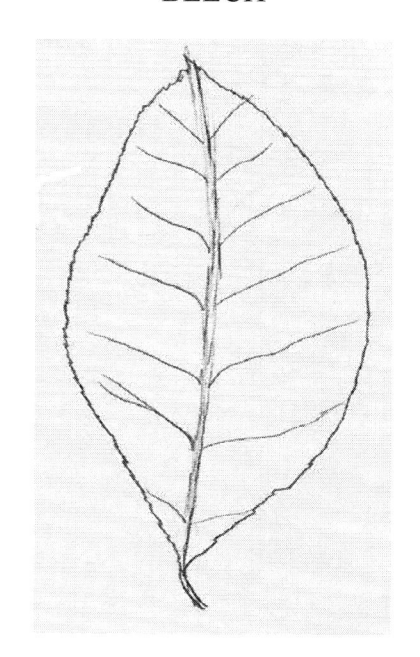

BLACK CHERRY

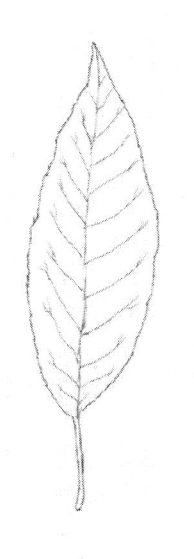

PIN CHERRY

BLACK OAK

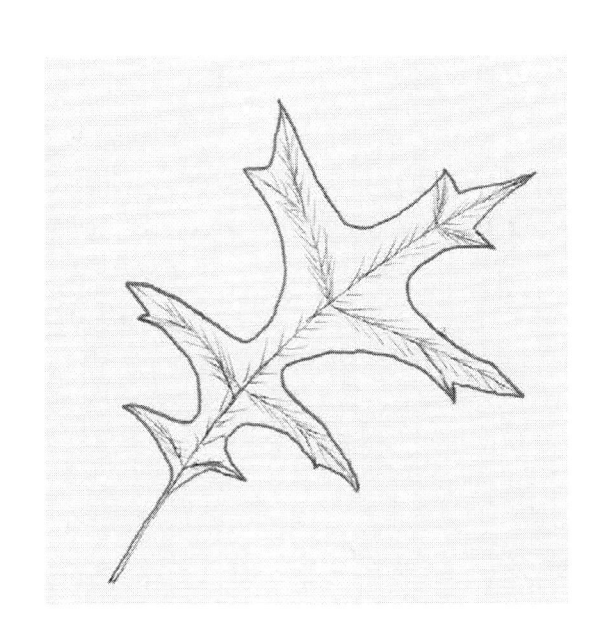

PIN OAK

SCARLET OAK

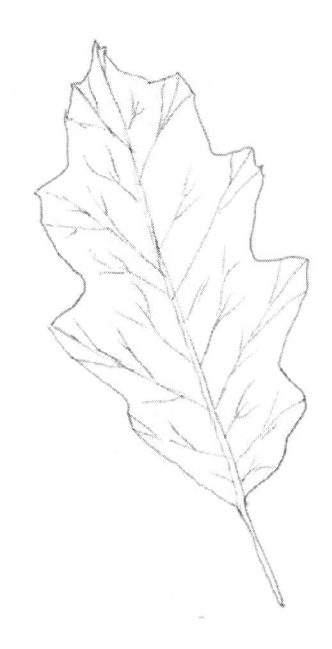

RED OAK (Rounded Lobes)

RED OAK (Pointed Lobes)

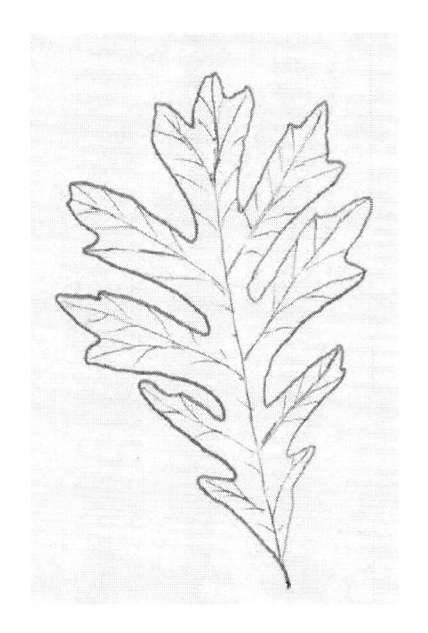

WHITE OAK

SWAMP WHITE OAK

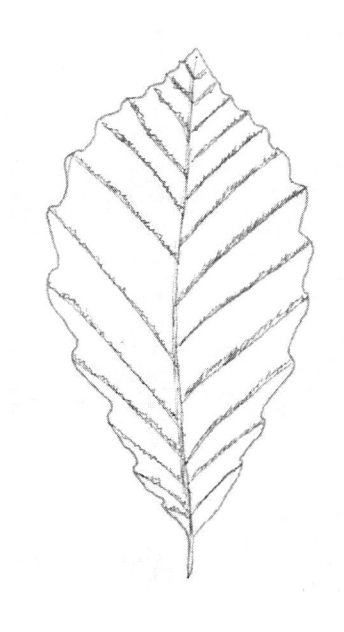

Chestnut Oak

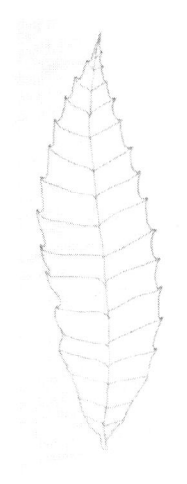

AMERICAN CHESTNUT

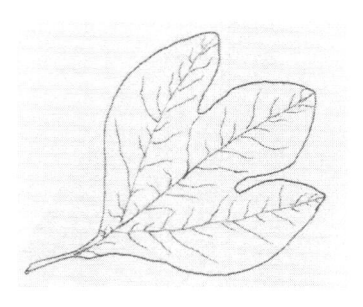

Sassafras (Glove Leaf)

SASSAFRAS (Mitten Leaf)

SASSAFRAS (Sock Leaf)

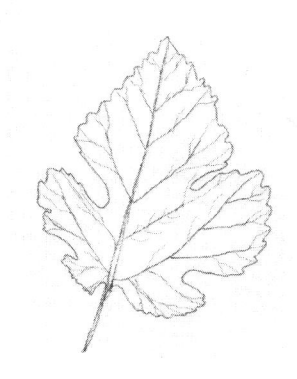

WHITE MULBERRY (Glove Leaf)

WHITE MULBERRY (Mitten Leaf)

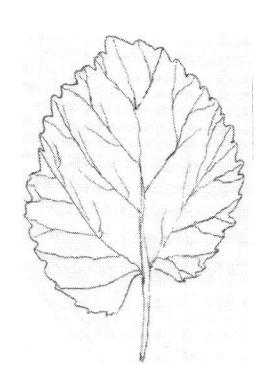

WHITE MULBERRY (Sock Leaf)

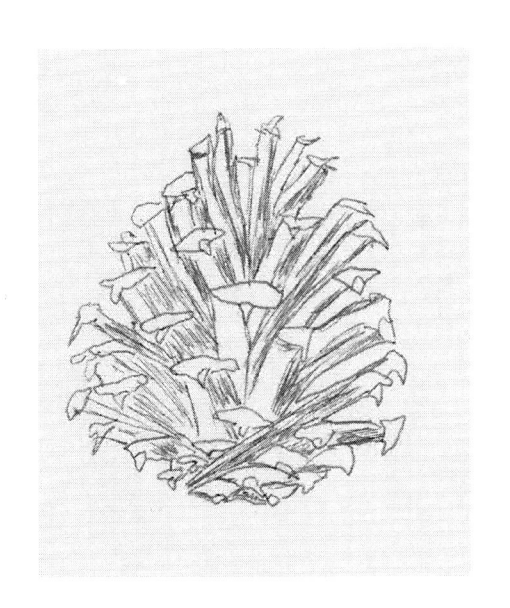

PITCH PINE CONE

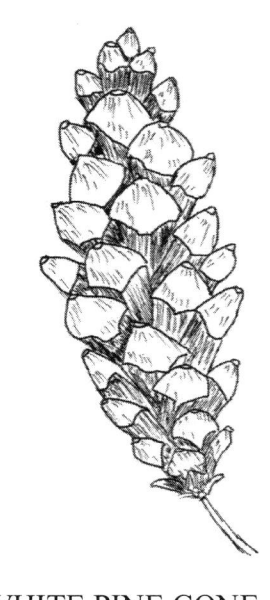

WHITE PINE CONE

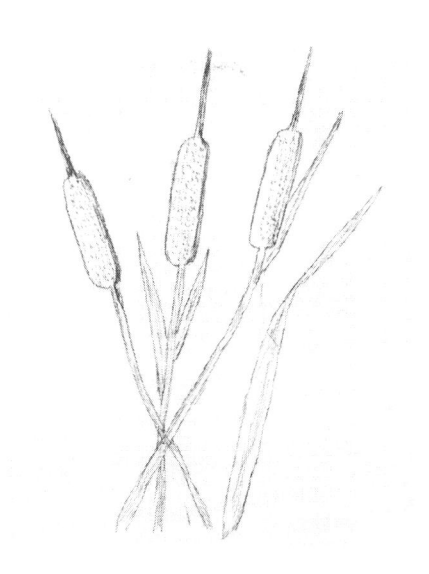

CAT TAILS

PHRAGMITE

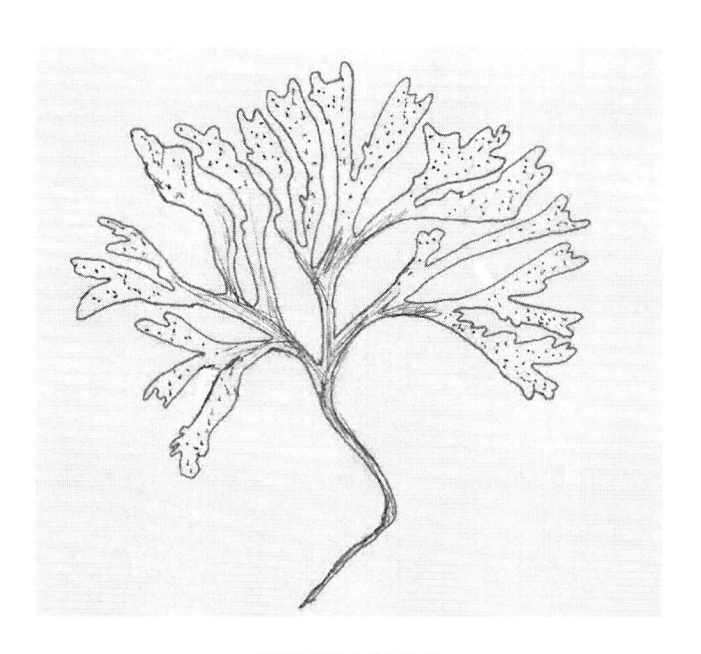

IRISH MOSS

GINKGO

HAWTHORNE

GRAY BIRCH

HICKORY

HOLLY

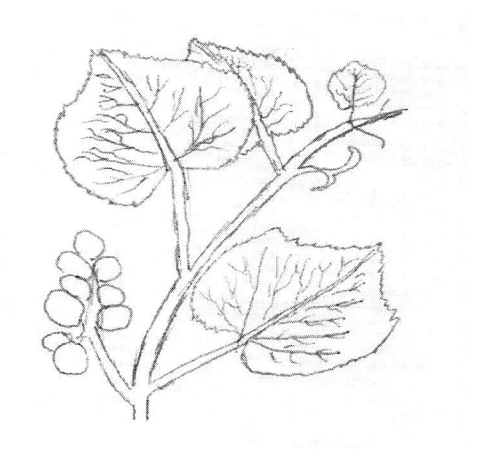

WILD GRAPE

WILD RASPBERRY

CATBRIER

POISON IVY

VIRGINIA CREEPER

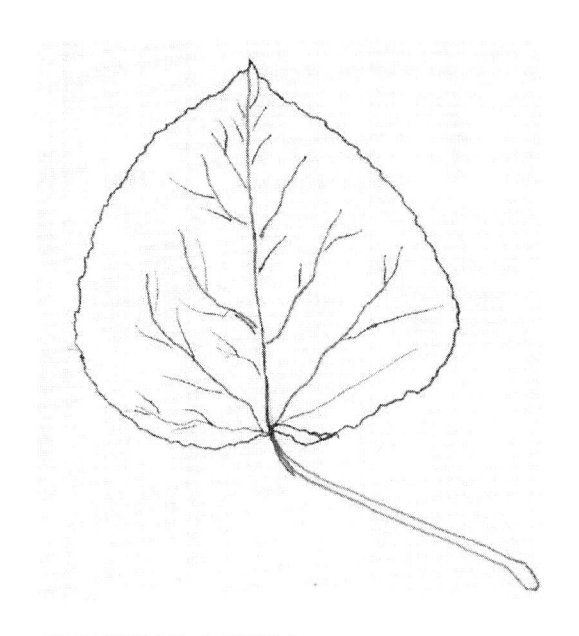

QUAKING ASPEN

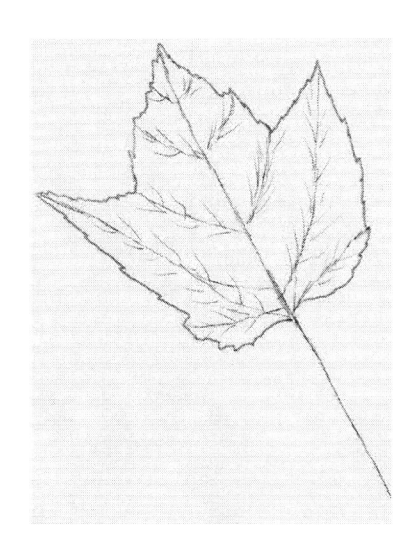

RED MAPLE

SUGAR MAPLE

SWEETGUM

SYCAMORE

TULIP TREE

HAPPY TRAILS

GROUND HOG

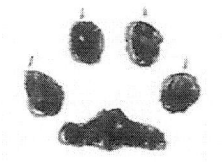

FOX

DOG

CAT

RIVER OTTER

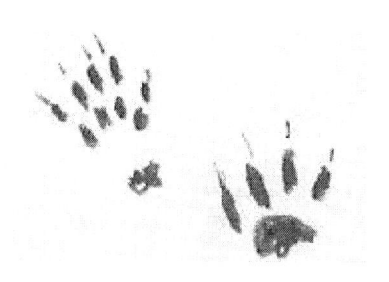

SQUIRREL

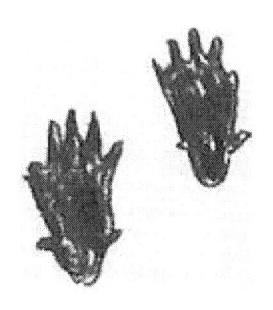

MUSKRAT

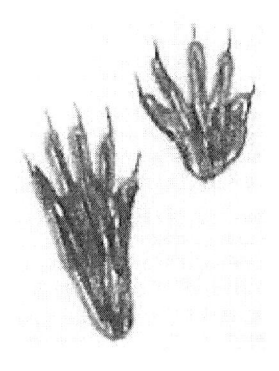

RACCOON

OPOSSUM

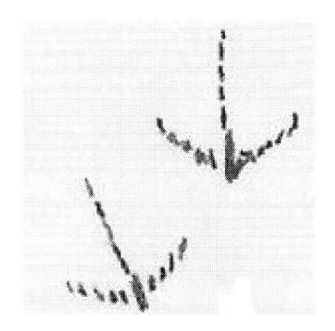

WILD TURKEY

The Great Spirit

The Great Spirit is in all things, He is in the air we breathe. The Great Spirit is our Father, but the Earth is our Mother. She nourishes us, that which we put into the ground, She returns to us.
-- Big Thunder

Index

Alewife Pond, 90
American Black Duck, 222, 241
American Coot, 241
American Chestnut, 88, 144, 153, 212, Leaf Illustration 277, Picture of Nuts 195
Amur Honeysuckle, 113, Picture 114
Apple Gall, 58
Arrowwood, 165, 183
Asiatic Day Flower, 141, 145
Aster 100, 106
Atlantic White Cedar, 18, 41, 63, 249, Picture 43
Aurora Pond, 164
Bank Swallow, 47
Bat, 84, 183
Bayberry, 37, 62, 89, 100, 149
Bay Scallop, 62, 172
Beach Heather, 62, 118, 123, 209
Beach Pea, 63, Picture 64
Beach Plum, 89, 268
Bearberry, 209
Beaver, 85, 90
Beaver Pond, 11
Bee Balm, 116
Beech, 68, 127, 144, 145, 174, 187, 195, 240, Leaf Illustration 272
Belted King Fisher, 161
Big Leaf Oak, 112
Black and White Warbler, 146
Black Cherry, 57, Leaf Illustration 272
Black-Eyed Susan, 107
Black Jack Oak, 62
Black Locust, 139
Black Oak, 112, 188, Leaf Illustration 273
Black Owl Trail, 248

Black Scoter, 218
Black Throated Warbler, 191
Black Tupelo, 58, 124, 154, 240
Bladderwort, 168
Blue Jay, 25, 201, Picture 202
Blue Spotted Salamander, 259
Boundary Tree, 187
Box Turtle, 57
Brant, 267
Brewer's Blackbird, 267
Buck Moth, 210
Bufflehead, 193, 237
Bullfrog, 81, 90, 217, Picture 23
Butterfly Weed (Orange Milkweed), 107
Canadian Goose, 38, 84, 154, 180, 263
Canadian Mayflower (False Lily of the Valley), 51, 52
Carman River, 56, 188
Caroon's Lake (Massapequa Lake), 78
Catbird, 74, 124
Catbrier, 14, 103, 124, Illustration 286
Cat Tails, 124, Illustration 281
Cherry, 68, 73, 112, 165
Chestnut Oak, 88, 112, Leaf Illustration 277
Chicory, 116, 141, 158, Picture 110
Chigger, 134
Chipmunk, 68, 85, Picture 71
Clapper Rail, 95
Clay Deposits, 216
Coastal Plains Ponds, 168, 231
Connetquot River, 24, 193, 235
Cord Grass, 47, 96, 100, 124
Cow Lily (Spatterdock), 79
Crane Neck Point, 266
Crow, 128, 174
Daffodil, Picture 27
Diamond Back Terrapin, 37, 38, 62, 222, 267, Picture 66

Dogwood, 154, 212, 230
Double Crested Cormorant, 61, 95, 100, 119, 140, 127, 154, 180
Downy Woodpecker, 158, 217, 240
Duckweed, 52, 73
Dwarf Pine, 208, 227
Earnst Marine Conservation Center, 267
Eider, 260
Elderberry, 141
False Lily of the Valley (Canadian Mayflower), 51, 52
Farwell's Water-milfoil, 254
Feral Westie, 183
Fiddler Crab, 95, 100, 101, 141, 160, Picture 104
Fire Island, 122, 148, 192, 204, 226
Flander's Bay, 158
Forest Lake, 240
Fowler's Toad, 134
Foxglove, 107
Gabler's Creek, 164
Gardiner's Bay, 61
Gardiner's Island, 62, 88, 260
Gerretsen Creek, 138
Ghost Forest, 158
Ghosts in the Graveyard, 32, 38
Giambrino Pond, 13
Ginkgo, Illustration 282
Glossy Ibis, 94
Goldenrod, 118
Great Blue Heron, 118, 237, 240
Great White Heron, 58, 94, 118, 140, 165, 240, Cover Photograph
Green Frog, 52, 174
Green Winged Teal, 241
Grey Birch, 223, Leaf Illustration 283
Grey Seal, 226
Grey Squirrel, 85, 128

Groundhog, 200, 201, 235
Groundsel, 149, 159, 191
Gypsy Moth, 38
Hairy Vetch, 63
Hallock's Bay, 61
Hallock Pond, 254
Harbor Hill Moraine, 212, 216, 221
Harbor Seal, 226, 259, Picture 227
Hawthorne, 63, Leaf Illustration 283
Hearts-a-bustin', 12
Heath Hen, 182
Held Pond, 146
Hemlock, 154
Hermit Thrush, 174, Picture 175
Heron, 58, 62, 222
Hickory, 85, 128, 212, Leaf Illustration 284
High Bush Blueberry, 118, 123, 258
Hog Peanut, 141
Holly, 39, 122, 124, 191, 204, 206, 258, Leaf Illustration 284
Honeysuckle, 37, 106
Honeysuckle Pond, 24
Hooded Merganser, 193, 241
Hoodoo, 254, Picture 255
Horseshoe Crab, 139, 140, 222
Howell's Spring, 254
Hubbard Creek, 158
Huckleberry, 57, 106, 209
Indian Paint Pots, 216
Indian Pipe, Picture 137
Irish Moss, 47, 89, Illustration 282
Jamaica Bay, 35, 138
Juniper, 112, 118, 127, 191, 201, 240
Kestrel, 174, 209
Kettle Hole, 174
King Tide, 222

Knob and Kettle, 212
Leopard Frog, 81
Lesser Scaup, 222
Lichen, 41
Lily Pond, 254
Little Neck Bay, 164
Long Island Greenbelt Trail, 24, 84, 103, 153, 191, 192, 222, 235
Long Tailed Duck (Old Squaw), 193, 218
Loon, 218
Low Bush Blueberry, 209
Mallard 20, 84, 140, 180, 241, Picture 21
Maple, 42, 20, 57, 68, 73, 80, 178, 204
Mary's Island, 78
Massapequa Lake (Caroon's Lake), 78
Massapequa River, 78
Mill Creek, 158
Miss Annie's Creek, 173
Mocking Bird, 117
Monarch Butterfly, 149
Moriches Inlet, 226
Mosquito, 165
Mosquito Cove, 216
Mountain Laurel, 20, 30, 31, 34, 53, 68, 107, 144, 262
Muskrat, 25, 85
Mussel, 89, 95, 102, 138, 141, 218
Mute Swan, 57, 58, 79, 154, Picture 252
Nannyberry, 154
Nassau Suffolk Greenbelt Trail, 67, 78, 111
Nissequogue River, 84, 99, 102, 153, 193, 221
Northern Fog Fruit, 155
Northern Harrier (Marsh Hawk), 175, 209
Northern Pintail, 156
Northern Shoveler, 241, Picture 242
Norway Spruce, 47, 52, 69, 127
Oak, 33, 41, 58, 68, 80, 158, 170, 174, 212, 230, 262

Old Inlet, 148, 150, 151
Old Man of the Woods, 134
Olive Hairstreak Butterfly, 47
Orange Chanterelle, 134
Orange Crowned Warbler, 183
Orient Point, 61, 88
Osprey, 47, 48, 58, 63, 94, 95, 120, 149, 158, 263, Picture 49
Ovenbird, 57, Picture 59
Oyster Pond, 257
Painted Turtle, 19, 57, 236
Paumanok Path, 88, 90, 132, 158, 167, 245, 248, 257
Peconic Bay, 88, 168, 172, 260
Peconic River, 168
Peregrine Falcon, 94
Persimmons, 53
Pheasant, 120
Phragmite, 37, 42, 95, 138, 192. Illustration 281
Pickleweed (Glasswort), 159
Pin Cherry, Leaf Illustration 273
Pin Oak, Leaf Illustration 274
Pink Lady's Slipper, 52
Piping Plover, 47, 63, 89, 99, 149
Pitch Pine, 41, 26, 57, 58, 80, 125, 132, 160, 169, 182, 230, 232, Pinecone Illustration 280
Plum Island, 61, 88, 260
Poison Ivy, 33, 107, 118, 141, 149, 191, Illustration 286
Porpoise Channel, 266
Prickly Pear Cactus, 38, 63, 81, 119, 160, 267, Picture 93
Purple Coneflower (Echinacea), 106, 107
Purple Milkweed, 106
Quaking Aspen, 112, Leaf Illustration 287
Queen Anne's Lace, 107
Rabbit, 113, 125, Picture 76
Rattlestone, 216
Red Bellied Woodpecker, 58

Red Breasted Merganser, 222
Red Cedar, 33, 47, 52, 62, 63, 89, 100, 108, 113, 119, 123, 160, 191, 254
Red Fox, 268
Red Maple, 237, 240, Leaf Illustration 288
Red Oak, Leaf Illustration, 275
Red Tailed Hawk, 47, 113, 127, 253
Red Winged Blackbird, 12, 94
Rhododendron, 107, 197
Ribbon Snake, 174
River Otter, 12
Robin, 240
Rock Crab, 119, Picture 130
Ronkonkoma Moraine, 249
Ruddy Duck, 241
Salt Spray Rose (Beach Rose), 100, Picture 91
Saltmarsh Loosestrife, 254
Sanctuary Pond, 175
Sanderling, 149
Sandpiper, 63, 89, 99, 119, 149, 193
Sassafras, 68, 80, 117, 124, 174, Leaf Illustration 278
Scoy Pond, 88, 90
Scarlet Oak, Leaf Illustration, 274
Scrub Oak, 182
Sea Lavender, 63
Seaman Pond, 240
Scrub Oak, 112, 208
Seaford Creek, 16
Semipalmated Plover, 119, 149
Shellfish Scented Rasulla, 134
Shelter Island, 88, 172
Shining Lady's Tresses, 63
Shipman's Point, 266
Skunk Cabbage, 12, 32, 242, 258, Picture 15
Smith Cove, 175
Smith's Point, 148

Smithtown Bay, 266
Snapping Turtle, 41, 57, 236
Snow Goose, 218, Picture 219
Snowdrop, 263, Picture 264
Snowy Egret, 78, 94, 95
Spatterdock (Cow Lily), 79
Sphagnum Moss, 41, 173
Spring Peeper, 20
Stony Brook Harbor, 266
Strack Pond, 213
Stump Pond, 153
Sugar Maple, Leaf Illustration 288
Sumac, 69, 100, 112, 117, 141, 165, 174
Sundew, 168
Sunken Meadow Creek, 99
Swamp Mallow, 125
Swamp White Oak, Leaf Illustration 276
Sweet Bay Magnolia, 159
Sweet Gum, 198, Leaf Illustration 289
Sweezy's Pond, 41
Sycamore, 145, Leaf Illustration 289
Telegraph Weed, 133
Tick, 74, 145, 149, 158, 191, 209
Touch-me-not, 107, 145, 153, 165
Trail View State Park, 68, 111
Tree Swallow (Unladen), 94
Tufted Titmouse, 58
Tulip Tree, 13,14,32,68, 117, 144, 145, 216, 262, Leaf Illustration 290
Turkey Tail, Picture 163
Turtle Cove, 258
Turtle Pond, 263
Virginia Bluebell, 51
Virginia Creeper, 144, 158, Illustration 287
Virginia Point, 164
Wantagh Nature Trail, 240

303

Wantagh Pond, 240
Watch Hill, 148
West Meadow Creek, 266
Westbrook Pond, 235, Picture 234
White Birch, 254
White Coral Mushroom, 134
White Fringed Orchid, 168 240
White Mulberry, Leaf Illustration 279
White Oak, 127, 144, 178, 195, Leaf Illustration 276
White Pine, 20,35,52,69, 112, 120, 133, 173, 187, Pinecone Illustration 280
White Tailed Deer, 26, 47, 53, 74, 75, 90, 117, 125, 160, 191, 200, 209, 230, 238, 244, 253, Picture 238, 259
Wild Turkey, 230
Witch Hazel, 187, Picture 189
Whitman Creek, 84
Wild Bergamot, 81
Wild Grape, 112, 117, 222, Illustration 285
Wild Raspberry, 84, 103, 108, 117, 128, 144, Illustration 285, Picture 86
Wildwood Lake, 245
Willow Oak, 39
Willow Pond, 84
Winterberry, 155
Wood Duck, 84
Wood Sorrel, 106
Woodcock, 259
Yellow Crowned Night Heron, 140
Yellow Owl Trail, 249
Yellow Shafted Flicker, 165
Yucca, 38

Made in the USA
Middletown, DE
17 July 2021